Also by Valerie Davis Raskin

Great Sex for Moms: Ten Steps to Nurturing Passion
While Raising Kids

When Words Are Not Enough:
The Women's Prescription
for Depression and Anxiety

This Isn't What I Expected: Overcoming Postpartum Depression

THE
MAKING OF
A MOTHER

THE MAKING OF A MOTHER

Overcoming the
Nine Key Challenges from
Crib to Empty Nest

VALERIE DAVIS RASKIN, M.D.

BALLANTINE BOOKS
NEW YORK

Copyright © 2007 by Valerie Davis Raskin

All rights reserved.

Published in the United States by Ballantine Books,
an imprint of The Random House Publishing Group,
a division of Random House, Inc., New York.

BALLANTINE and colophon are registered trademarks of Random House, Inc.

ISBN 978-0-345-47598-5

LIBRARY OF CONGRESS CATALOGING-IN-PUBLICATION DATA
Raskin, Valerie D.
The making of a mother : overcoming the nine key challenges from crib to
empty nest / Valerie Davis Raskin.
p. cm.
ISBN 978-0-345-47598-5
1. Motherhood. 2. Mothers. I. Title.
HQ759.R37 2007
306.874'3—dc22   2006049720

Printed in the United States of America on acid-free paper

www.ballantinebooks.com

2 4 6 8 9 7 5 3 1

First Edition

Book design by Carol Malcolm Russo

Experience is a hard teacher because she gives the test first, the lesson afterwards.

—ABRAHAM LINCOLN

Contents

Introduction — xiii

1 **Identity:** *The First Key Challenge* — 3

2 **Unloving Moments:** *The Second Key Challenge* — 40

3 **Honoring the Father:** *The Third Key Challenge* — 58

4 **Separation:** *The Fourth Key Challenge* — 84

5 **Setting Limits:** *The Fifth Key Challenge* — 108

6 **Imperfect Institutions:** *The Sixth Key Challenge* — 129

7 **Revised Dreams:** *The Seventh Key Challenge* — 150

8 **Adversity:** *The Eighth Key Challenge* — 173

9 **Saying Good-bye:** *The Ninth Key Challenge* — 193

10 Conclusion — 221

Bibliography — 225
Acknowledgments — 231

*The stories in this book are either from
interviews conducted with mothers
who volunteered to be included in this book,
or from highly disguised clinical studies.
In all cases, names and identifying information
have been changed to protect the privacy of
the women and their families.*

Introduction

In my clinical practice, I specialize in the problems of motherhood. I'm also the mom of three kids, including one out of the nest, and I've been writing about parenthood for almost twenty years.

I know, personally as well as professionally, that the job can bring you to your knees. But you don't need to be an expert to realize that mothering is hard, maybe the hardest thing you've ever done.

You don't need a book to tell you that motherhood is marked by a series of tough challenges. You already know that sometimes it feels like an endless roller-coaster ride: just when you come up for air, you have to grab back onto the rails because there's another dark and scary patch immediately ahead.

And you surely don't need a psychiatrist to tell you that you will grow and change, developing as a mother as you move through these challenges, most likely for decades.

You might, however, need to be told that you don't have to worry so much. After all, we live in a culture of parenting that implies that you probably aren't doing enough for your child. We're absolutely flooded with messages about the dangers that threaten our kids, including being a major cause of the things that can go wrong in their lives. We're taught to hover over the tiniest developmental change in our children, encouraged to fret almost incessantly about how they'll turn out.

You also might want to find out more about what *you* need, how *you're* turning out. You might crave more truth about the inner lives of mothers, long for credible, unsentimental accounts of how women become mothers. You might want to know more about how all moms make mistakes and get second chances, and that experiencing growing pains doesn't mean you're failing.

Parenting experts rarely attend to the growth of mothers, focusing instead on the development of our children. But just as children develop physically, cognitively, morally, socially, and emotionally, so, too, do mothers grow and change over the course of mothering. This is a book of real women's struggles with each of the nine key challenges that show up predictably, repeatedly, and often uncomfortably, in the mothering life cycle. The forty women whose stories form the basis of this book come from two sources: case studies from my clinical practice, and women from all walks of life whom I interviewed about their experiences as mothers. In every story, at every stage of motherhood, you'll discover how moms, from pregnancy to the empty nest, face remarkably similar emotional milestones.

Brianna and Amanda, for example, are mothers who at first glance have little in common. Brianna, who didn't finish high school, became a single mother in her late teens, while Amanda was in her forties when she adopted a baby girl from China. Brianna lives at the poverty threshold, according to federal guidelines; Amanda is a college professor who resides in a middle-class suburban home that she and her husband own. Yet they echo each other's sense of the bittersweet changes in their lives as moms of babies. Both feel naïve when they look back on how they underestimated the changes that motherhood would precipitate.

Brianna mentions the negatives: "I can't hang out with my

friends like I used to, can't come and go as I please. I have no free time, and all my money goes to the baby." But she likes the good ways that she's grown up, how becoming a mom affects the important issues that teenagers struggle with: "I'm not silly anymore, and I don't get into petty fights. I'm more responsible."

Amanda also mentions the losses that accompany new motherhood: "I still can't believe I thought I'd get all this work done while the baby slept. I'm behind on three projects I've promised to colleagues, and I'm so tired I can't imagine when I'll catch up." But when the baby, fussing, makes it clear that Amanda is the one she wants to be soothed by, she glows. Just as Brianna uses other teens as a point of reference, Amanda refers to a fundamental issue that concerns her midlife peers as she soothes the baby. "This is it, right here. *This* [mother-child bond] is the meaning of life."

Only a few months into motherhood, both women feel fundamentally different than they did before, and while richer for it, they know there's a price. Both are actively facing the first of the nine challenging milestones I'll be writing about, that of forming a new identity. Sorting pluses and minuses, they reflect on what it means to "be me, now that I'm a mother."

What makes this a key challenge? In hindsight, saying that you weren't prepared for how motherhood would change your life borders on being trite. (No kidding. *Duh.*) But for Brianna and Amanda, it's huge because it's the first time they realize that mothering is inherently unpredictable, a path one cannot entirely plan out. This is a lesson parenthood will continue to demonstrate: stuff happens. Knowing that you didn't quite know what you were getting into can make you feel anything from a little wet behind the ears to foolishly incompetent, perhaps, depending on how much you expect or like to be in control.

And it's a big moment because it immediately requires adapting to the gap between what motherhood is actually like, and what we believe or have been told it *should* be like. Brianna and Amanda aren't different from the rest of us: they compare their insides to other mothers' outsides. Other mothers talk about how wonderful motherhood is, and they leave off the exhaustion, the things you can't afford anymore, the freedom you no longer enjoy. If I breezed into their living rooms and asked how they liked being new moms, I am certain both women would give me the glossy eight-by-ten. But once they trust that I will not judge them, we spend several hours picking apart their experiences of parenthood. I admire mothers, and I hope that my appreciation of the work that goes into mothering is what allows the women described in this book to tell their truths.

Perhaps I even told Brianna or Amanda that I view the making of mothers as being like the making of Marines: the toughest job you'll ever love. There is a Marine Corps motto that describes exactly how, by facing tough challenges, new recruits are made into Marines: "Improvise, Adapt, Overcome." This book is about how women learn to improvise, adapt, and overcome the nine developmental milestones that make them into mothers.

These challenges force internal shifts in how women think and feel about themselves. They trigger self-appraisal, and a mother's emotional muscles may ache in the beginning. The outcome of each—positive growth, stagnation, or disappointment in oneself—has an impact on the changes that lie ahead, as well as how a mother views herself and the emotional experience of mothering. They provide opportunities to reflect on the journey, and, quite possibly, to experience a sigh of relief.

A few children hop on a bicycle and ride with grace the first time; most skin their knees in the beginning. Most of us scrape our knees the first time we encounter the nine key challenges of motherhood, and yet we keep going. Our scraped knees may mean that we feel clumsy, inept, flustered, disappointed, overwhelmed, self-conscious. Or we may feel worse: anxious, deficient, guilty, remorseful, sad, angry, even miserable. We know we're at a maternal milestone because our knees hurt; unfortunately, we can't always tell when we're riding with no hands. This book is about recognizing the milestones, and it's about how to know when you're thriving, even if you have no role model.

Perhaps it would help to know why I think I have something new to say about the experience of mothering. In part, it's because it's my job to study motherhood. My practice specializes in mental health issues for mothers, and I need to be able to reassure when appropriate, and confront when necessary. Time and again, I find that mothers are, well, simply terrible when it comes to appraising their own maternal performance. I've treated numerous terrific mothers who are panic-stricken that they aren't doing a good enough job, mothers who lack an internal compass that reassures them that they're headed in the right direction. I have also worked with mothers who *were* heading off course, and helped them find their way to break the chains of a legacy of seriously flawed parenting. While grossly bad mothering is usually easy to recognize, conscientious mothers find that "good enough" is as hard to hold on to as the slipperiest greased pig at the fair.

In the course of conducting therapy with hundreds of moms, I developed a theory of the nine key challenges that put mothers to the test. Since many of the moms in my practice were poorly mothered themselves, and lacked an adequate role model, while others had burdens that made motherhood more difficult, such as postpartum depression or a disabled child, I wanted to find out whether their challenges held true for all mothers. In order to test my theory that these challenges were universal ones, I conducted longitudinal and comparative case studies with mothers in my community, using the grounded-theory techniques I learned in my postdoctoral fellowship at the University of Chicago Committee on Human Development. My results confirmed that these key challenges transcend age, ethnicity, socioeconomic and marital status, and even whether or not mothers wish to reject their own role models.

The forty women I will describe in this book are all mothers who have spent considerable time thinking about parenthood's challenges. Some I came to know in the therapy setting. Others specifically volunteered to participate in the study and haven't felt the need for professional help. As a group, they're women who became mothers at sixteen, others who adopted in their late thirties. The moms are Caucasian, African-American, Latina, Jewish, Catholic, born-again Protestants, and multicultural. They're single, divorced, married, and cohabiting. Some receive public assistance, some are working class, some students, and others are highly educated, accomplished, and affluent.

These mothers' stories reinforce the truth every mother knows: motherhood changes you forever, and you can't know how it changes you until you're there. You'll hear moms relate the challenges of the early years, stripped of sugar coating; the loss of time and money and freedom that accompanies parenthood; the discrepancy between what a mom thinks she should know and what she actually knows; the conflict that arises when baby intrudes on a romantic relationship; and the shock of discovering that there are moments when you don't *like* the toddler you love dearly.

I'll describes the challenges that show up in the early school years, when one woman can't bear to be away from her kindergartner, and another has to find a way to get away from her job in order to be at her son's side while he is in the ICU for asthma. I'll show why moms sometimes find it difficult to set limits, and how it happens that an otherwise capable woman cannot get her child to pick up after herself. I'll tell of moms' painful encounters with the imperfect institutions that educate their kids, and how moms are tempted to push their own dreams onto their children. You'll hear about secondhand blows: a mom immobilized by how her teenager copes with the popularity battle, and another crippled by guilt when her child inherits the family's genetic illness. Finally, I'll describe how women empty the nest and build relationships with their young-adult kids, including a mom whose son became a solider in Iraq, another who left for college in fits and starts, and one with a so-called boomerang child.

Because first encounters with the key challenges are generally awkward and difficult, that's when moms are especially susceptible to the sinking feeling that their best isn't good enough. These are the times when psychotherapists get a very close look at what's really going on inside our patients, and we know how important affirmation is when a person hits the rough spots. As I share what I've observed about the inner world of mothers, I'll also tell you what I've learned about taking your own maternal pulse, more accurately assessing your performance.

Many, perhaps most, women enter motherhood with an idea about what kind of job they want to do: a perfect one. Some plan on compensating for what they missed or wished had been different for them growing up. Women who were poorly mothered are especially sensitive to the cultural idealization of motherhood, as they hope to avoid repeating the past by attaining perfection. But these days, no new mother gets off lightly.

Truly, no mom always feels sure of herself. You may have impeccable parenting credentials, but when your child refuses to go in the big-girl's potty, wipes your kiss off in disgust as he marches into second grade, slams her bedroom door in your face, or sits behind the steering wheel with a brand-new driver's permit, you're unprepared. When it's your first encounter, chances are you improvise, wondering a millisecond later about what you said or did, or what you should have said or done. Uncertainty, years of second-guessing yourself, comes with the territory. There is no surefire way to figure out if you're doing it right, no performance appraisal, no answer sheet at the back of the book to compare your results with the correct choices.

The myth of the perfect mother is rampant, the stakes so high, that any mother can succumb to the insecurity that accompanies the never-ending ambiguity of human mothering. Fortunately, the chorus of voices telling us to reject the modern mythology of motherhood is growing. In *Perfect Madness: Motherhood in the Age of Anxiety,* Judith Warner asks us to resist the "widespread, choking cocktail of guilt and anxiety and resentment and regret. . . .

[that] is poisoning motherhood for American women today." Psychotherapist-writer Janna Malamud Smith notes, "Messages from the culture encourage mothers to feel bad, and, in turn, they may believe that their only route to parenting virtue is to do until they overdo."

Warner attributes the extraordinary pressure on mothers to attain what she terms "über-motherhood" to our competitive, winner-take-all mind-set. She notes that we fear that "if we don't do everything right for our children, they may be consigned, down the line, to failure. To loserdom." Mothers toil under this pressure, while, as Anne Crittenden points out in *The Price of Motherhood: Why the Most Important Job in the World Is Still the Least Valued,* "The job of making a home for a child and developing his or her capabilities is often equated with 'doing nothing.' "

Another reason you might be feeling worn down, Susan J. Douglas and Meredith W. Michaels observe, is that you're being told that motherhood is "an individual achievement, something you and you alone excel at or screw up." In *The Mommy Myth,* they describe the new "momism," with "impossible ideals about child rearing," that "insinuates itself into women's psyches just where we have been rendered most vulnerable: in our love for our kids."

In addition to turning motherhood into an unwinnable rat race, we have come to idealize motherhood beyond recognition. As Naomi Wolf notes, "[A]ll too often, women are offered sugar-coated niceties to guide them on the journey, misleading information, half-truths, and platitudes." After *Misconceptions* was published, Wolf discovered that "expressing fatigue, loneliness, or sadness, or even at times feeling overwhelmed . . . ." was labeled, by some, as "whining."

These books go a long way to help women reclaim motherhood as a comfortable endeavor that sensible people can actually carry off and feel good about. They help us reject what Anna Quindlen coined the "Hallmark version" of motherhood. I hope to contribute here by sharing what I know about the psychology of maternal vulnerability, about feeling defective when we encounter the hard stuff. Toxic notions about motherhood encourage women to greet normal maternal growing pains with self-condemnation: if you feel bad, you must be messing up. My hope is that this book helps you soothe yourself when you feel overwhelmed, incompetent, frustrated, or defensive about good-enough, improvised parenting. I hope that when you find yourself feeling shamed by human imperfection, you opt instead to identify the key challenge that is making mothering tough at that moment. My wish is that the reader finds here the affirmation she lacks, recognizes that just because it's hard doesn't mean she isn't doing it right.

We will need to be honest, authentic, and gentle in our self-appraisal. If we accept growing pains as part of the deal, we will view mistakes less harshly. In general, those least well mothered are the ones who are most worried about how they are doing, but it doesn't always work that way. What I have found in my work with mothers is that rejecting perfection as a concept isn't as easy as it looks.

Part of what makes the myth of the perfect mother psychologically hard to abandon is the trap of comparative mothering. There's a saying that it's foolhardy to compare your insides with other people's outsides. Another mom's exterior may look perfect, while inside she's just as uncertain as you are about how she's doing, and may even think *you're* the one who never stumbles. Mothers who try to judge their own performance by observing the actions of others often sell themselves short.

Why isn't it enough to instruct mothers to lighten up, resist the forces that ruin motherhood, stop believing that you're the only one who ever slips? Unfortunately, I believe the problem of maternal self-esteem is as challenging for women as body image issues are. It's darned hard to overcome cultural pressures to feel inadequate if you have the smallest doubt about yourself, and who doesn't? To complete the analogy, we know in our heads that size-two-age-seventeen is an absurd standard for beauty, but in our hearts, almost all of us would be happy to weigh less than we do and look younger than we are. We may know in our heads that there is no such thing as a perfect mother, but we keep trying anyway. There are too many beautiful women who hate their thighs, and too many capable mothers who feel flawed.

To our chagrin, psychotherapist-mothers know that the idea that mothering should, or could, be flawless has deep roots in the history of psychoanalysis and psychotherapy. Sigmund Freud, the founder of modern psychotherapy, taught us to look to early childhood to locate the foundation of the patient's problems. In the model under which I was trained as a psychiatrist, there is no relationship as formative as the one between mother and child. It's where you hit psychological pay dirt. This is such a widely accepted truth these days that we almost don't hold individuals accountable for bad adult behavior, moving too quickly to examine the early childhood trauma that must explain it.

Even if we've taken this concept a bit too far, I doubt anyone could mount a serious argument that early childhood experiences, particularly around issues of nurturing, are not deeply important to subsequent mental health and well-being. Who could argue that your child's experience of being mothered doesn't bear heavily upon his or her identity and functioning as an adult? Undeniable—but it's not the whole truth.

The whole truth is that while the emotional life cycle begins with one's earliest experiences, human beings never outgrow the possibility of change and maturation. After I completed a clinical psychiatry training program, while pregnant with my second child, I was fortunate enough to learn an entirely new way of looking at what makes people tick than is typically taught in American psychiatry programs. After residency, I entered a fellowship in which I studied human development. My eyes were opened to a new way of approaching the human condition, a new way of helping people change. The faculty (made up of psychologists, anthropologists, scientists, and educators) cared less about how humans are stuck in the past than about the ways in which we constantly evolve, grow, mature, and adjust to ongoing challenges. From the perspective of a developmental psychologist, the only thing that is permanent is change.

As a mother and a student of mothering, this is incredibly reassuring. Like most mothers, I'd like my mothering to be enriched by the best pieces of my childhood, would be happy if my own strengths could be set in stone. And yet, I'd also like to be able to grow and change when I stumble, to better myself, and to shake off the mistakes that I've made. Developmental psychology offers a promise most mothers greet with relief: you get to grow into, and *from,* the role of mother. And there's more good news: your children keep growing and changing, too, even if *you* misstep.

Sometimes I stumble as a mother, and I'm disappointed in how I do. Sometimes it's awkward and uncomfortable. And yet I know I'm a good mom. If you put my feet to the fire, I'd confess that I'm a very good mom. I'm not a perfect mom, and here's the great news: you aren't either.

Why am I so certain that there are no Perfect Mothers out there? Because mothering is not a fixed trait. It's not like eye color, something you're born with that doesn't change. The stories the women in this book tell demonstrate that mothering is a constantly evolving condition, with a predictable set of big moments accompanied by growing pains. The women in this book prove, beyond a doubt, that motherhood *can* be learned on the job.

It's a journey, not a destination.

THE MAKING OF
A MOTHER

1

Identity
The First Key Challenge

*In a sense, a mother has to be born psychologically
much as her baby is born physically.*
—Daniel N. Stern, M.D., and Nadia Bruschweiler-Stern, M.D.,
The Birth of a Mother

Cecilia, age thirty-eight, and her husband, Michael, performed six separate home pregnancy tests, each showing the two little pink lines, and still they doubted that she was pregnant. The signs were there: nausea, sensitivity to odors, fatigue, hunger. But they'd been told by Michael's cancer doctor a dozen years ago that after the experimental chemotherapy he underwent, he was infertile. They had never used birth control, and fourteen years of unprotected sex without a pregnancy seemed to settle the matter.

When they married, they assumed their life would be childless, and they compensated as best they could. They became the aunt and uncle the nieces and nephews love best, the ones with the "fun house." They filled their life with travel and play. "We'd show up at the family birthday parties dressed to the nines. We'd stop in, but we were always on our way somewhere else for dinner or dancing." They traveled at the drop of a hat. "Michael would say, 'Hey, honey, do you want to go to Vegas next weekend?' and we'd be off."

In one of those examples that proves Life Isn't Fair, Cecilia herself got breast cancer six years ago. They caught it so early that she didn't need chemotherapy, but the surgery removed her milk ducts. When her cancer doctor told her that she'd never be able to breast-feed, she replied, "That's for sure, Michael can't have children." Her cancer, following his, left her with a permanent sense that bad things can and do happen, that you can't tell yourself "that would never happen to me."

In some sense, the fact that both were cancer survivors helped them adjust to being infertile—there are worse things than not having a baby. She never spoke of her longing for children to Michael, not wanting him to feel bad or guilty. He didn't bring it up with her, thinking that she would only feel worse if they dwelled on it.

When the doctor confirmed her pregnancy, they were ecstatic. Their world flipped upside down, and now they love it. The baby is named Jessica, because it translates to "God's grace," and that's how they feel: blessed. They also understand John Lennon's statement that "Life is what happens when you're busy making other plans." They bought their first house a month before they learned she was expecting, and hadn't even moved yet. The room they'd planned to make into a party room with a deck overlooking a swimming pool was suddenly to become the baby's room. Cecilia immediately wished she'd considered the school system when picking a home, and began saving for Jessica's college fund.

Cecilia is a planner, quick on her feet when it comes to shifting directions. She responded to the sea change in her life by becoming an expert. "My sisters laughed at me at my baby shower. My wish list only included things the American Academy of Pediatrics approved. I know what the safest car seat is, what dishes a baby can't throw off the high chair, and how to try to avoid SIDS." In general, she likes to be prepared, and she joined countless new-mom chat rooms, read articles, and talked to mothers she respects about what to expect. In this, she's like her mother, who advises, "You always need a Plan B." Her husband says she frets too much, suggesting that since Jessica is only four months old, there is no need to stew about where she's going to high school.

Cecilia attributes her tendencies to be a planner, as well as a worrier, to her childhood. She's the oldest daughter of three, and her mom and dad suddenly divorced when she was six, because her father had been unfaithful. Her mother, of Mexican descent, moved the family back from a distant suburb into a tight-knit urban Italian community where her former mother-in-law lived, so she could go back to work with the help of her ex-husband's family (her own mother was deceased). Cecilia grew up feeling the weight of the world on her shoulders. She was often anxious about whether they'd have the rent money when the landlord knocked on the door, and worried that her mother sometimes looked sad. Overwhelmed, her mom lashed out in anger on occasion. As the oldest of three, as soon as Cecilia was ten, she supervised her younger sisters after school until her mom came home from work.

She doesn't fault her mother, whom she describes as "wonderful." She experienced her as "devoted," always making the girls her priority. She recalls that her mother fed them first, eating what remained. If she had some leftover money, she spent it on the girls. She taught them pride: "It doesn't matter if your clothes are new; it matters if they're clean and pressed." She also taught her to be proactive, saying repeatedly, "If there is something in your life you don't like, you are the only one who can change it." When her two sisters had children, she appreciated her mother's devotion with adult eyes, noticing how she gives her all to her grandkids.

When Cecilia became pregnant, she felt confident that she could repeat the best pieces of her mothering without idealizing her mother's human flaws. She, too, intends to put her daughter's needs first, and feels certain that she'll be able to convey to her daughter that she'll always be taken care of. She is certain that she'll repeat the maternal dedication she herself experienced growing up.

Her mother wasn't perfect, and Cecilia wants to do a few things a little differently. She says, "I want Jessica to be a child of her age. I don't want her to be aware of the pressures that the adults in her life have." She also rejects the importance her mother placed on appearances. Perhaps culturally driven, in response to stereotypes about Mexican-Americans in those days, her mother was preoccupied with making her girls look pretty all the time. Cecilia says, "Don't get me wrong. On Easter, Jessica was gorgeous in her little dress and patent leather shoes, but when I buy clothes, I think, 'Is it comfortable? Is it warm? Will it last?' " One of her sisters is just like their mother that way, but Cecilia says, "I don't obsess about how Jessica looks."

Cecilia views her mother's shortcomings through the lens of maturity. She doesn't fault her mother for being overwhelmed at times. "I've got new props* for single moms now. I can't imagine how I would have been when I was teary and couldn't sleep and had indigestion if I'd been on my own with no husband, no mother, no money." She gives her mother credit for wanting to do the best she could by her children, even if she sometimes stumbled. Her heart was always in the right place, and, in her way of thinking, that offsets any mistakes her mom made.

At almost forty, Cecilia entered motherhood with a strong sense of identity as a nonmother. Her work in accounting and bookkeeping is important to her, and she says, "I always try to be the best: the best employee, the best sister, the best wife." She differentiated herself from her mother long ago: her marriage is thriving, she is financially self-supporting, and knows that she'd never be as broke or helpless as her mom was when her world turned upside down because of her father's unfaithfulness. When Cecilia became a mother, she was at peace with the ways she's like her mother

---

*Slang for proper respect

("my kitchen table suffers from mom syndrome—it catches every paper that comes in the house"), and the ways in which she isn't destined to be like her.

As a childless couple, Cecilia and Michael had their lifestyle well mapped out. They were very free and spontaneous, and yet they don't miss that existence. "Maybe it's because we got enough of it. We weren't in our early twenties, stuck home with a baby while everyone went out and partied. We'd had that, and we feel that Jessica is, literally, a miracle baby."

Anticipating parenthood, Michael and Cecilia modified parts of who they were pre-baby. In addition to happily giving up the party room, they've switched careers. Michael, formerly a freelance construction worker, took a lower-paying union job with benefits so that if Cecilia needed to leave her job, they would have his insurance and job security. Just this week, after eight years at one company, she quit to stay home when the friend who was watching Jessica decided to go back to work herself. After visiting numerous infant care centers, Cecilia decided, "I can't drive up and drop her off with strangers like she's a package." She'll work part-time in the evening when her husband gets home, and downplay other people's worries about how her career might be adversely impacted when she's ready to go back full-time. "I'll cross that bridge when I get there. Right now, I have to watch the cars in the road that are here." Her identity as a professional conflicted with her identity as a mother. Motherhood easily triumphed, because, as a mom, the most important thing to her is to do what her mom did: be devoted, put the baby first. "We'll just have to manage on less money."

Cecilia entered motherhood with a track record of being capable in her former roles. She doesn't like the feeling of incompetence that comes with new motherhood, and thus she prepared herself with all her energy. "I think I might be the only first-time mom who actually knew when her mucous plug came out because I had read every little thing about pregnancy." Her one nightmare was when, a few weeks postpartum, she accidentally fell asleep on the couch and dropped Jessica eight inches, onto the carpet. She immediately called the pediatrician for reassurance, and he ran her through the danger signs, none of which were there. She still says, "I could have killed my own kid," although her husband gave her the perfect soothing words: "Honey, you're exhausted, and you're doing the best you can. The baby's fine." That day, they set up blankets and cushions on the floor so that it could never happen again.

I notice that Cecilia holds herself to a higher standard than she does her own mom, whose parenting mistakes she now overlooks. And she holds herself responsible for an injury to Jessica that didn't even happen. I suspect she'll get past this. Newborns are exceptionally vulnerable, and one way new moms cope with the awesome responsibility is to try to be superhuman. I think she'll grow into knowing that, like her mother, she can only do her best, because she's at peace with good enough mothering. Empathy toward your own mother's flaws is a good place to start learning to accept being only human yourself.

Truth Be Told, I Didn't Want This Pregnancy

Gretchen, the single mother of a fourteen-month-old girl named Diantha, was as shocked as Cecilia to find herself pregnant. Much of her background mirrors Cecilia's. She's also half western European ethnicity, with a mom born in Mexico. Her parents divorced when she was young, and she and her mother remained geographically and emotionally close with her paternal grandmother, growing up in a tightly knit ethnic community in urban Chicago. (She still lives on the block she grew up on, where she says people are not only mostly from Mexico, they're from a particular town.)

The similarity ends there. Gretchen was crushed when she learned, three days before her twenty-first birthday, that she was pregnant; she was completely unprepared mentally. She was single, living at home with her "hard-core Catholic" mom, and enrolled in college, which she paid for entirely by herself through scholarships, grants, and loans. She was on the dean's list, and worked part-time and summers. To spare her anguish, she lied when her mom asked her if she was sexually active, since her mom couldn't accept premarital sex.

Third in her class in high school, Gretchen is no dimwit. She always used birth control, but this one time, she "knew" she was safe. She'd just had her period, so "there was no egg there, nothing to be met." Her next-door neighbor, Marisol, was a full month late getting her period, and she was worried for her. One day, Gretchen noticed a billboard that said in big letters "Are you pregnant?," and she had her first fleeting thought that she might be. She dismissed it, saying, "Oh, you're just paranoid because of Marisol." She had the slightest nagging feeling because she had slept twenty hours one day, and her appetite had skyrocketed. But she hadn't even missed her own period yet. To support her neighbor, and get it off her own mind, she offered to do pregnancy tests together.

Marisol pretty much knew she was pregnant, and asked Gretchen to go first. She did, and was stunned by the positive result. She recalls saying, " 'Oh my God' at least a hundred times." She simply couldn't believe she was pregnant. She told Marisol, "This is yours. This isn't mine." She immediately called her boyfriend Ryan, "hysterical." She kept saying to him, "This shouldn't be me." Her self-concept didn't include motherhood. She was a young woman with a great future, an honor student at a competitive university, and a good daughter who planned to buy her mom a house once she established her career. She didn't do unprotected sex, so how could this be her? Her response was "complete and utter disbelief."

Her family had planned a big birthday celebration, so they put off letting everyone know for a few more days. When she and Ryan told her mother, it went as badly as she feared. She was furious and ashamed, especially because they weren't married. She blamed

Gretchen's boyfriend for taking advantage of her, was angry at Gretchen for lying, and then blamed herself for something "she did or didn't do that must have made this her fault." She nursed her grudge for months. At church, she told people the news as if someone had died, even when Gretchen was standing right there. Her mom cried a lot, and asked her repeatedly, "Why did you get pregnant?" She demanded that she and Ryan get married immediately.

Gretchen told her, "Look, Mom, you were married when you had me and that didn't even last a year, so maybe it's not so great your way." This didn't sink in, so Gretchen sometimes had to leave the room when her mother wouldn't let up on the criticism and doomsday predictions. She went to the shower to cry in private. Everywhere she turned, she encountered negativity. Her father assumed that she wouldn't finish college. Her university was a Catholic institution, where "you just don't see a lot of pregnant girls running around." Few of her classmates were supportive, and took it for granted that she wouldn't be graduating with them a year later.

She pushed back at people's expectations for her. She declined the dean's suggestion that she take a semester off during her pregnancy, and proved her dad wrong that she would drop out. She was back in school (part-time) one week after the baby was born, while breast-feeding, and at the time of our interview had just received her bachelor's degree in psychology. Gretchen also refused her mother's demand that she and Ryan marry. They live together in the apartment that is downstairs from her mom. She says, "I was thrown into motherhood, or you might say, self-propelled," but marriage was something she could remain in control of. She won't get married until she feels more stable, and won't get married for her mother's sake. "We'll see."

Pregnancy was a bad shock, a moment of recklessness that changed her life plan forever. Abortion was not an option she considered; she was becoming a mother and that was that. Gretchen coped well with this sudden change in her identity by differentiating the parts of her self she was forced to give up or change from those she wasn't. She didn't have to quit school, didn't have to be ashamed of her pregnancy at a Catholic university, didn't have to get married, and didn't have to please her mom. She even continued to work out at her gym until the day before labor, although since Diantha's birth she can no longer find the time. She *did* need to prepare to provide a loving home for her baby, and she's stepped up to the responsibility. She hung on to all that she could of her old self while making room for the new.

Women who are pregnant, planned or not, commonly note that their emotional attachment to the fetus grows as the baby becomes more real. Gretchen noticed this when she first felt the thrill of the bubblelike sensations of the baby's movement. Her loving feelings increased when she saw the ultrasound, and she and Ryan learned that they were having a girl. She brought the photo home, and the ultrasound technician had typed in "Hi Mom, Hi Dad" on the scan. This turned her mother around. They went shopping for pink baby clothes that day, and her mom began to shift from outrage into understanding that her daughter was really going to be a mom and it was time to put her disapproval behind her.

Gretchen is a very loving mother, and her interactions with her toddler give no hint that this isn't how she always meant it to be. During our interview, she's watching a friend's son along with her own daughter. When she tells them to wait a moment for a snack or a drink of water, they do, which is a sign that they expect her to be good for her word and see to their needs. The room overflows with baby paraphernalia. The living room doubles as the baby's room, and in it I see a crib, a dresser, a stroller, a baby swing, a red wagon, a child-sized bench, a humidifier, a bin of diapers, children's books including *The Giving Tree,* a pile of stuffed animals, and toys that sing, make animal sounds, and pop up when touched or wound. It screams "well-loved child lives here." She chose the name Diantha because it means "God's flower," and she now feels blessed by her daughter.

Gretchen and her boyfriend aren't the only ones who have come full turn. Her mother denies how angry she was, and now calls her granddaughter "*my* baby." She hugs and kisses her all the time, and they can run upstairs to wake her up in the middle of the night if they need help with teething pains or aren't sure what's bothering the baby. Gretchen isn't finished giving her mother grief about her first reaction, not entirely ready to forgive her hysterics. But she saw something in the labor room that helped her put her mother's negative reaction in perspective: her mom is a full-fledged drama queen. She was so overwrought during the delivery, accusing the doctor and nurses of failing to watch in case the baby slipped out of the womb, that they had to repeatedly insist "Grandma" calm down. Her overly theatrical response to unmarried pregnancy was completely replaced with overly theatrical protectiveness. She hasn't uttered a word of criticism since the baby's birth.

During her pregnancy and in the first few months after the baby was born, Gretchen did what all mothers should do: she immersed herself in a supportive network of friends. There are nine mothers with babies around Diantha's age in her neighborhood, and the moms help one another out. They swap babysitting, clothes, and, in an emergency, formula. Mostly, she says, "we call each other for help. All of us get to a point where we don't know what to do, and one of us has been through it." As an example, she mentions commiserating about a child needing stitches. The mother of the four-year-old boy that Gretchen is watching is the "head mother," since she went first. "You can go to her and she'll figure it out with you." She is proud of their honesty about motherhood. "You can't sugar-coat anything when it comes to the kids. If you did, that mother wouldn't be prepared when they find out how hard it is." Gretchen hated sympathy, hated the response "you poor thing." What she got from her pregnant and mothering friends was realistic encouragement: Yes it's tough, but it's great, too, and we're here to help.

Motherhood Is an Idea Before It's a Reality

Gretchen's honesty about the fact that her beloved baby was, at first, unwelcome news is refreshing but rare. She's not like her mother, who can't admit her early lack of enthusiasm. She shows psychological maturity by acknowledging that good, loving moms didn't always greet the positive pregnancy test with joy. The way she feels now about the person who Diantha is has nothing to do with the way she felt when the baby wasn't yet real, was just an obstacle to be overcome.

Transforming parenthood from an idea into a part of one's actual identity is a major piece of the first key challenge that women face as they become mothers. This process may begin before conception and surges during pregnancy and in the first few postpartum months. "Who am I now? Who will I become?" are questions each prospective and new mom must address. Since most girls grow up with ideas and fantasies about becoming a parent, women step into the role with expectations, fears, myths, and hopes for what this new identity will mean. And it's uniformly transformative: any mother will tell you that she is no longer the same person she used to be.

Cecilia quit imagining herself as a mother the day she married Michael. That was just how it was going to be. She didn't *not* want to be a mom, but it just didn't seem to be in the cards. Unlike many women with infertility, she didn't go through a long period of trying to get pregnant, didn't suffer the agony of will-I-or-won't-I? As a result, the idea of motherhood was long buried, and so she had only seven months in which to undergo a huge shift in her identity. She succeeds in part because she feels that she's won a cosmic lottery, and it's just easier to adapt to sudden changes in identity when they're welcome. She also is flourishing because she's had twenty adult years of competency, and she applies what she knows about how to be successful in other roles to how to be successful in this role. Do the best you can, she says, and "if I don't know something, I'll find it out." That and, she says frankly, "don't give a shit about what people think" if they criticize how you're doing things.

Since half of all pregnancies are planned, many women have more time than Cecilia and Gretchen did to anticipate motherhood. But like a bride walking down the aisle, or a college graduate buying an outfit for her first "real" job, people in transition wonder "Can I do it?" They naturally look to others to help allay their fears. As prospective mothers, women contemplate what parenting will be like for them, and use their maternal role model as a point of reference.

As hysterical as her mother was, Gretchen could see ways in which she'd be happy to be like her. She admires all the fortitude it took for her mother to come to Chicago with only a third-grade education, and establish herself as a legal immigrant with a steady job and a caring community. She can now read English, which Gretchen notes is not the case for many people with her mom's background. Gretchen could be describing herself, in managing to finish college, when she says of her mother, "She doesn't realize all that she's done in her life." Her mom is very affectionate, noting "we're an 'I love you' type of family." When Gretchen sees Diantha play with her baby doll, rubbing her tenderly, she knows that she's repeated the type of warm mothering she had benefited from.

The Unmothered Mother: Rejecting the Role Model

For some women, however, the prospect of being like your mother is very troublesome. Sharon, a high school English teacher, worried about becoming a mother since the first time she really thought about it, at least twenty years ago. No one who knows her mom would want to be like her. Sharon knows only too well that her fascination with Hollywood-Mom exposés, from Joan Crawford à la *Mommy Dearest* to whether Britney Spears always uses an infant car seat, is directly related to her own upbringing. Like the daughter of a beloved starlet with a secret, Sharon lived inside the upside-down world of a revered society matron who never showed her alcohol-fueled rages anywhere but at home.

Sharon's list of things she doesn't want to do or be is long. She doesn't want to be a mom who has two personalities, one public and another private. She wants a family with no deep, dark secrets. She doesn't want to raise her voice, let alone slap her child. She won't permit alcohol in her house, and she doesn't even take aspirin for a headache in case it might be a slippery slope to substance abuse.

She is so afraid of becoming like her mother that she tried to marry a man whom she could count on to step in if she does something wrong, a form of insurance against her past. She believes that her husband is someone who would never pretend everything is fine when it isn't, lose himself in his work, or abdicate fatherly responsibility. Still, she can't help being afraid that fatherhood could change him.

Most of all, Sharon wants a role model for motherhood. She constantly compares her imagined self to other women. At parent-teacher conferences, she finds that she analyzes her students' parents, wondering how she would handle the sullen teenager who isn't meeting her potential, the child with attention deficit disorder, or the artsy superstar with a gift for writing and a taste for gender-bending apparel. She categorizes her imaginary reactions to what she sees other mothers do: "bad," "disastrous," "perfect." She watches women at the grocery store, trying to discern the secret of calming a toddler at the checkout line, wondering how tired mothers find the patience to soothe tired children, knowing that she herself was never soothed in this way.

Sharon can't turn to her older sister Janet for help because Janet has decided that having children is too risky. Janet wouldn't get married until her fiancé agreed to remain a childless couple, and, eight years later, she shows no sign of changing her mind. Unlike Janet and Sharon, Sharon's younger sister Suzanne got pregnant, and then married, at an early age. Sharon feels that Suzanne, in an attempt to avoid duplicating their mother's extreme behavior, has gone too far the other way. Sure, she doesn't yell or hit her six-year-old son, but she never sets a limit, either, and Sharon can barely stand to be with her spoiled nephew. The idea of ending up like her sister is only a bit less distasteful than the idea of ending up like their mother.

Women like Gretchen and Cecilia, who look at their own mothers with admiration, feel more or less equipped for the job. Their experience of being parented, while not perfect, was good enough to allow them the freedom not to sweat the small stuff. Gretchen, for example, fundamentally believes that she can do about as well as anyone else when it comes to parenting. In fact, her description of herself is a testament to maternal self-esteem. When Diantha was born, she says, "I was an inexperienced good mom." Motherhood is challenging, but she feels up to the task. She saw her own single mom manage; so will she. She's become a contemplative mother, because it's in her personality to engage in self-examination, but she isn't destined to drive herself crazy with worry.

Mothers like Sharon regularly fear failure. No mistake will be acceptable, no failure easily dismissed. Self-doubting mothers often share a common worry: becoming their mothers. Who rejects the model provided by her own parent? These are the women who in this book will be called "unmothered mothers." While the umbrella labeled "good enough" is a mile wide, there are outliers, women so ineffective that their daughters left childhood without any sense of what competent mothering looks like. These inadequately mothered daughters, when they become moms, lack even the flimsiest guide that most women take out of childhood.

How does a woman know if she is an unmothered mother? Surely, daughters of good-enough mothers sometimes reject parts of their upbringing but it's the distinction between wanting to *do* differently and wanting to *be* different. Many well-mothered women say "I shouldn't do that," or "I will handle that issue differently," just as Cecilia and Gretchen do. The unmothered mother says "I must not be like her." Her repudiation of her mother is deep; it reaches into her core self. For her, the heart and soul of her identity as a mom must be fundamentally different. These women typically know who they are because a primary parenting goal is to avoid reproducing what they themselves experienced.

They may be the daughters of women who were abusive or neglectful, where the need to do things differently is obvious. Others are daughters of could-have-been-worse mothers who manipulate through guilt, shame, blame, and self-pity while providing for the basic physical needs of childhood. They may have been mothers who criticized but could not praise, who required an emotional payback for every gift, or who lavished attention on a favored sibling. Perhaps they made their children feel burdensome, or taught their daughters to loathe their bodies as they did. They may have been so emotionally or physically fragile that they "parentified" their daughters by forcing them to act as if they were the adult caretaker, the "little mama," too early.

Women who emerge from wounded childhoods enter their own journey through motherhood with an extra burden in today's culture of perfectionism. Without lived experience to guide the way, the tunnel is pitch black. And they have firsthand knowledge of the damage inadequate mothers can inflict. It takes guts to mother when you know that you wish to reshape motherhood. For once you get the job, you can't cancel the contract. Much is at stake—the health, happiness, and well-being of those loved most passionately—without any chance to truly anticipate the journey until you're already at sea. If you discover, as countless novice and experienced mothers do every day, that you have only a vague idea of how to navigate the territory, culture insists that you keep silent, lest you be marked with the scarlet letter that signifies Bad Mother.

Any mother who rejects the model she grew up with enters motherhood intending to create a new blueprint. If she wasn't well-mothered, she aspires for more, believing that nurturing *can* be learned, that she can grow and develop as a mother, literally on the job. Daunted, perhaps anxious, but also brave and determined, she resists the idea that nurturing is only inhaled at a critical developmental time, or that once missed, the deficiency cannot be undone. By the very act of giving birth, she renounces the notion that mothering is innate, fixed in the past.

New Mothers Need Affirmation

Most new mothers feel inept at times, unable at first to conquer all that is awkward, complicated, mystifying about caring for a newborn. A sympathetic mother tells her daughter that things will settle down, that she'll figure it out along the way, that mistakes are to be expected. Early on, women often see their mothers in their words and actions, in a process of identification. We all know the truism about turning into your mother. It's soothing, a form of affirmation of your future as a fellow capable mom, to know that she, an admirable mother, also felt like a complete idiot at the beginning.

For the woman who rejects her role model, this aspect of her new identity is more complex. She will need to master motherhood as an identity with intention and care, without being able to turn to her mother for the validation every new mother craves. She may find herself emulating and identifying with other caretakers. Some women get validation from their mothers-in-law, who may be the most supportive nurturers available, while others turn to sisters, neighbors, a nurse, fellow Lamaze students, or a lactation consultant.

Intuitively, it would seem that an unmothered mother would be the first to reject the myth of the perfect mother, to embrace the identity of being good enough. As long as she stays sober, for example, or notices when her child is feverish, she's surpassed her own upbringing. But fate conspires with culture for these mothers. Today's cultural mythology of Perfect Mothering hooks a vulnerable mother like Sharon by the extravagant promises that a person can undo her past by getting it exactly, perfectly, right. She is likely to be the mother most in need of ongoing affirmation.

Denise is a mother who intends to be unlike her own mom. She has found a community of mothers who validate her identity by agreement and encouragement. Her unexpected pregnancy at age twenty made being different from her mother a certainty at the outset, since her mother, a college professor, had her first child in her thirties, after getting her doctorate and launching her career. Denise intends to be a different kind of mother in every way she can think of, although she imagined that she, too, would be older when she had her first child.

Mothering as an identity is something that occupies a central role in her mental life. Denise had a rocky adolescence, which she remembers being unusually painful, in part due to bulimia. She describes the family picture one often finds in women with eating disorders: a picture-perfect family on the outside, with an inner emptiness that others don't perceive. Despite her mother's professional success in a mostly male world, at home Denise's father was a tyrant who made every decision. Denise notes that her mother wasn't terrible—she says twice in our interview that her mother didn't hit her or tell her she was ugly or bad—but she felt a pronounced lack of warmth. As an example, Denise mentions that she never had a single conversation with her mother about her first period—her mom wordlessly provided the sanitary pads, but Denise's information and support came entirely from her cousin.

Denise felt emotionally starved, unable to turn to her mother for nurturing. Barely out of adolescence now, she recalls the struggle for teenaged independence as being over before it began. She lacked the freedom she saw others having, citing how crushed she felt when she won a radio contest for backstage passes to see her very favorite band—a teenager's dream come true—and her father refused to even listen to her request to attend. Her mother "never" took her side, never challenged her "control freak" father's domination. Indeed, she mentions that her father was preoccupied with his wife's physical appearance, prescribing exercise for his slender wife, purchasing a wig that he wanted her to wear, "like she was a Barbie doll." Her disappointment in her mother centers on a lack of emotional sustenance, describing her as "incomplete," which she attributes to an excessive wifely devotion to pleasing an impossible-to-please man at the cost of not having emotional reserves for her children.

Denise describes herself as "a little nonmainstream," which is quite an understatement. She is by nature a caretaker and advocate for the underdog, dreaming of operating a no-kill animal shelter one day. Her walls are covered with photographs of animals and proclamations of peace. She became a vegetarian at age thirteen, a vegan by age seventeen. An advocate of holistic approaches, she rejects medical forms of birth control, and became pregnant when natural family planning (using temperature monitoring to detect ovulation) failed.

There's unplanned pregnancy and then there's sort of unplanned pregnancy. A month before she became pregnant, Denise mistakenly believed she had become pregnant. A college student, she'd been dating her boyfriend for less than a year. Her first response was panic, stating "it wasn't part of the plan." By the time she got her period, however, she was disappointed, having begun to adjust to the idea rather quickly. Not surprising, then, that when she actually got pregnant the next month, she was pleased. She soon married, because "it was the right thing to do."

Denise describes her lifestyle as "primitive," by which she means old-fashioned, retro. In bygone days, people married if pregnant, never considered divorce, baked their own bread, and delivered babies at home. This natural lifestyle pervades her mothering.

She consulted a lay midwife for her prenatal care, never considering a nurse midwife or obstetrician. She labored at home, attended by four lay midwives who massaged her back, delivering her baby in a pool of warm water. Now the mother of a fifteen-month-old, she intends to breast-feed until her son chooses to wean, even if that occurs years from now.

She is a proponent of a specific mothering style called "attachment parenting," an approach popularized by pediatrician William Sears, although she points out that she had a mental blueprint before she learned there was a movement of like-minded mothers. "Attachment parenting" is characterized by long-term breast-feeding with child-led weaning, co-sleeping (also described as a "family bed," although some, including Denise, place a crib next to the parental bed), and as much baby-holding as possible (sometimes called "baby-wearing"). Mainstream child-rearing practices such as letting a baby cry himself to sleep; reliance or even supplementation with formula; circumcision of boy babies; disposable diapers; the use of pacifiers, strollers, or swings to soothe babies (as opposed to holding or nursing); and popular mothering advice books including the *What to Expect* books and *Secrets of the Baby Whisperer* are anathema to proponents of attachment parenting. While some mothers who ascribe to attachment parenting work outside the home, most do not, in part because the role of the mother in comforting her child is central. Denise herself has not been away from her son for longer than three hours—in fifteen months.

Denise is succeeding in her effort to create her own identity as a mother. She is clear about her intent to be highly emotionally responsive, and she is. I interviewed her at home, where she lives in the back two rooms of her in-laws' modest rural home. Her son is a happy the-world-is-my-oyster toddler, and I see her repeatedly attend to him, seemingly effortlessly. Her style is remarkably gentle, and he is unusually secure in my presence. It occurs to me that this is the first toddler I've met who has not experienced being separated from his mother, and perhaps it simply doesn't occur to him that the arrival of a stranger could mean that Mommy is leaving. I am no threat to his comfort, and it shows.

I've had patients who nurse their children into kindergarten. Moms who nurse for years typically package this with beliefs that seem quaint, Amish-like: home schooling, natural fibers, highly traditional family roles. Many pay a significant economic price, because the mothers usually don't work, and it costs more money to buy organic produce and natural-fiber baby clothes. Discount stores don't carry the foods you'd feed your child, or the clothes you'd dress your baby in. Denise knows, for example, that if she was employed outside the home, they could afford their own place, but it's an easy decision for her to live with her in-laws in order to be with her baby all the time.

Absolutely no one in my circle of family and friends would even consider this approach to raising children.* Most people I know consider having a child sleep in your bed to be a somewhat shameful secret, best not mentioned to the pediatrician, and would call very devoted breast-feeders those who don't wean before a year. I also know that most mothers would feel defensive about the idea that their more conventionally reared children are somehow less optimally bonded, and some would see attachment parenting as an approach devised by right-wingers to keep women barefoot and pregnant.

I don't agree with the belief that this system of selfless devotion is necessary to raise emotionally secure children, and I hope that Denise is right in her assertion that this intense interdependency ultimately will allow her son, Noah, to master independence without anxiety, on his own timeline. I worry about the risk of maternal burnout, wonder how Noah will come to tolerate frustration, and can't imagine how he will cope with the siblings his parents plan to produce. Usually, I'm in the role of encouraging mothers to have

---

* In fact, a girlfriend who read an early draft of this book accused me of making up Denise's story, which she found unimaginable.

balance in finding their own time and space, and believe that excessive dedication to a child takes its toll on tired, guilty, depleted, and/or resentful mothers.

But I wouldn't dream of pushing my beliefs on Denise. This alternative lifestyle sustains her, because the single most important thing to her definition of being a good parent is to be a responsive, available, nurturing mother. In repudiating, on an hourly basis, the emotionally aloof childhood she experienced, Denise *is* taking care of herself. No one would describe her mothering as detached, and that is what matters most to her.

Her approach to creating a maternal identity radically different from her own mother's identity may be relatively easy for her, because she has a long history of marching to a different drummer. But Denise lives off a gravel road in rural Indiana, not in Boston, where she could attend one of four support groups for advocates of attachment parenting, or northern California, where there are twelve. No one in her extended family practices mothering like she does. Still, she has located role models for her kind of mothering, and has found a community to affirm her new identity. She entered motherhood with a room full of nurturing midwives who also believe that traditional, natural ways are best. And she has a network of Internet friends who share her views and support her struggles. The first of her peers to become a mother, Denise went through her pregnancy as a member of an Internet bulletin board of women with delivery dates close to hers. When she realized that she was the sole member of her pregnancy board who intended to stay home with her baby indefinitely, she ran a search for a new Web site, landing at a Christian mothers' site called gentlechristianmothering.com.* Here, as with her community of holistic healers, Denise finds validation and support for her created identity as a distinct type of mother.

---

* Not all attachment parenting is faith-based, but some proponents feel their approach is "God-given."

A person who wishes to mother very differently from the way her own mother did may feel overwhelmed by the enormous challenge. Denise, however, is not anxious; she's proud of herself, pleased with how she's doing. I believe that Denise's strategy works so well for her for several reasons. First, the way she conceptualizes the mothering identity is so black and white that it's easy for her to figure out how she's doing. There is no confusing gray space. Perhaps more importantly, she is as gentle with herself as she is with Noah in appraising how she's doing. She says, "I have high mothering standards," and yet she doesn't chase perfection. She doesn't feel perfect—she still struggles with binge eating at times, and fails in her goal of abstaining from wheat, which she feels upsets her son when it is transmitted in her breast milk. But since she is able to reassure herself on a daily basis that she is achieving her goal of not being like her mom, she feels good enough.

Denise is guided by an ideology that some would find rigidly dogmatic, if not cultlike.* In my opinion, the model is more like an evangelical or orthodox religion than it is a cult: a strong set of beliefs and values that are shared by a like-minded community. Her favored Web site, for example, discourages critical postings by those completely opposed to their practices, but invites participants who don't share all their views to feel free to join the bulletin board discussions. Still, they hope you come around to their way of seeing things, and they want to help mothers overcome the practical problems associated with the approach. I don't believe in one-style-fits-all mothering any more than I do one true religion, and I certainly wouldn't encourage the undernurtured to feel that they must adopt so stringent a code. I would, however, encourage any

---

* For more about the controversy regarding attachment parenting, see Amy Brill's piece in salon.com's "Mothers Who Think," and the letters to the editor that followed. Polar views are expressed in Peggy Robin's *When Breastfeeding Is Not an Option: A Reassuring Guide for Loving Parents,* and her vehemently opposed detractors, who defiantly use the domain name militantbreastfeedingcult.com.

mother who is consciously attempting to mother differently to find affirmation, as Denise has, however she defines "nurturing."

All new mothers need psychological affirmation. Affirmation is a process by which a person validates the worth, competence, effort, and goodness of the other. It says "you are not alone" and "what you are doing is okay." Affirmation must be experienced as authentic, and meaningful—it can't be platitudes or false reassurance, as Gretchen points out. Women who belong to the Web site Denise likes describe the affirmation they get there: "[This site] armed me with the confidence to follow my instincts when it comes to raising my son." "It's a wonderful place where I can go with my concerns and questions and know I will get love and understanding." An entirely different mother might find affirmation in knowing that she's not alone, as at www.imperfectparent.com, where one blogger notes, "When you've got the 3 a.m. postpartum weepies, every cell of your body aches, and you're trying to quiet a colicky, sadistic infant, the last thing you need to hear is that Cindy Crawford was back at yoga in one week." The message of these two very different parenting Web sites: we're here for you, and with you.

New Mothers Need Good Boundaries

"Boundary" is a psychological term used by modern psychotherapists. A boundary is an imaginary line that allows an individual to delineate him- or herself from others, and which defines appropriate interactions within relationships. Boundaries are popularly described as one's own "space," as in "stay out of my space." When boundaries are crossed inappropriately, we might say that someone has "stepped on my toes."

A mother with good boundaries may take counsel from others, but will not internalize advice as criticism or reproach. She recognizes that another person's opinion is not fact and she feels entitled to her own psychological space. She knows what she wants for herself, and respects the rights of others to make different choices or hold different beliefs. Healthy boundaries allow the individual to embrace what psychologist Carl Rogers called the "quiet pleasure in being oneself." They also help us define how we expect to be treated as unique individuals. Mothers with good boundaries naturally seek affirmation, but do not need constant approval to feed their self-esteem. In other words, they feel good when another mother says "me, too," but do not reproach themselves when she says "not me."

When boundaries are too permeable, mothers are susceptible to feeling shame or anxiety about difference, because you can always find someone who does things differently when it comes to parenting. When you take the baby out for a stroll in October, there may be someone who tells you that your baby is dressed too warmly; one block later another stranger suggests that your baby is cold. If you have poor boundaries, you might feel guilty when you hear that someone breast-fed her baby for six months, because you gave up after six days, or you might feel bad when you hear someone breast-fed her child until he began kindergarten, because you weaned your three-year-old. The individual with poor boundaries may frantically try to match her mothering with others, because she defines herself by the expectations of others. The mother with good boundaries is more likely to tell herself, "I did the best I could under my particular circumstances."

Boundary issues often emerge when people are assuming new identities. For example, students leaving for college the first time, or people taking on a new profession, often try on, imitate, practice, and ultimately modify for themselves what that new identity entails. New mothers are like medical students donning their white coats for the first time: excited, awkward, wanting to look like "real" doctors but afraid of the new responsibility. Even the slightly anxious new mother may feel self-doubt when her baby cries frantically in public, and it seems that every expert within a three-mile radius thinks she should feed/stop feeding/burp/change/jiggle/not jiggle/take the baby home for a nap or simply stop spoiling her two-month-old. The experienced mother, confident in her maternal identity, doesn't internalize the suggestions as worthy criticism, doesn't allow the comments to penetrate her boundary. But that same experienced mother may panic the first time she hears that someone's fourteen-year-old has already visited two college campuses, uncertain about what mothers of teens ought to do in order to be good moms.

Boundary issues pop up across the life cycle for all mothers; you can expect to encounter many opportunities to firm them up over the next two decades. The average mother who first responds with embarrassment when a stranger criticizes her baby's attire (and thereby her caretaking skills) will likely grow a thicker skin—she simply must. She exhibits adaptation to this aspect of forming the mothering identity by recognizing her own expertise and authority. Cecilia's advice about protecting your boundaries—"Don't give a shit about what people think"—is sometimes harder than it looks. When her baby was in the hospital, her mother-in-law criticized the way Jessica was swaddled. "She looks like she's squished in there." A baby nurse informed her, "That's what comforts her. It's how she was in the womb, and it makes her feel secure." That helped Cecilia feel more confident in rejecting the "old way" of doing things that her husband's mom was pushing. "The last thing you want is a confrontation over a newborn with your mother-in-law," but she felt encouraged to trust her own judgment, which was that tight swaddling was indeed best. "Sometimes I'll use my doctor as a line of defense," she says, citing the advice from family members she's rejected: sugar for baby hiccups, syrup or food in the formula for better sleep, juice at three months. Those giving well-intentioned suggestions are entitled to an explanation of why Cecilia isn't taking their advice, but she's doing it her way all the same.

The examples in the following table are the kinds of weak boundaries that can be seen in any mom, and do not signify the need for therapy. Rather, they are characteristic of the growing pains precipitated by this critical challenge—times when you feel uncomfortable, or perhaps wish you'd handled a situation differently. When there are weak boundaries because a mom is inexperienced or stressed (physically ill, worried about work issues, or at one of her first parent-teacher conferences, for example), they are normal, a place one visits from time to time. Lifelong struggles with boundaries are more commonly found among unmothered mothers, who may live with an impaired sense of self-determination.

> ### Examples of Healthy Mothering Boundaries
>
> 1. Meredith's pediatrician advises that she let her four-month-old baby cry for twenty minutes to help him learn to sleep through the night. After ten minutes, she can't stand it, and she decides to modify the schedule to a maximum of ten minutes.
>
> 2. Lynn, the mother of three, pooh-poohs her sister Roberta's decision to feed her ten-month-old organic baby foods, noting that her kids are perfectly healthy and *they* grew up on ordinary baby food. After dropping her baby at Lynn's for a few hours one day, Roberta is not pleased when her sister hands her her organic baby food jars, unopened. She announces that she bought some "regular" baby food at the store and, look, the baby is just fine. Roberta lets her sister know that while she recognizes that Lynn has a lot of experience with babies, this is her decision to make for her child. She tells her that she'd like to continue to leave her baby with Lynn from time to time, but she needs to know that Lynn is willing in the future to respect her parenting decisions. When Lynn agrees, she lets it go.

3. At Annie's son's parent-teacher conference, his third-grade teacher says that Jimmy is having some issues getting along with one of the boys in his class, and sometimes seems to pick on another child. Annie asks for advice on how they can work together to help Jimmy be his best self at school.

4. When Joy, of Japanese-American descent, tells her mother that her fourteen-year-old son, David, placed second in a junior high school math competition, her mother laughs and says, "Well, that's the Japanese in him. He sure can't claim he got that from his father's side." Joy points out that she believes that this is prejudiced, and that while her mother is entitled to her opinion, she expects her to keep her beliefs about David's Japanese and/or African-American heritage to herself. When her mother hangs up on her, Joy doesn't call her back until she apologizes.

Examples of Weakened Mothering Boundaries

1. Meredith is ashamed that she didn't follow the pediatrician's advice, and she lies to the doctor at the next checkup.

2. Roberta never says a word to Lynn, but she's so angry that she refuses Lynn's future offers to watch the baby, making excuses about the drive across town.

3. Annie immediately becomes defensive, noting that the other boy is probably starting it. She then attacks the teacher, saying that since Jimmy is an angel at home, she must be doing something wrong.

> 4. Joy boils inside, but cuts it short by saying, "Oh Mom, there is someone at the door . . . gotta run." She cries for hours. When she talks to her sister later, her sister encourages her to "tell Mom to cut it out." She states that she can't because Mom is Mom, and she can't help having "old country" beliefs.

Women with extremely permeable boundaries may struggle repeatedly with comparative mothering, because they have a lifelong tendency to feel inferior or defer too much to others. They are at risk of becoming maternal doormats, excessively dependent on approval or afraid to trust their own judgment. They may become mothers who, defining their self-worth in terms of their children, put too much pressure on their kids to succeed so that they themselves feel good enough as parents. While they aren't doomed to a life of misery, women with very weak boundaries will find mothering harder than it has to be unless they repair the infrastructure, which might be done through professional therapy, self-help (such as that found in books, support groups, and twelve-step organizations such as Adult Children of Alcoholics), spiritual growth, or magnificently supportive girlfriends.

Good boundaries make happy mothers. Denise's boundaries help her feel satisfied with the job she is doing. She is able to recognize the clear differences between herself and her mother, and as a result, she is not afraid of becoming like her. I have never met a woman who, in defining who she is as a mother, hasn't considered herself relative to her own. We do it before we have language to describe the process, beginning as toddlers when we imitate our mothers in our play (as Gretchen observes in Diantha). We do it as teenagers, when in our search to differentiate ourselves as individuals, we begin contemplating the complexity of the woman previously experienced in functional terms, what she does—or doesn't, can't, won't do—for us. We do it before we become mothers, while we are pregnant or preparing for adoption and, especially, during the first few months of motherhood. And we do it throughout the course of our mothering lives, asking ourselves, "How did I do compared to her?" as we work and rework motherhood's challenges. If you have a clear sense of a personal boundary, if you understand where you end and others begin, recognizing your mother in your words and actions is amusing, poignant, an endearing sign of generational continuity.

Hand in hand with seeing your mother as a separate person comes seeing your mother as a fallible human being. Some women feel a shift in their psychological alignment with their mothers during their first pregnancy. At birth, many women are like Cecilia, who experienced a burst of empathic identification, recognized that, as it must have been for her mother before her, this is the hardest thing she's ever done. For some, the criticism they feel about their mother's mistakes, however justified, is softened by an appreciation of the difficulty one only really grasps firsthand. Many new mothers have sudden insight into the ways in which they have it easier, or deeply recognize for the first time how hard it must have been for their moms: "I can't even imagine how she did this at age twenty," "My dad was stationed in Germany when I was born and I don't know how she survived," "How did women figure out what to do without the Internet?" or "I always knew that her dad died just after I was born, but I just didn't understand what that must have been like until now."

Mothers who have carried resentment toward their mothers may find that stepping into the shoes of adversity releases some negativity. Motherhood looks much easier to the child than it does to the mother, and some women are like Ellen, who says, "My mom was depressed a lot of the time I was a kid. I have so many memories of her lying on the couch, withdrawn, uninterested. She's better now, finally has medications that help her, but I never gave her problems much thought. When my baby was born, she came to help me during the first few days. Instead of seeing her as this incredibly incompetent mom, I was amazed at all she knew: how to give a newborn a bath, how to keep a sleepy baby awake during feeding, what to do with the umbilical cord. I really hadn't seen her like that, as someone capable, certainly not as someone more capable than I."

Boundaries for the Unmothered Mother

Before she became a single mother at age forty-one, Naomi was a highly accomplished professional. She found that becoming a mother increased her sense of outrage about the way she had been parented. Like Denise, she rejects her mother's model, but with even more vehemence. Unlike Denise, Naomi had a terrible mother. "Verbal abuse" is a term that is so overused as to have become diluted, but in Naomi's case verbal abuse is exactly what she experienced. Her narcissistic mother constantly tried to quiet her own insecurity by putting others down. She was relentlessly demeaning, competitive, jealous of her children's intellectual accomplishments, belittling her daughters from morning to night.

Naomi's first memories include her father's frequent admonishment "don't make your mother mad." This paternal response to angry, alcoholic, and/or abusive mothering is one I hear often. Children are already psychologically and cognitively inclined to blame themselves for family dysfunction, and this seals it. Their hope of having the craziness validated by a nonabusive, better-loved father is dashed, as he subtly shifts responsibility to them, suggesting that if they'd only be perfect children, mother would be kinder, better. Naomi also remembers a very early awareness that her goal was, simply, "get out of here," modeled by two sisters who fled the family home at the first opportunity.

Naomi hesitated to become a parent for years, because she was terrified that her child might not like her, just as she did not like her own mother. She dipped her toe in the mothering waters when she explored a foster parent training program for children who were HIV orphans, many of whom were also HIV positive. Subconsciously, Naomi was drawn to children who were so profoundly needy, so terribly difficult to place in the child welfare system, that she couldn't fail; better than nothing was a standard she felt able to meet. But in the course of the training program, she became more confident and, paradoxically, came to feel that she'd do best with an uncomplicated child with fewer overwhelming needs.

Artificial insemination of single mothers was gaining medical and social acceptance, and Naomi began to have friends who were pursuing this, including one partnered lesbian couple she knew who had a daughter just at the time Naomi conceived. Naomi hesitates to say that she also wanted to have a girl, because she is incredibly grateful for her son. Tentative mothers almost always want girls, because they seem less daunting. The woman who is conscious of how challenging doing mothering differently will be finds a like-me baby easier to imagine nurturing. In Naomi's case, she felt prepared to nurture a strong, confident girl. She was "not as clear" on how to raise a boy, and had more ideas about what kind of boy she would *not* wish to raise. She also knew that as a single mom with no brothers she'd have fewer male role models. In hindsight, she feels her worries were foolish, saying "it's not a matter of some abstract unborn male child, it's my son Josh, what *he* needs."

Naomi feels mothering as a single mother is different, harder. She's tired all the time. While her son is healthy, he has some significant differences that demand more than the usual child, and Naomi is the sole provider of the time, energy, and money that support Josh's private school and therapy aimed at his deficits. He is off the charts in advanced math skills, but delayed in acquiring social skills and sensorimotor integration. Naomi has a wonderful sense of humor, and she says, "I think it would be better for Josh if he could trade a couple of standard deviations from the norm in math for the ability to know how to join a game other kids are playing, but that's not how it turned out."

At the same time that Naomi carries all the parenting weight, being a single parent allows her to identify more with her father than with her mother. In her family, her dad was the nurturer, the one who got on the floor and played, who delighted in the academic successes that characterized her childhood. She was a "huge source of conflict" between her parents, because her self-centered mother was violently resentful of the attention her father gave her. Naomi knows that many single mothers who opted for artificial insemination in their late thirties and early forties felt a painful relinquishing of the dream of having a nurturing relationship between two adults who in turn share nurturing of a child. But she says she never imagined being with a partner as a coparent, even though she has had many intimate relationships. I believe that this is one way in which Naomi created an identity boundary from her mother: she established an exclusive parent-child relationship that would not ever be subject to jealousy, resentment, or interference by anyone else. She had confidence that she would not be the harsh mother she knew, but she couldn't count on anyone else to nurture her child unconditionally.

Naomi and one of her sisters have a pact: "Shoot me if I ever turn out like Mom." But unlike her sister, Naomi temporarily established the most rigid of boundaries with her mother: she cut off contact for almost two years. This came about after a visit by her parents, when Josh was three. Her mother announced, in Josh's presence, that he was spoiled and needed a father. She stated that getting married was the best thing Naomi could do for Josh. Needless to say, Naomi was emotionally devastated. Suggesting that Naomi needed to be married in order to have a happy child is just plain mean. It hit Naomi where she is most vulnerable, since she knows it's likely at some point Josh will want to be just like the other kids. But the worst part for her was that her mother's cruelty had touched Josh, who watched while his grandmother put them both down. Naomi said, "I cried for three weeks. Then I wrote a letter letting her know that I wasn't going to be in touch for a while, and I immediately felt better."

For a year, she had no contact with her mother. Then her father became ill, and for another year, they spoke every few months on the phone about his condition. Eventually, Naomi and her mother saw each other at a family bat mitzvah. When Naomi "went back," she felt that she had an internal boundary she hadn't had before, one that allowed her to deflect the verbal blows. She says, "I wasn't trapped anymore, I was detached. I could tolerate her; even feel a glimmer of compassion and tenderness toward her." She isn't entirely clear how she developed the emotional boundary as a result of the interruption in contact. In part, she saw a social worker for therapy for several years, which she credits for helping her internalize a deep sense that "my mother was just wrong about me, and about my son." I believe that in order to heal old wounds, she had to put a stop to the new ones, had to let the scar that would protect her from more pain grow without her mother picking at it. She came to feel whole in spite of her mother's lack of affirmation of her individuality, and it naturally followed that she was then able to feel whole even if her mother would never affirm her mothering. I also suspect that her mother, who hadn't previously experienced so solid a boundary, got the point.

Naomi feels that mothering itself has helped heal her childhood pain. She knows that what brought her to erect the brick wall that cut off her mother from herself was her son: "I did for him what I could never do for myself as a child. I kept him safe from her." She's grateful, because when the brick wall came down, she kept a firm boundary in its place, which allows her to be with her mother more peacefully than ever before. She also feels that watching her mother interact with Josh was enlightening. She remembers seeing her mother botching play with Josh when he was two, trying to engage him in her interests rather than joining in his. She said, "I realized she was completely unable to interact with a child on a child's terms, even when she wanted to. I thought, oh, so *that's* how I was parented." For Naomi, realizing that her mother could not engage her grandson softened Naomi's pain—there were things her mother did not do because she could not, rather than would not, do them.

Naomi's twinges of compassion for her mother emerge from her hard-won psychological boundary. By finally "getting" that her mother was wrong in her behavior toward and her beliefs about Naomi, she is free to look at her mother with objectivity. What is obvious to everyone else becomes obvious to her: how greatly her mother suffers being the way she is. Her mother's treatment of her is inexcusable and cannot be undone. But Naomi takes the first step in forgiveness, finding a new empathy that lets her acknowledge that her mother failed out of incompetence rather than spite. Being less angry, feeling less shamed in the presence of her mother, brings her a calmness that she has not previously known in that relationship. Detachment takes a lot less energy than rage, and detachment by its very nature allows her to see clearly that she is not destined to become her mother.

Grief and Forgiveness

Forgiveness is the benefit you get from doing the emotionally draining work of grieving the wounds of childhood; it's a state of grace that you've earned. Forgiveness is a hot topic in psychological circles these days, as growing research increasingly demonstrates the benefit to the forgiving party. An ancient Chinese proverb says that the person who seeks vengeance digs two graves, and the study of forgiveness supports its important role in emotional and physical well-being. Key healing components include the role of time in softening the hurt, which is never brushed aside or minimized—forgiveness is *not* forgetting.

Naomi's other sister refuses to discuss their upbringing. She claims to have put it behind her, which Naomi scoffs at as wishful thinking. Premature forgiveness is seductive, seems to offer a quick fix out of a lot of pain. "Get over it" is the mantra of the hurting adult who wishes to slam the door shut. But forgiveness can't happen through denial, won't really occur if the wronged party believes she has no right to her pain. Denied pain lingers, forgiven pain lessens its grip. Harvard psychiatrist and Pulitzer Prize–winning author Robert Coles, cochair with Archbishop Desmond Tutu of the Campaign for Forgiveness Research, notes, "If we don't somehow forgive, whatever it is that's ailing, troubling, angering, enraging or shaming us, or getting us in any way worked up, is going to live longer. . . ." My belief is that the denial of being poorly mothered is wishful thinking that interferes with the new mother's developing identity.

Conclusion

At the best of times, taking on the new identity of motherhood brings great fulfillment and joy. No question, there are countless Gerber baby moments. But pregnancy and new motherhood are also accompanied by losses for many. Other roles are crowded out, time, money, and independence evaporate, as does the sense that you know what you're doing. We're also told that "you'll feel so close to your mother," which is certainly true for some. For others, becoming a mother actually widens that gulf, increasing the sense of outrage at having been wronged, or activating conflict with a mother who criticizes or intrudes anew.

Part of the transformation in identity is rooted in one's sense of competence, as a new mother struggles to accept all that is new, difficult, and at times overwhelming. For mothers with a personal history of skills, talents, and prior accomplishments, which is to say most adult mothers, the very nature of new motherhood challenges the sense of a competent self. Unmothered mothers are especially challenged when it comes to feeling good about themselves as caretakers in the absence of a strong personal history of being nurtured.

Assuming a new identity is often a comparative process: How am I compared to other wives? What do other college students do? New tasks of any sort are stressful as one tries to incorporate the new, not-yet-mastered role into one's self-definition. Mothers naturally compare themselves to their own mothers, to images of mothering, and to real mothers they know. Coming to experience oneself as capable, able to meet the task requires relinquishing a fantasized model of perfect mothering. For some, this is easy. For others, a fear of sinking into the quicksand of the past or an inability to reject outrageous standards is a source of distress. Most mothers find peace when they embrace their individuality, know that there are many perfectly reasonable choices and ways to raise children, and seek affirmation to reinforce their own personal beliefs, choices, and expertise.

Signs of Poor Adaptation to Forging the Mothering Identity

1. Preoccupation with perceived strengths of other mothers.

2. Marked insecurity about being "fit for duty." This might appear in a straightforward manner, when a woman never trusts her own instincts, or can't weed through conflicting parenting advice to choose what best suits her and her child. It may be masked as overconfidence in the mother who, insisting she already knows everything, is overly sensitive to parenting suggestions, which she perceives as an attack.

3. Belief that one is destined to repeat mistakes made by one's mother.

4. Denial or minimization of the significance of a neglectful or abusive childhood in one's experience of motherhood.

Strategies for Successful Adaptation to Forging the Maternal Identity

1. Recognize that one's identity as a mother is not fixed. Remain aware of the truth that, good or bad, one's identity as a mother is not predetermined. Believe that you can grow and change as you need to, and that mothering can be learned even in the absence of a perfect role model.

2. Seek support and affirmation from worthy role models. If your mother can't be that person, seek out alternative models, who might include your father, a stepmother, a sister, an aunt, a friend, or others from your community. When seeking affirmation, try to connect with truthful, authentic women. Resist the urge to compare your insides with other mothers' outsides, and run from those who deny that parenting is challenging.

3. Clarify the rules and expectations for how your mother or other critical observers may treat you, becoming aware of the power of personal boundaries to diminish the impact of ongoing criticism by judgmental individuals.

4. Thoroughly and honestly grieve unmet nurturing needs, moving toward forgiveness of the mistakes made by one's mother. Be clear that forgiveness does not mean excusing, exonerating, or condoning failures.

2

Unloving Moments
The Second Key Challenge

> But, as my neighbors can tell you, I get mad at my kids. . . . I also say things I regret on occasion. I try to make sure I apologize, but I didn't stop being emotional or fallible when I gave birth.
> —Muffy Mead-Ferro, *Confessions of a Slacker Mom*

Unloving feelings arrive for all mothers just on the heels of motherhood. It's an early challenge, and one that reappears time and again.

Some mothers cannot acknowledge unloving feelings. Leslye is one such mother. She recalls a glorious pregnancy, her first, and felt that the birth experience she had under the care of her nurse-midwife was, all things considered, quite positive. She came for treatment of postpartum depression three months after delivery, about six weeks after she first began feeling down. She cries on and off all day, feels like a failure, and finds it difficult to make it through the day without calling her husband four or five times for support. When he gets home from work, it seems like he's been gone for weeks, and she hands him their baby and takes to bed the instant he's home. Not that she sleeps in bed—it's just a way to escape the mess she sees when she looks around the apartment. Although she and the baby are meticulously dressed, she tells me that most days she doesn't even get out of her pajamas. Leslye is an unlucky statistic, the one out of every four new mothers who develop postpartum depression.

Despite her obvious suffering, Leslye insists that motherhood is "the best thing in the world." She remembers the first six weeks with rose-colored glasses, claiming, "I have never been so happy in my life." Until the postpartum depression set in, she announces, "life was perfect." Leslye repudiates any feelings of anger and frustration before I so much as ask. For half of her maternal career, Leslye has been clinically depressed, yet she cannot voice how let down she feels.

Pediatrician and author T. Berry Brazelton notes that the normal mother's belief is that her infant is unusually cute. The corollary isn't true: it isn't normal for a mother to believe that she's unusually content. Indeed, only first-time mothers regularly make that claim. If an experienced postpartum mom, depressed or not, tells another experienced mom that she's never felt better, she'll likely be greeted with a snort.

It's important to distinguish whether Leslye's claim to bliss is preemptive, a gloss applied in response to a belief about what she is *supposed* to say. She is afraid of my judgment if she owns up to her distress about motherhood itself. Embarrassed by her postpartum depression, she is especially eager to make a good impression as a mother. But when I tell Leslye that I see that she is delighted by the birth of her baby, feels incredibly connected to him, I also say that mothers usually feel mixed at times, and that it might be scary to acknowledge the negative feelings that society tells mothers to keep to themselves. Pushed a bit, Leslye admits that she did feel discouraged, and sometimes demoralized, from the moment she got home from the hospital. She is relieved to relinquish her secret. I tell her that my own children periodically love to give me grief about the time I admitted on the *Oprah* show that while I hadn't personally experienced postpartum depression, I certainly know what it's like to want to throw your baby out the window. (Oops.)

When unloving feelings surface, it's usually when what the child needs or wants is much more than the mother can readily give, or when a mother's human patience is depleted. For me, these feelings first came when my babies acted like babies: waking after two hours, crying the inconsolable tears of colic or emerging teeth, fussing nonstop on a four-hour flight cross-country. They come when children act like children: demanding, whining, talking back, dumping shoes by the front door for the thousandth time. And when teenagers act like teenagers—offering withering looks of disdain, insisting that they're bulletproof, testing limits time and again—unloving thoughts are likely to rise, too. The mother who thought she'd never survive after her son left for college may find herself counting the days until spring break ends after he comes home drunk and vomits on her Oriental rug.

Almost always, new mothers are taken aback by their unloving thoughts. Childbirth education classes prepare you for the easiest part. Labor is trivial compared to the physical burden of caring for a newborn. Almost no mother is prepared for the overwhelming task of mothering an infant, and second- and third-timers often declare that they'd forgotten how hard it is. It *is* always harder than we imagined or remembered, more demanding than the most demanding profession, and I can personally compare it to being an intern in the ICU. The sheer brutality of caring for an infant, night after night of sleeplessness, the unquenchable demands of the helpless baby accounts for the shocking discrepancy between what we fantasized about maternal feelings and what the realities are. The highs are high, no doubt, but the lows can be very low.

The Price of Sustained Denial

Some mothers never admit to feeling anything shy of exhilaration. The new mother who, despite obvious evidence of exhaustion, maintains that she never has a negative thought about motherhood is stuck. It takes an enormous amount of energy to lie to yourself, and false cheerfulness is especially hard to maintain. As Shakespeare said, "The lady doth protest too much, methinks." No one protests as much as a mother who cannot tolerate her unloving thoughts. Alas, one price of the culture of Perfect Motherhood is the guilt we feel when we're only human.

Kathy is one mother who won't give up the mythology. She first sought treatment for panic disorder, after a successful pregnancy that followed a miscarriage by six months. Kathy had been relinquished for adoption by her biological mother. Her adoptive mother suffered from alcoholism, and in a sense, Kathy has two models of motherhood to reject. Like many children of alcoholics, Kathy is bound and determined to please, and has an overdeveloped sense of responsibility. She becomes defensive and noticeably more anxious when I try to elicit any ambivalence about motherhood, insisting that, if not for the panic attacks, she'd be on cloud nine. She says that after a miscarriage, any mother would be grateful to stay up all night with a baby, and besides, she made a deal with God to do everything right if she was graced with a healthy baby.

She may sustain the denial for a period of time. But she deprives herself of the support of others, because she can't stand to be with other new moms, whom she perceives as whining. Kathy also robs herself of an opportunity to develop a more reasonable standard for herself. Her denial says, "If I admit to unloving feelings, I might become like my biological mother who abandoned me, or my alcoholic mother who neglected me and screamed at me. The only way to avoid that is to be perfect." Medication for panic disorder may relieve the symptoms, but it won't address the anxiety brought on by denial, perfectionism, and impossible expectations. If she didn't insist on burying her head in the sand, she could give herself permission to create a perfectly reasonable model of acceptable mothering, one in which good and loving moms have unloving feelings, without acting on them or harming their children.

If Kathy remains stuck, she will be unable to acknowledge her irritation at her child when he throws a huge temper tantrum at the grocery store, gets into fights at the schoolyard, or slams a door in her face. If she doesn't make peace with her unloving thoughts, she can only maintain her denial by ignoring unacceptable behavior (see no evil, feel no evil), or by disavowing her own tendency to moments in which she erupts with excessive anger, a steam kettle left to boil too long. She may remain too-cheery-Mom, allowing her son to mistreat her over the years, the price she pays for denying natural annoyance. She may have the world's most spoiled child as a result of her inability to own up to her reaction to her child's unpleasantness. Or she may lash out, erratically, when her child fails to play the part of the world's most lovable child. Ironically, Kathy may become the mother who, in disclaiming unloving thoughts in an attempt to undo her past, fails her child when the fragile defense of denial shatters in an explosion of pent-up rage.

Denial is hard to sustain, and, more commonly, mothers know they have dark moments, but may feel isolated and ashamed of their thoughts. It's normal to feel guilty when you've just lost your cool and yelled. Yelling, per se, is not a sign of denial or abuse. Nor is a little guilt necessarily a bad thing. Guilt about maternal behavior that one regrets is a powerful motivator to change, to soften a tone of voice next time, to remember that Suzy needs a nap before a trip to the grocery store, to apologize when her child is old enough to understand "I'm sorry." Shame goes beyond guilt in that the mother condemns not her behavior or her unloving thoughts, but her very being. She feels defective, judges herself to be a bad mother, simply for what she thinks.

Sharing Unloving Thoughts

Because admitting to unloving feelings with just anyone is risky, it is natural for new mothers to turn to their own mothers as confidantes, for reassurance. Many women find just that. Vivian, for example, felt relieved when her mom confessed how completely revolted she, too, had been. She recalled how grossed out she was by Vivian's umbilical cord stump, and said that she never, ever found baby poop to be anything but disgusting. Vivian understood that she was saying, "I've been there."

Unfortunately, when a poorly mothered woman confides such feelings to her own mother, she is often emotionally slapped. My patients have been told: "You girls have it so easy nowadays. Disposable diapers, dads that help, you just think you can have it all." Or, "grow up," "buck up," and "quit whining—you wanted this baby." There is, "At least *you* can go back to work," "I told you not to marry him/have a baby now/breast-feed/go back to work/stay at home," etc., and "What made you think it would be easy?" The request for support, as so often happened in childhood, is met with disapproval, criticism, an absence of empathy.

While I'm tempted to add my own critical two cents ("Why on earth did you turn to *her* for sympathy?"), I also understand the ongoing urge to hope that a mother who has failed twenty thousand times before might come through this one crucial time. I, too, continue to be baffled by the tendency of critical or self-absorbed mothers to belittle their adult daughters' struggles with motherhood. What's in it for them? Sometimes it seems as if a narcissistic new grandmother is jealous of her daughter's attachment to her baby, and lashes out at the first opportunity. Or she may be defensive, knowing somewhere down deep that her daughter is trying to mother differently, which threatens her own self-esteem, her version of how *she* mothered. Often, it seems part of a global inability to put herself in her daughter's shoes, to have any idea about how to respond to distress lovingly. She doesn't support her daughter as she struggles with motherhood because she cannot.

Mothers may meet with greater success when they turn to more reliable role models. A common prescription I give: join a new-mothers' group. Whether it's a support group for women with postpartum depression, a moms-newly-at-home group, a brown-bag-lunch group for employed mothers, or even a book group of women who mostly happen to be mothers, new mothers are often amazed at the confessions of other women, especially those who don't live in fear of being judged, for whom shame is not an ever-lurking shadow. The mom who arrives at a book group and declares "Thank God for a break—Sarah was really on my nerves today!" or the new mother who jokes about how much her baby would be worth on the black market, is a great source of support. And it only takes one to give permission for everyone in the room to acknowledge their maternal stress.

Another source of validation or support can be found in one's husband. He may also admit to being at the end of his rope when all three are up for a two a.m. feeding. Sometimes a husband models the use of humor, joking about his own escape fantasies, suggesting that they leave the baby at home and go find an all-night bowling alley. But it can also go the other way. A defensive mother may be irritated, horrified by the casual way in which he mentions feelings she is trying to suppress. Or she may see his attempts at humor as juvenile, bad-boy goofing off that increases her anxiety that neither one of them is up to parenthood.

Some tentative mothers find encouragement on the Internet. Parenting Web sites include multiple postings in which mothers who are too afraid to ask someone they know about their unloving feelings are reassured by anonymous strangers. For example, a mother on one site headed her posting "Please tell me this gets better." She went on to say that at two weeks postpartum, she told her husband that she doesn't think she can do it anymore, that she is "very frustrated." Within a week, she received fourteen comforting replies, including "it gets better!," "I suffered also," "don't lose heart," "it really does improve," "hang in there," and "this too shall pass." Strangers told her, in many ways, we've been there, we get it. Comments included, "no one prepares you for the reality of a newborn. All you hear is how sweet they are, how precious, how miraculous." Another noted how isolated she felt in her frustration. One Internet buddy confessed that a few months prior to the posting, she, too, fantasized about leaving the baby with her husband with a farewell note, and offers a vision of better days ahead: "I can't believe it now [that the feelings diminished]." She noted: "You have an entire board of parents here to help you."

The anonymity of the Internet allows new mothers to take the risk of acknowledging painful feelings that might not find a voice in any other situation. This e-community extends well beyond the baby years. Between postings laden with practical advice about sleeping, eating, fevers, marriage issues, and school problems, mothers posting on boards for older children occasionally drop comments about frustration, anger, annoyance, but far less often than do new mothers. It's as if they are no longer so surprised, or perhaps it reflects the relative ease of the elementary-school-aged child. Parents' message boards begin to pick up steam again with teen-parent postings, in which messages say "Will I make it until she's 18?" or note, "I can't stand to be with her and it makes me feel like a bad mother." Here, too, mothers tell one another, "You aren't alone."

Admit It, It's Kind of Funny

Finding humor in the midst of unloving thoughts provides great solace. As psychoanalyst Glen O. Gabbard states, humor is "the ability to poke fun at yourself and the situation you're in—an invaluable part of mental health." Motherhood jokes offer the promise of letting go of the idealization of how a mother should always feel. When Phyllis Diller said, "Always be nice to your children because they are the ones who will choose your rest home," she poked fun at the idea that a mother *could* always be sweet to her children, or would absent consequences. Mother humor has gotten edgier of late. Anne Lamott, in discussing the mothers who never acknowledge an unloving thought in the "Mothers Who Think" section of salon.com, writes, "A few mothers seem happy with their children all the time, as if they're sailing through motherhood entranced. However, up close and personal, you find that these moms tend to have tiny little unresolved issues: They exercise three hours a day or check their husband's pockets every night looking for motel receipts."

Humor falls into what psychoanalysts call high-level defense mechanisms. These are healthy ways to remain calm and to continue to like yourself in the face of ideas or impulses that you find unacceptable or even abhorrent. When Dawn is frustrated with her colicky baby, she decides, consciously, to put it out of her mind. She blasts her old Rolling Stones music, and suppresses the anger. Unlike unhealthy denial, Dawn lets her feelings in, pronounces them unwanted, and releases their hold, distracting herself. Dawn also combines humor with altruism, sometimes writing a note to herself that she places on the mirror—"You are a saint"—other times reciting the Lord's Prayer until she regroups. Later, she might also use sublimation, redirection to a more acceptable outlet. When she gets furious at her toddler, she punches a pile of pillows until she feels better.

When to Get Help

There is one psychiatric disorder in which the very problem is an extreme flooding of unloving thoughts—obsessive compulsive disorder (OCD). Pregnancy and childbirth are the most common triggers for OCD in women, which can affect adequately and inadequately nurtured mothers alike. Postpartum obsessive compulsive disorder is characterized by repeated, horrifying thoughts, almost always about the new baby. Images of dropping an infant down a flight of stairs, accidentally poking the baby in the eye with a needle while sewing, cutting the baby with a kitchen knife, putting the baby in the microwave, and/or pushing the stroller into traffic are repeated symptoms of this bizarre illness. Panic attacks and depression soon follow, and mothers with postpartum OCD are usually afraid to be alone with their infants.

Like Heidi, whose illness began at three weeks postpartum, women with postpartum OCD are aware that these images are a product of their own mind. They are experienced as senseless, unwanted, perturbing, recognized as one's own thoughts, in contrast to the bizarre thoughts of a psychotic mother who may experience infanticidal ideas. Though Heidi swore that she would never harm her child (and infanticide is, in fact, never caused by postpartum OCD), she became so frightened of her thoughts that she hired a nanny to be around "just in case." OCD is a brain illness characterized by an overactive imagination, an inability to turn off a worry loop. It is easy to imagine why nature would make new mothers more vigilant to potential dangers, but in this illness, the vigilance goes so far as to include oneself as an imaginary threat. Heidi was unable to reassure herself that she wouldn't do something terrible, because the very nature of the grotesque images seemed to prove her unfitness for motherhood.

Heidi, as some OCD patients describe, came from a particular type of unmothering: suffocating anxiety. Although one in fifty people in the general population has OCD, one in ten children of a parent with OCD will develop OCD, a fivefold greater risk, due to the strong hereditary nature of the disorder. Heidi's mother may herself have suffered from OCD, but she won't discuss it with her daughter. One cannot make a psychiatric diagnosis of a person not in the room, but Heidi describes many features of her upbringing that strongly suggest that her mother suffered from OCD, too.

Heidi recalls a vigilance for safety that went well beyond the ordinary. She wore sweaters in June, sunscreen in December. She was made to take private driving lessons in addition to the school driver's education, and even then could not drive unaccompanied by a parent for a year after she got her license. She was not allowed to go on school field trips because the buses had no seat belts, couldn't play in the backyard without supervision at any age, was not permitted to ice-skate because she might hurt herself, and couldn't date until she went to college. She remembers her mother taking her to the emergency room for minor scratches and slight headaches, and learned to hide any symptoms of a cold that might trigger her mother's anxious hovering.

When Heidi experienced her first symptom of postpartum OCD, she was overwhelmed with anxiety. Heidi lives in a high-rise apartment building in Joliet, Illinois. Sitting on her balcony, she suddenly had an image of dropping the baby to the ground, and she rushed herself and her baby inside. She insisted that her husband return home from work that instant, although, at first, she refused to tell him of her symptoms. The images developed with a raging force, and soon she was having panic attacks several times a day. She would not be alone with her infant, and brought all of her knives to the basement storage locker.

Heidi knew that she was mothered with crippling anxiety. She had promised herself that she would raise her children to believe that the world was a safe place, to mother with conventional precautions while conveying a sense of calm security and courage to her children. The horrifying images of OCD are highly distressing to any new mother, but Heidi was devastated by her inability to mother without anxiety, so quickly after childbirth. She feared that she would never be able to do it differently.

Many women with postpartum OCD hide their symptoms from everyone, including their doctors. Fortunately, those who only acknowledge panic attacks or postpartum depression usually get better with the typical medications prescribed for these conditions: serotonin enhancing antidepressants. Unfortunately, those who hide such extremes of unloving thoughts never learn that they have a diagnosable condition, an illness reproductively triggered that has no basis in their competency as mothers.

When a woman has postpartum OCD, she usually will not believe that she is a safe mother until her medication kicks in. Because Heidi, like other new mothers, had normal unloving thoughts in moments of fatigue, she felt punished by the illness, as if she brought it on by wishing the damned baby would sleep at night.

The impact of serotonin takes weeks, sometimes even a few months, to act. In the meantime, the reassurance of a therapist, a woman in a postpartum group who has recovered, or a personal narrative posted on a Web site, may help her believe that she will recover. Heidi's baby accompanied her to my office, and I was never surprised by the fact that the baby was impeccably dressed, content. I observed Heidi respond quickly and appropriately to her infant, showing the unique knowledge a mom has about which cry means "hungry" and which means "wet." My confidence in her mothering provided mere transitory relief. Only when Heidi's symptoms responded to medication was she able to feel completely comfortable being alone with her infant.

Missteps

Unkind thoughts are distressing; unkind actions can be devastating to developing maternal self-esteem. One of the worst moments for many mothers is losing control of unloving feelings. *All mothers lose their temper at some point.* Loud, angry reprimands with harsh words more or less come out of most every mother's mouth from time to time, including my own. It is difficult to explain to a nonparent quite how enraging certain repetitive behaviors can be. Until you've been there, it's hard to imagine how easy it is to lose one's cool when a preschooler repeatedly darts into intersections, a child simply will not stay in her bed at night, siblings bicker in the backseat on every road trip, a preteen will not get out of the bathroom during the morning rush, or a teenager baits his younger brother for sport. You, however, know.

Words that go too far include hateful words, regular outbursts, words that would shock you if you heard another mother utter them, words that cause a child to cringe or cry. It's the difference between a child who may think "Mom is so mad at me" and "Mom hates me." It's the difference between yelling at a teenager caught playing Nintendo instead of reading Shakespeare, with the words "Fine, don't study, see if I care. I've been to college and I don't give a damn if you end up flipping burgers," and "You lazy asshole. I'm calling the principal tomorrow to get you moved to Special Ed."

An even more frightening moment for many is an unforeseen spanking done in a moment of anger. You will be hard-pressed to find any parenting expert who endorses spanking. The American Medical Association, American Academy of Pediatrics, and the major professional organizations of psychiatrists, psychologists, social workers, and elementary school principals—even Ann Landers—all oppose spanking as a means of discipline. I vehemently oppose spanking, and yet I've done it once, in the midst of the terrible twos.

I'm not alone. Statistics suggest that as many as 90 percent of parents have spanked a child. We don't know how many of those have swatted a child's well-padded bottom once or twice, in a moment of dys-control (what the American Academy of Pediatrics terms a "spontaneous spanking"), versus the number who practice regular, hard, punitive spanking as a means of child-rearing. At least once or twice a year I get a panicked call from a mother who has, to her horror, smacked her child's hand or bottom. An isolated instance of unforeseen, personally unacceptable spanking lurks in the dark closet of many a capable mother.

Renee is one such panicked mom. Orphaned as an infant and raised by a single, alcoholic, manic-depressive aunt who refused medications, she's a true survivor of unmothering. She is extremely conscious about her mothering: she reads three parents' magazines each month, has a shelf of books on raising kids, attends parenting workshops at her local community center, carefully observes mother-child interactions at the playground. Because she knows she grew up without a role model, she is a voracious consumer of information, determined to provide a nurturing environment for her sons. Her background makes it especially hard for her to fall short of perfection.

One of her five-year-old twins, Michael, loves playdates. He is so eager to play at someone else's house that Renee's feelings are sometimes hurt when he seems disappointed to be stuck at home with her and his twin brother, Madison. Michael is a good host when friends come to his house to play; he shares well. But lately, Michael is almost impossible to extricate from a playdate elsewhere. He runs and hides when she arrives to pick him up, pretends that he can't hear her calling him, won't cooperate with putting on his shoes and jacket. Sometimes she's bribed him with a promised trip to the ice-cream store just to get it over with, even though she knows darn well that she shouldn't. On the day she spanked him, Michael was especially unpleasant, and Renee was embarrassed in front of the other mom. He stuck out his tongue and called her a bitch, a term she knows he doesn't understand and was trying out for the first time. Without thinking, she grabbed him, yanked him toward her, and smacked him on his rear end, once. He looked astonished, and quietly got himself ready to leave.

Renee's swat was not hard enough to make Michael cry, but *she* feels like crying. I run through my checklist: Did she hit him in the face? Punch him in the gut, draw blood, make a bruise or mark? Did she grab something with which to hit him? Her nos reassure us both. She hasn't abused Michael, but she did something she swore she'd never do, spank her child.

She wants to know what to do, what to say to Michael. I encouraged her to apologize, tell him it was a mistake to lose control, and let him know that they will sit down later to talk about the behavior that got Mommy so mad. She understands: "Just like when I tell him to 'use his words' when he's mad on the playground, I'll tell him that Mom is also supposed to use words when she feels like hitting." Our next sessions focused on behavior modification strategies to manage

Michael's refusal to end a playdate, including developing natural consequences to his misbehavior and applying them consistently.

Judge Yourself Kindly

Many a mother has found herself too angry to feel sympathy for children who have been hurt by their own disobedient behavior. When Linda lost her temper at her daughter Ashley, she did not spank or hit her. Still, her angry outburst shamed her deeply. Linda was in her kitchen, preparing dinner, looking out over the counter while Ashley played in the family room. For what seemed like the hundredth time that day, Linda told Ashley to stop jumping off the couch. She warned her repeatedly that she was too close to the coffee table, and might hurt herself.

Linda was as busy as any other mother making dinner after a long workday. The phone was ringing and the dog was barking at the back door for no reason. In between washing lettuce and stirring pots on the stove, Linda was sorting mail and looking through the preschool papers sent home in Ashley's backpack. She was distracted, but she was watching her daughter. Still, it happened: Ashley took a dive off the couch, landing her chin right on the corner of the table. As her mouth slammed shut, she bit her lip, and blood flowed. The cut wasn't serious, but it was messy and frightening. Ashley began sobbing hysterically.

Linda did what many mothers would do in a moment of frustration: she lost her cool. She already had ten things to do, and now she had to stop for a perfectly avoidable accident. She scolded Ashley, "I told you over and over again not to jump off the couch by the table! Are you surprised that you hurt yourself? Do you think you might want to listen to Mommy next time?" Then she said something she really wanted to take back: "Stop crying this second if you want me to help you." No surprise, Ashley's sobs escalated, and suddenly Linda saw herself through Ashley's eyes. Ashley was scared and hurt, and she needed her mom to soothe her. As if a switch clicked on, Linda calmed down and went to help Ashley regroup.

Linda was mortified, and she kept replaying the scene in her mind. She couldn't put her angry response in perspective: failing to calm her daughter, even for a moment, felt as if she had caused the injury herself. Ashley *should* have heeded her mother's advice, but, like all children, she learns from experience. It is normal for children to disregard helpful information, to acquire repeated bumps and bruises as they tend to think themselves invincible. And it is normal for mothers to vent their frustration, particularly when feeling mad, scared, or guilty in the face of an avoidable minor injury.

I ask Linda to think back on times when she's observed mothers get angry when a child is scared or hurt. She does so easily: last week, a neighbor's two-year-old suddenly darted into the street, and was almost hit by a car that wasn't even going fast. The mother's first response was to scream at her toddler, who didn't even know what he'd done wrong. Or the time at the grocery store when she saw a child unfasten the safety belt and start climbing out of the cart, and the mother lost her temper as the child teetered on the edge. And the mom who yelled before soothing the child who got smacked at the playground when he walked too close to another child on the swing set. I ask her to consider how often this happens in private, given how frequently we see it in public. And I ask her to consider whether these mothers' angry outbursts may actually help impress safer behavior on their children.

Linda realizes that she's done it again: she's expected perfection for herself. While her outburst is embarrassing to her, most children survive repeated bouts of this maternal version of "I told you so." She articulates her goal for next time: first soothe, help her child get to a place of emotional calmness, which would actually allow her to take something away from the experience, and gently review what Ashley herself has learned from this incident. I articulate my goal: judge maternal missteps gently, too.

Conclusion

Let's face it: motherhood can be very disappointing. When an emotionally resilient woman realizes that much of what she thought new motherhood would be like was a preposterous myth, she typically lowers her expectations. Her self-esteem allows her to accurately locate the problem: the lies she was told by culture, the hardship of the situation. If she is lucky, the mother she admires most, her own, confesses how hard it was for her, too. She can forgive herself for the fleeting nasty thoughts she has, the moment in which she wants to put her screaming baby outside in the hallway, the brief fantasy she has of running off to Tahiti with the pizza delivery boy. When she feels closer to losing it than she would ever have believed possible with someone so adorable, so innocent, so loved, she is gentle in her self-assessment. She will use these same coping skills when her children periodically get on her nerves, understanding that her ambivalence is a normal response to a trying event, not a sign of personal inadequacy.

The filter of the past amplifies the secondary distress that poorly mothered mothers experience when they feel or act angry, frustrated, annoyed. It makes it more difficult to dismiss these moments as understandable human lapses, fundamentally "not me," and therefore of no significant threat to maternal self-esteem. The poorly nurtured mother is more likely to blame herself, exaggerating the mythical powers of the saintly mother. Chasing perfection, she regularly fails to live up to her expectations for how she *should* feel.

Signs of Poor Adaptation to Unloving Moments

1. Inability to acknowledge unloving moments.

2. Belief that unloving thoughts make one a bad mother.

3. Frequent verbal outbursts that result in shame in mother or child.

4. Regular spanking or other impulsive physical punishment; any punishment that causes physical suffering or injury to a child.

Strategies for Successful Adaptation

1. Recognize that unloving thoughts are to be expected, and that they do not usually lead to unloving actions. Establish reasonable expectations for oneself, and grade yourself on a curve.

2. Confide unloving thoughts with caution, choosing your audience carefully. If you encounter superiority, criticism, or outrage upon revealing unloving thoughts, disengage from the conversation. If you find validation and constructive support, cultivate the relationship.

3. Employ healthy coping mechanisms, including humor. Consider whether unloving thoughts indicate a need for more self-nurture or alone time, and make it happen.

4. Use remorse pro-actively rather than self-punitively. Consider episodes of dys-control as data that indicate a need for a new course of action, rather than as evidence of defective mothering.

3

Honoring the Father
The Third Key Challenge

Mothers need fathers more than babies need fathers.
—Ian Sansom, *The Truth About Babies*

Denise, the mother in Chapter 1 who practices "attachment parenting," is at high risk for a difficult marital adjustment. For starters, since she rejects her parents' formula of dominant husband-father/submissive wife-mother, she has no role model to emulate. And because she and Terry married when she was pregnant, they went straight from the honeymoon to the chaos of a new baby, with no time to build a foundation for getting through tough times as a couple. Furthermore, Denise's consuming style of mothering leaves even less time and energy for Terry than the usual mom has. In fact, she has spent only three hours alone with her husband since their son was born.

When I ask if he feels left out at times, I expect her answer. "Of course—he's jealous. I can't be an attentive mother and an attentive wife at the same time. I can only focus on one person. I can multitask a lot of things, but not attention; it doesn't work that way." Even the baby seems to put him last. When Noah is upset in any way—hungry, hurt, sick, tired—he only wants Denise, rejecting his father as an inferior substitute.

Babies don't, of course, worry about the feelings of the rejected parent: they are the ultimate narcissists, demanding the preferred primary caretaker, who is usually the mother. It's often euphoric to be on the receiving end of such powerful love—how could anyone resist basking in the glow? Adoration by one's baby is pretty darn good if you've been extremely well mothered. Unmothered mothers, however, can be so overwhelmed by the worship they see in their baby's eyes that nothing, or no one, else matters. For some, it's the first experience of unconditional love.

It's as normal for a mother to savor this love as it is for a dad to feel pushed to the side by it. Still, some women are annoyed when their husbands complain about feeling left out, quick to accuse them of immaturity. In contrast, Denise handles her husband's feelings with grace. It's good to be queen, and she knows it. She acknowledges that the bond she shares with Noah makes her husband feel rejected at times, and she imagines how she might feel in his place. She tells him, "It is just that the baby has learned where his comfort is, knows what will make him feel better," which she attributes to breast-feeding. She reassures her husband, "It won't always be like this, it will get better." Denise is quick to notice, and praise, how Terry and their son play together "in their own way."

Denise realizes that her husband is entitled to expect *some* attention, even though often she'll need to attend to the baby first. She says, "I have to catch myself and remember that I'm not my husband's mother, and I'm not my baby's wife." In part, this means that she feels he has a right to expect an ongoing sexual relationship, and that he naturally misses the carefree days before the baby was born. She doesn't begrudge his unchanged sex drive, as some new mothers do when they notice a postpartum drop in their own libidos. Neither does she expect that she can be Superwoman. Because she accepts the impossibility of always being the wife she was and the mother she wants to be, sexually and otherwise, she isn't defensive, doesn't counterattack when her husband grumbles or tries to initiate lovemaking.

It's How You Fight, Not What You Fight Over

There is no such thing as a perfect marriage, especially after children arrive. Studies consistently indicate that marital satisfaction goes down in the first year after the birth of a baby, and most new parents find themselves arguing more than usual. It isn't surprising that tired and cranky people are cranky with one another. The key is *how* they argue, including whether it's "clean" fighting, and how rapidly conflict escalates. Aside from the stress of a new baby, it is a simple fact of life that any two individuals will not always agree on everything from what to have for dinner that night to how to handle curfew for a teenaged driver. Two parents, be they blissfully married or bitterly divorced, will not escape parenthood without needing to accommodate each other.

Couples like Denise and Terry, who tolerate differences between the partners, are said to be "well differentiated." They don't require one hundred percent endorsement of their interests, beliefs, hobbies, and preferences. Their operating principle is separate but equal, and they accept difference as a given. These couples usually have less conflict, because they don't start with the premise that happy couples always see eye to eye, and they are less likely to believe that the other partner is responsible for their happiness.

When differentiated couples argue, they are quicker to realize that both members are struggling, more able to use humor to detach themselves from a battle over, for example, which parent is more tired, or how often other new parents Do It. They don't mistake fusion for intimacy or commitment, and thus don't embrace conflict with a demand that a good spouse quit thinking the way he or she thinks, quit being the way he or she is. Instead, they look for a way to accommodate the difference, assuming that compromise is a natural part of marriage between individuals. Denise and Terry, for example, have compromised about sex. She doesn't always say yes to lovemaking, but she says yes more than her body signals. He doesn't pout, label her "frigid," or resent her passionate mothering, and she doesn't label him self-centered or insensitive.

Denise and Terry are negotiating the new family construction with the strengths seen in adaptive couples. She doesn't pull back because he is unhappy at times, and she tolerates his disappointment without becoming defensive or judgmental. She tells me that he does the same. The couple has what family therapist Murray Bowen, M.D., called "a positive emotional climate." They remain optimistic that things will eventually be better, and don't dwell on the negative or nurse wounds. They have a strong sense of loyalty that the other is doing the best he or she can under the circumstances.

New mothers deescalate parental conflict when they:

1. Accentuate the positive.

"I know we argue a lot lately, but you have to admit, this is one terrific baby." (Or, "I'm pretty sure things will settle down when we aren't both so tired all the time.")

2. Provide emotional strokes.

"You are a terrific dad" (or partner/lover/provider/cook/thank-you-note writer/grocery shopper/baby mattress).

3. Find common ground.

"I know there are things about the old days that we both miss." (Or, "Sometimes I talk like I'm the only one working so hard, but I really do know how tough it is for you, too.")

> 4. Screen their comments.
>
> Withstand the impulse to insist that your husband do child-rearing tasks exactly the way you do. If he isn't drowning the baby, let him bathe her as he sees fit, for example.
>
> 5. Avoid contempt.
>
> "Can I hold the baby for a minute longer while you wash up?" is much more peaceful than "What kind of idiot would pick up a baby when he's filthy?"
>
> 6. Avoid labeling.
>
> "You are so clueless" is far more likely to escalate to an argument than "Would you be okay with me showing you a way I think works well?"
>
> 7. Acknowledge his concern.
>
> "I know I never seem to want sex these days, but I know that's true for a lot of new moms. Maybe instead of having sex at night when I'm so tired, we could try to make love on Saturday afternoon during nap time" is more successful than "New moms never want to have sex, and most grown-up husbands just deal with it."

In contrast, Diane is annoyed by her husband Mike's sexual overtures. Since her baby was born seven months ago, she hasn't "ever thought once about having sex." She feels entitled to a sexless marriage, at least for now, and finds her husband's overtures irritating. If she doesn't want sex, he should respect that and leave her alone. She is bothered by "the pressure," and thinks he's selfish to ask her to make love when she's tired all the time. "When I give in, he is nicer than usual for a few days, which really pisses me off. Why does it take sex to make him sit down and talk with me? He's become the biggest baby. I want him to grow up already. No one I know has a husband this selfish." At some level, Diane believes that if Mike really loved her, he'd sacrifice his desire for her.

Undifferentiated couples, such as Diane and Mike, expect conformity. They tolerate difference poorly, pushing for emotional fusion, a shared inner world. When differences emerge, undifferentiated couples often become highly reactive, turning to anger, distance (the "silent treatment"), and/or entrenchment at the battle line. The conflict is not experienced as "ours," but rather *"your problem."* When couples fight nonproductively, each member seeks to be judged right, rarely remaining calm enough to think dispassionately about the issue. The undifferentiated couple is very vulnerable when experiencing the stress of a new baby, with partners regularly fighting over who is working harder, suffering more, getting less. The absence of a sense of common ground is a big red flag for poor marital adjustment to new parenthood.

Diane doesn't feel sexual, and she believes that a "good" husband shouldn't either. She can't tolerate differentiation at this point, believing that spouses should think and feel alike. Since it's important for her to feel that she's being a good wife, she demands a solution that minimizes her own buried guilt: *he* has to change because he has a problem. If he wants sex a lot more often than she does, he's either selfish, or a sex maniac. From her husband's point of view, it's as if she gave birth and then suddenly changed religions or political parties, demanding that he do so, too, in order to be judged a good spouse.

Chances are Mike is also responding in an undifferentiated manner, labeling her lack of sex drive as pathological, maybe even demanding that things be exactly as they were in their sex life (in an abusive marriage, a new father may even force his wife to have sex). He may even criticize her devotion to the baby, which only makes matters worse. If Diane conforms to Mike's sexual expectations, he's warm and friendly, but he abandons her emotionally when she won't be bullied or guilt-tripped into having sex. When members of a couple can't tolerate and respect each other's different sex drive, labels, conflict, and hostility (sometimes expressed as doors slamming, pouting, withdrawal, forgetting to pick up diapers, staying late at the office) emerge. The mismatched libidos aren't experienced as a couple problem, but rather each feels the other is the one with the problem.

Sexual intimacy is the one thing a mother can't get from her baby, and that may be why it's so important to new fathers. It may reassure him that he has something important, other than a paycheck, to give to her. Many new fathers are more than willing to overlook the mother's preoccupation with the baby, to take an emotional backseat for a while, and to step into the role of major or sole provider with pleasure, as long as the sexual connection remains somewhat intact.*

Father's Special Importance

In families where mothers do most of the early caretaking, optimally the father also has a special role that confirms his emotional worth in the new family.† Sometimes time itself promotes marital harmony as the mother-baby cocoon opens to include the father, often as the playmate of choice for his child. Somewhere around the first twelve to eighteen months of age, the baby begins to walk, literally or figuratively taking the first steps away from the mother, toward Daddy. Fathers typically have a unique role with babies, as the only adult trusted enough to throw the giggling child in the air, play vigorous games, chase the toddler at the beach. This is what Denise means when she describes what is special about Terry's relationship with their fifteen-month-old son: their play. A newborn has no need for play, but toddlers thrive on it. As the baby's need

---

* One in ten couples have not resumed lovemaking by the time their child is one, suggesting that many new parents lack the emotional connection that sexual intimacy provides.
† U.S. Census data for 2003 indicate that compared to 6 million stay-at-home mothers, there were 100,000 stay-at-home fathers. Even when both parents work, sociologists find significant gender disparity in child-care responsibilities between most spouses.

for socialization and play become stronger, the father's value and importance increases, and his sense of belonging in the threesome increases. At the same time, ideally the mother willingly relinquishes the exclusive romance she has with her baby, further stabilizing the threesome.

The birth of subsequent children, while logistically more challenging, is often easier on the parental relationship. The father has a crucial role: helping the older child adjust to the mother's preoccupation with the new baby. When his bond with the firstborn is strong, his role in the family is validated. Knowing that the exclusive mother-baby twosome will eventually be replaced by a rebalanced set of attachments and responsibilities cushions the transition next time around. With less anxiety about what the future holds, even poorly differentiated couples are generally less alarmed by discord.

Regardless of how they managed the first baby, mothers will revisit the challenge of balancing mothering with marriage after subsequent babies. Hindsight may heal buried wounds, as Jenny, who has recently had her third baby, notes: "You wonder what you got so upset about before. It's just so predictable that it looks like you're on the verge of divorce, then, poof, everything settles down." She describes that this time around, they sometimes laugh when they catch themselves fighting over the same old issues: whether she's the only person who ever changes the diapers, if he is staying late at work because it's a drag to come home, if she will ever ask him how *his* day went again. In the worst-case scenario, the past doesn't soften the present, and couples endure another year of bickering and distance. Each parent thinks "here we go again" with bitterness and disappointment. Jenny doesn't feel as impossibly stretched between the baby and her spouse because she knows it doesn't last forever.

The Unacknowledged Sexual Gulf

Alma, a twenty-two-year-old mother of a nine-month-old son and a six-year-old girl, grew up in Chicago. Because her mother worked two jobs, she was primarily raised by her grandmother. Alma is determined to be a hands-on mom, creating a new model of motherhood. That part is going well, but she has a big problem: her husband, Ernesto, moved out of the house a month ago. Their often-stormy relationship (which began in their teens) has endured similar separations in the past, but she isn't confident that they'll patch things up this time.

The model of marriage she was shown as a child is atrocious. When her grandfather emigrated from Mexico, he took up a second "wife," maintaining a relationship with her even after Alma's grandmother also immigrated. Her mother divorced her alcoholic father, who died when Alma was seven. She then had a common law marriage with a man who, unbeknownst to her, was married to someone else. Alma believes that her mother and her grandmother were terribly unhappy, and she hasn't seen up close what a good marriage looks like.

Alma first reviews what Ernesto says is his reason for leaving: she isn't a satisfactory housekeeper. I'm in her condominium, and anyone could see that her home is sparkling clean. But his mother dusts the back of the television set on a daily basis, and who could keep up with that standard? His mother doesn't hesitate to express her disapproval in a passive-aggressive way: saying nothing, she immediately sets about housecleaning whenever she comes to visit. Alma mentions that Ernesto is annoyed by her sloppy bookkeeping, since she sometimes forgets to pay their bills on time. She concludes, "That's BS, too."

Suspecting that she's right, I ask her whether sex might be a problem that neither wants to acknowledge. Immediately she concurs. Alma is in college full-time preparing to become a teacher, and she's very busy. She says, "Maybe he senses that he's always on the back burner." She tells me there simply isn't ever the time or the space to make love. Their daughter "won't" fall asleep before eleven-thirty p.m., and sometimes is up as late as one a.m. She tried getting her to bed by nine p.m. but it didn't work. The baby is in bed with them, and wakes easily, especially if they try to move him back to his crib. She attempted her pediatrician's advice to let him cry it out, but "I couldn't last more than ten minutes." She's a very capable mother, firm with other limits, but she has thrown in the towel on getting her children on a sleep schedule that works for her. She expects to "wait it out" until their sleep schedule improves.

I ask if the couple could go to another room before the children wake up in the morning. She explains: it's a three-bedroom condo; the baby is in her bedroom, her six-year-old in another, and the crib and a rocking chair are the only furniture in the third. Is there any other place you could go? I ask. She points to the couch where we're sitting: this is where Ernesto's cousin from Texas, who has been living with them for four months, sleeps. Could they make love in the shower? The bathroom is three feet from the couch, and she says, "I just couldn't."

I'm almost stumped, but I tell her babies were produced in one-room cabins, and I know it can be done. As I see it, she has a few options if she wants to create sexual opportunity: a portable yoga pad or some type of floor cushioning to use in the baby's empty room, or scheduling lovemaking at a time when the kids are at school or day care, asking her husband's cousin to clear out for a few hours. Latin culture honors loyalty and duty to the extended family, and asking the cousin to find a new place to stay so that they could have their privacy back is unthinkable. I am struck that even as Alma describes the obstacles to intimacy, she doesn't believe *this* issue is "BS." She knows sex is important in marriage, and she doesn't resent him wanting more. If he can be similarly respectful and tolerant of her concerns, and if they get the issue on the table, stop fighting about her alleged housekeeping problems, I'm optimistic that this, too, will eventually blow over.

When There Is No Middle Ground

Sometimes decisions on parenting are anticipated prior to marriage or childbirth: Will the baby be Jewish like Dad or Catholic like Mom? Who will care for the baby—will one or both parents cut back at work? Will they be city kids or will they be raised in the suburbs? But many conflicts about raising kids aren't or couldn't be predicted, and, divorced or married, coparents will regularly face difficult decisions until the child becomes an adult. The critical challenge for a mother is to make parenting decisions with considered input from her partner and to develop successful strategies for managing conflict. When conflict erupts, as it will, she should neither allow a dominant husband to veto her opinion, nor play the womb card, giving a father second-class status simply because he is not the mother.

Successful families may delegate responsibilities—you teach driving, I'll choose the summer activities. Having separate roles for mother and father is different from having separate status. The issue here is equal weighting of each parent's perspective and preferences.

Denise and Terry hit an area of major disagreement—"a huge problem"—about their son even before he was born. Denise believes very strongly that circumcision of male babies is wrong, a barbaric practice that causes unnecessary pain and unnatural disfigurement. In contrast, her husband is like most American men, circumcised. Most of the penises he's seen in the locker room and bathroom are circumcised, and he has come to view circumcision as natural, something you just do. He knows that teenaged boys can be brutal in their teasing, and doesn't want his son made fun of because he looks different when he's older. There was no compromise here: both viewed their position on the procedure as the "natural" thing to do, and one of them wasn't going to get his or her way. As Denise said, "It was black or white."

Denise did not have an ultrasound or know the sex of her baby until he was born, but she wanted the decision made in advance. She recalls driving with Terry, early in the pregnancy, and having an argument about what to do if they had a son. It heated up quickly, became harsh and hurtful, and the fight became about the fight, not the issue of circumcision. They did what marriage expert John Gottman prescribes: they exited the argument when it escalated. They agreed to come back to the topic when their tempers had cooled. As it turned out, they almost went too far in the other direction: they avoided the topic for months. As her delivery date approached, it came up again. Each partner tried to convince the other "but neither of us wanted to give in." Again, there was no resolution, but this time, less surprised by the passion that the other felt about the issue, they remained calm. This discussion, too, ended in a stalemate, with the mutual decision to take it up later when each had a chance to think it over. A few days later, she recalls with an affectionate rather than gloating smile, her husband, "caved." He decided that since someone had to give in, he would respect her "authority" as the mother. For Denise, whose mother never challenged her overbearing father, her husband's concession meant that she was in a different marriage. She could be a different mother, one whose opinion mattered, who sometimes prevailed when it came to important parenting decisions.

Curious about whether this decision was based on special status accorded to the mother in this retro family, I asked her how she thought it might go next time they disagreed about how to raise their son. Would she imagine that there would be times when Terry's "authority" prevailed? It turns out that they've already been down that road. Denise is a vegan, a choice made out of a deep reverence for living animals. As a vegan, she eats no animal products, not even eggs from a free-range farm, or organic milk.

She remembers "knowing" that she could never marry a hunter, and she demonstrated against guns while she was in college. Famous last words: Terry is a hunter, fisherman, "near Olympic-level marksman," and gun collector who believes that guns may be necessary for citizens to protect themselves from government interference and/or to survive in the event of a national disaster or terrorist attack. He first shot a gun at age five, and he considers it crucial for his son to learn to use a gun with expertise and safety. He plans to introduce guns when their son is about as young as he was. She is horrified at the idea that her son would go near a gun, let alone shoot and kill an animal. Again, there is no middle ground on this issue—one of them has to give in.

This time, Denise plans to give in. They've already found a way to compromise in part. Terry has become vegan also, but he still hunts and fishes, giving deer meat to his parents, or using fish and meat for their pets. When her son is older, she knows it will be very difficult for her, but this time *she* will "cave," in part because she recognizes that he did so on the last major split. She also feels that health and comfort issues—the circumcision—are her domain as the mother, but "politics" are his, and guns are a political issue in their family, where men view them as a necessary preparedness for the uncertainties of modern life. She prevailed on the circumcision not because she is a more important parent, but because they divvy up parenting domains.

How Did We End Up Fighting About Honey-Nut Cheerios?

Most parents won't have to face negotiating such diametrically opposed parenting views as survivalism versus pacifism. Still, they will inevitably face disagreements about what is best for the child. Sometimes the point of friction is surprisingly mundane. We know couples fight about sex and money. I would add that parents also fight about how to feed their children. A mother who has been urged by her pediatrician to defer solids until four to six months may disagree with her husband, who thinks cereal at night would help the baby sleep longer. Years later, they may argue about how much Halloween candy is too much, whether you should eat what is served to the family or be permitted individual food preferences, what to do about a teenager's atrocious snacking habits. Issues may erupt around how often a child is permitted to eat dinner at a friend's house, how long a child must sit at the dinner table, what to do when a child criticizes the meal, or handling a child who is overweight.

Gary and Vicky had no food problems with their first child, but their second is a picky eater. Gary, who frequently works ten-to-twelve-hour days, feels that Vicky should put her foot down and make four-year-old David eat what the family is having. Vicky, who works as a paralegal three eight-hour days per week, resents Gary insisting on the rules when he's not around to enforce them. The issue is potentially explosive, and could easily spill into a long-standing grudge that Vicky will have about Gary's tendency to be bossy, and what she views as his workaholism. Gary could see this as another example in which Vicky overindulges the kids, and, by the way, he works long hours so she can spend more time with their kids.

Fortunately, Vicky and Gary keep the food issues in a narrow focus. They talk about David's eating habits, and only that. Vicky consults their pediatrician, talks to a few mothers she trusts, and scans some Web sites about picky eaters. She proposes a compromise: she's not going to wear herself out by making a separate meal for David or by fighting this battle night after night, but she will let him have microwaved cheese on bread as his entrée if he refuses what they're having. However, he has to eat the evening's vegetables if he wants dessert, period. Left to her own devices, she would let him eat plain lettuce every night to be sure that he "earns" dessert, but she believes Gary has a right to participate in the plan.

Gary is pleased because since they found a compromise they can both live with, he's not always stuck being the bad guy. Vicky knows how important it is to present a united front, which means that sometimes the parenting decisions won't go her way.

Conflicts over family rules about food are common, and they're complicated by any number of factors. One is the child: some are highly adaptable, willing to try new foods and eat what is offered. Other children are obstinate about food choices. More than the occasional good mother finds herself giving her four-year-old a bowl of Cheerios for dinner because she is just too tired to put up with the temper tantrum that will ensue if she insists on chicken casserole.

Food is a powerful symbol in families. Feeding can resonate with issues of soothing (a lollipop after a shot), self-control (learning to eat in moderation and choose healthy foods), parental authority (eat what you are told to eat), discipline (no dessert as punishment), ethnic or religious identity (eating soul food, saying grace), generational continuity (your grandmother's recipe for matzoh ball soup), and cultural conformity (when children of immigrants insist on "American" food).

For many women, food symbolizes nurturing. When a father says, "Why can't the kids eat regular cereal and not that sugary stuff?" a woman might hear, "Why aren't you a good mother?" Being good feeders—good nurturers—matters to mothers. Sociologists have described an issue for modern mothers, called "gate-keeping." Gate-keeping refers to mothers' belief that they are uniquely suited to meet certain needs of their children, even among women who endorse egalitarian parenting. Gate-keeping explains why the pediatrician's wife, herself an accountant, thinks it's her job to soothe their feverish child, why it's almost unthinkable that anyone but you would buy your daughter's first bra. Those are just things that mothers do. Food issues are often gate-keeping issues: you decide when to stop the bottle, you shop for school lunches, you're the one who bakes for the school fund-raiser.

Gate-keeping is a complex and controversial idea; some critics feel it is outrageous to account for men's generally lower participation in caretaking tasks by claiming that men don't do more in the family because women don't want them to. Nonetheless, many women have an "omigod that's me" reaction to hearing certain behaviors characterized as gate-keeping. Gate-keeping duties may be willingly surrendered by fathers, who may not see buying shoes for the first day of school as an important parenting function, for example. But when two parents disagree about a gate-keeping decision, it is easy for a mom to take a hard-lined "I'm the mom and you're only the dad so what I say goes" stance. If conflict touches a nerve about whether you feel or look like a good mom, it can be difficult to stay logical.

Mothers not only want to *be* capable mothers, we want to be *seen* as being capable mothers. Quadruple that for employed mothers of young children, who often feel on the defensive. How we are seen to feed our children is on the mind of many mothers. Allison Pearson opens her novel of working motherhood, *I Don't Know How She Does It,* with an example of the angst an overextended woman feels about the way in which food reflects her mothering: she's distressing purchased pies with a rolling pin in order to appear to be the kind of mother who baked for her daughter's school party. If you've ever been on a field trip and peeked at what other kids have in their lunch bags, scanning to see how the lunch you made for your child compares, if you've looked to see who bought doughnuts and who make homemade cupcakes for the Girl Scout bake sale, if you've obsessed about what to serve at a party for four-year-olds, food may not be just about food for you. If you felt relief, guilt, or superiority when you compared the contents of your child's lunch bag with what another kid brought, you have succumbed to the worried mom's tendency to judge her interior— her mothering—by other people's exterior.

One group of mothers have a constant sense of being on stage, observed, criticized, found faulty by other moms: poorly mothered women. And food is associated with bad memories for many. In Lisa's family, meals were always risky business: at any time, a drunken parent might lash out at one of the kids, verbally and sometimes physically. Jeanette's always-on-the-couch mother was so neglectful that Jeanette began packing her younger siblings' lunch bags when she was eight. Shelly remembers the times her mother was too depressed to get a turkey for Thanksgiving or Christmas. Mary remembers stuffing herself when her parents screamed at each other, trying to soothe herself with food. These unmothered mothers are profoundly emotionally invested in making the experience of food different for their families.

The emotional value of food means that parents aren't necessarily arguing about the same thing. When Ann's first child arrived home at nineteen for semester break, wearing her newfound vegetarianism like a badge of honor, Ann thought she'd blow a gasket. She was managing, sort of, to hide her irritation at her daughter's superior attitude, even when Megan made snide remarks intimating that the rest of the family were the moral equivalent of mass murderers. She'd describe how chickens are made to lay eggs by forced molting, give graphic renditions of pork farming conditions. When Ann's fifteen-year-old sister also passed on the meat entrée at dinner one night, Ann was ready to send Megan back to college early. She snapped at her, telling her to cut the Holy Mother Teresa act.

When Ann's husband asked her, in front of the children, to "chill," she was furious. Dinner was, indeed, chilly that evening, and later Ann had it out with Robert. He defended himself by saying that Megan had a right to eat the way she wanted to. Ann replied that he had humiliated her in front of the kids, and that her complaint was how sanctimonious Megan had become. She didn't want their other daughter to feel pressured to change her eating just to please her revered older sister. Ann was very angry that he, who maybe made dinner five times since they were in grad school, was being the Cool Parent, while she was cast as The Bitch.

Ann reported the fight to me in her next appointment. It's tempting to take sides with your patient. Her husband doesn't have a chance to report what he saw, to explain why he thought Ann was too hard on Megan. At some level, Ann wants me to say "Wow, what a jerk," to soothe her as she is pushed to the side in an apparent father-daughter alignment. At another level, she knows that's not what she's in my office for. Ann is an unmothered mother, and she uses therapy to help her achieve a higher level of parenting. We often review recent incidents, as she seeks reassurance about how she's doing. Today's task is to try to understand why she became unglued at a relatively common phenomenon: a child coming home from college as a vegetarian.* This, I hope, will also help us understand what was so hurtful about her husband's words.

Ann is aware that she's exquisitely sensitive to criticism. Her mother was a miserable person. Ann doesn't recall her mother ever taking her side—if Ann complained about a teacher everyone hated, she demanded to know what Ann was doing wrong to annoy the teacher. She criticized everything from her posture to her choice of boyfriends, never satisfied. Praise was never offered. As a result, Ann is jumpy and defensive, sometimes seeing criticism when it isn't there. We've worked for some time to help her modify her filter, to question her tendency to assume that her husband is putting her down when he merely begs to differ.

In the course of closely examining Ann's emotional reaction to Megan's arrival home, I remind her of how bereft she was at Megan's departure. She sent Megan off with tears, only to greet her now with annoyance. In dissecting her reaction, Ann realizes that Megan's vegetarianism felt like a personal rejection of her, an indictment of the way in which she was fed under Ann's tenure. Ann has a clear role in the family as the supplier of food, and she

---

* Fifteen percent of students become vegetarian during college; countless others experiment with it. Be prepared.

felt that Megan was implying that Ann had failed. That is one of those fears that light dissipates: she doesn't need me to say that of course Megan's vegetarianism has nothing to do with her mothering. I ask her to consider why the final straw was her fifteen-year-old refusing lasagna, and something clicks for her: it was also about loss, about grieving the time when both kids would be out of the nest, changing in ways that she wouldn't even know about until they came home for a visit. For her husband, it was no more complicated than Megan becoming a vegetarian like other kids at college. He saw it as just another example of how teens can be like lemmings, and figured it might or might not stick.

As she reviews her husband's words, she realizes that another interpretation is possible: perhaps he was offering his opinion, and maybe even hoping to help her dig out of a parenting hole. They both know that teens can back you into corners you don't want to be in, irritating you to the point of irrationality when they assume that air of moral superiority. His tone wasn't angry or annoyed. Still, they need to talk about how to handle conflicts between them as Megan flexes her growing independence. There are predictable areas of conflict: If she brings a boyfriend home, do they agree that he sleeps on the couch? What if she comes home with her eyebrow pierced? Suppose she chooses a major that one or both parents feel is not sensible? And there may be issues never anticipated but potentially divisive: academic problems, depression, a request to study abroad in a third-world country.

My advice remains the same when parents disagree: avoid criticizing or challenging each other in front of your child, or maligning the parent who isn't in the room. Avoid forming two sides of a triangle against the other parent. At the same time, recognize that good coparents will sometimes passionately disagree about what's best for their child. The goal is not a fusion of parental beliefs, but coming to a consensus each parent can support.

This advice goes for divorced families, too. Parenting decisions become more complex as children age, when the stakes and potential fallout of issues such as smoking, academic performance, and sexuality are so very high. Married mothers sometimes have a fantasy that it would be better if they were divorced: they wouldn't have to take anyone else's opinion into account, could make the judgment calls by themselves. Divorced mothers sometimes have the opposite fantasy: Wouldn't it be great to have a coparent with whom you always agreed?

Both are fantasies. The tough decisions are hard because they're hard, regardless of marital status. The grass isn't greener on the other side. Knowing when your child is ready for overnight camp, what to do about attention deficit disorder, deciding how to handle curfew violations for your seventeen-year-old are simply difficult. Married coparents may, in theory, have an advantage when facing complex decisions because they don't carry over resentments about divorce, custody, remarriage, or money, which can easily spill into and rapidly ignite discussions over parenting decisions. But divorced parents who operate at high levels of cooperative coparenting may have an advantage if they've previously agreed to defer important decisions until they both talk it over. Their system of consulting one another means that they never decide curfews, driving rules, academic expectations, in the heat of the moment. So, too, for the married woman who routinely says, "Let me talk to Dad and we'll get back to you."

Honoring the Father After Divorce

Mary is divorced, and her child support agreement states that her financially successful ex-husband has to pay for any "unusual" child-related expenses. Their sixteen-year-old daughter is going downhill fast: she's already been pregnant, and the highest grade she got on her last report card was a C-minus in art. Mary wants to enroll her in an alternative school for troubled teens, but it requires private tuition. She feels "screwed" by her husband financially, and is convinced that he objects to the school because he's a tightwad. That may be so, but he may have other concerns, such as being worried that the other kids at the alternative school would exert even more of a negative influence on their daughter. They are so combative that neither can listen to the other's opinion. No issue is too small to argue over, and big ones are disastrous. He has sent child-support payments late to punish her and once maliciously called the police alleging that she was violent; she retaliated by moving farther away, making it more difficult for him to visit the kids. Both regularly disparage the other parent to their children, and it's no wonder their teen is acting out. Mary and her ex-husband will likely never successfully negotiate a difficult parenting decision because they lost—or perhaps never developed in the first place—a parenting alliance when the marriage failed.

It's hardly surprising that divorcing couples lash out at each other. Many mothers in an ugly divorce simply aren't saintly enough to "honor their child's father" when what they mostly feel for him is hate and anger. It takes time and a period of readjustment, and mothers who occasionally err shouldn't be too hard on themselves, especially in the beginning. Even moms who mostly manage to keep their overheated emotions in check slip up now and then, but regularly denigrating him, even making repeated subtle criticisms or small verbal jabs to your children is always a sign of poor maternal adaptation.* If the father really is worse than pond scum, the child will come to see that through his own eyes, on his own timeline. The divorced mother who cannot withhold criticism is promoting an unhealthy coalition—us against him. And there's no excuse for it.

The appeal is understandable—divorce is very painful, and being validated as the better parent by one's child can seem to

---

* Of course, plenty of married coparents express negative emotions about the other parent. Married moms who regularly put down their children's father in their presence are also poorly adapting to the critical challenge of honoring the father.

soothe the aches, balance the scales. But such relief comes not only at the ex's expense, but also at your child's expense. Except in extremely rare circumstances—and yours probably isn't one of them—children love both parents and feel terrible when a parent is criticized. A divorced mother, as part of her emotional adaptation to divorce, must do whatever it takes to remain, at a minimum, respectfully silent about her child's father, even if he does not do so himself. Even better, she welcomes her children's special relationship with their father, knowing that's good for the kids. She may need meditation, prayer, sex, a support group, a journal, therapy, music, girlfriends, or a shelf of books on raising happy kids in divorced families to find a way to divert her anger and hurt away from her child. Some couples find that divorce therapy (couples counseling after the marriage fails that focuses on child-rearing) helps them learn ways of resolving parental conflict, possibly for the first time.

Sandra and Henry maintained an excellent parenting alliance after divorce. They divorced when their son was almost two. All divorces with children are painful, so the fact that they coparent well cannot be attributed to a "clean" or "nice" divorce. It's due to their mutual insistence on respect and communication. Both sought individual therapy at the time of the divorce, knowing that this is a time in which it's normal to need extra support. They've read countless books on how to help kids flourish after divorce, and they try to mirror bathing, feeding, potty-training, and bedtime rituals at both homes. When they first divorced, Sandra was the primary caretaker, with the joint custody, once-a-week and every-other-weekend schedule that many families adopt for the noncustodial parent. Initially, all three had dinner together once a week prior to a transition from mom's house to dad's house, but they stopped that when they realized it was better to be genuinely cordial for a brief switch than to try to force a longer period of false pleasantry. Their son, Dylan, is delightful, by all appearances thriving under their parenting.

When Henry remarried, Dylan was in kindergarten. Henry wanted to move to a fifty-fifty shared parenting arrangement, because he felt Dylan would benefit from an equal amount of time with both parents. He believed his son was old enough to be away from his mother for a longer period of time. Sandra was suspicious of the timing, and she wondered briefly if Dylan would simply be spending more time with his stepmother, given Henry's long hours. She also worried that it was a scheme to reduce his child-support payments.

But she made a conscious decision not to go there. One of her strategies in cooperative coparenting is to try always to see her ex-husband's viewpoint in the most favorable light, and to stop herself when she starts looking for the dark side. Sometimes she writes in her journal what her fear is, and what the other possibilities, the less resentful ones, might be. She'd be the first to say that Henry is a good dad, and that it's best for kids to have both parents involved.

Sandra clarified her concern about child support: Henry reassured her by e-mail that this wasn't a money issue, and, on her lawyer's advice, she tucked a copy away in her files. She asked for time to consider his proposal, even though her gut instinct was that a week at mom's and a week at dad's was premature. She agonized about it, wanting to do what was best for Dylan. Ultimately, she decided it was too soon for her five-year-old to be away from his primary caretaker for so long. Henry's only alternative would have been to go back to court, and neither wanted to reopen those wounds. Sandra offered to reconsider the issue in a year, in the meantime extending Dylan's weekend with his father and stepmother to three days.

A year later, Henry came back to her with a new proposal, one that he'd found by searching the Internet. His proposal involved equal parenting time, but rather than alternating weeks, the longest stretch of time for each house would be five days. He found qualified divorce mediation experts who felt that this 5-2-2-5 configuration was developmentally appropriate for elementary-school-aged children, assuming peaceful coparenting. He would work fewer hours when Dylan was with him, longer days when he was at

Sandra's. Sandra wondered if people would think she was an irresponsible mother? Would Dylan miss her and be afraid to say so? What if Henry went back to his old long hours? She remained worried, but she decided to try it Henry's way. She gave the most weight not to her anxiety or feelings of loss, but to honoring his fathering. She decided to leave it up to Henry to rise to the occasion, trusting that they would ultimately both put Dylan's best interests first if the arrangement didn't work.

Conclusion

The mother-baby relationship is often compared to a romantic love affair—and no wonder. It's consuming, passionate, exclusive, magical. But sooner or later, the mother must make room in her life for her actual romantic partner. The developmental challenge each new mother must surmount requires making emotional space for one's child as well as one's partner, and for honoring the relationship between baby and father. The mother who has mastered this first step sees the big picture, realizing that unhappy periods during times of high stress don't signify a dysfunctional marriage, or a defective spouse, but may just be the ebb and flow of marriage and parenthood.

The culture of Perfect Mothering can make the challenge of honoring the father more complex. A natural consequence of anxiously trying to be perfect is micromanagement, and fathers easily can feel put down by "do it my way." It also makes for exhausted mothers, who simply lack energy to invest in their marriages. And since it's an impossible standard, mothers who chase perfection are often on the defensive, quick to blow up at perceived criticism rather than be open to shared problem solving.

Women may find themselves struggling to honor their child's other parent over the entire mothering life cycle. The challenge may first appear as tension around sexuality or attentiveness. It potentially surfaces whenever a baby insists on being held by mom only, or when that baby becomes a toddler and deepens his attachment to his father. It may erupt at times of parenting conflict, when a mother may feel deep down inside that her way trumps his, by virtue of being the mother. It may surface when a teen asks his mom not to tell his dad about the speeding ticket he got. It may extend into the adult years of that child, when parents disagree about college, wedding, or lifestyle plans. For many, this challenge will surface with a vengeance at divorce.

The mother who truly honors her husband in his role of father will find that she has a solid foundation that will support the challenges motherhood places on her romantic relationship, even if that relationship ends in divorce. In a foreshadowing of the enlarging circle her child will eventually develop—which may include siblings, extended family, teachers, babysitters, peers, and ultimately a genuine love interest—a mother must begin to let go of her exclusivity almost from the start.

Signs of Poor Adaptation to Transitioning from a Couple to a Family

1. Inability to experience baby- and child-related stress placed on a marriage as a family problem to be solved together, resulting in highly reactive fights that escalate quickly or result in emotional standoffs.

2. Belief that a mother's rank or status belongs on a higher plane than a father's (unless the father has relinquished responsible parenting).

3. Belief that the marital relationship should always be trumped by the wants, desires, or whims of the children, which may be mistakenly labeled as the "needs" of the children.

4. Divisive parent-child relationships in which parents regularly emotionally exclude or take sides against each other by forming alliances with the children.

After divorce:

5. Inability to maintain respectful silence about and accept your children's love for their father.

Strategies for Successful Adaptation

1. Savor the intoxication of the mother-baby bond while remaining empathic to the probability that a new father will feel left out at times.

2. Welcome the ever-growing importance of the father as he forms his own relationship with your child, continuing to support the father-child bond regardless of the nature of your relationship with him.

3. If married, keep the relationship, including sexual intimacy, on the bottom of the list only as long as absolutely necessary, knowing that a strong and loving bond between parents is good for kids, too. Even if they demand all of your energy and time, set sufficient limits to free up what you need in order to stay connected with your spouse.

4. When disagreeing about parenting issues, stay narrowly focused on the specific issue, compromise even though you're the mom, and present a united front to the children whenever humanly possible. Remember, it's *how* you fight that matters.

4

Separation
The Fourth Key Challenge

> The mother-child relationship is paradoxical and, in a sense, tragic. It requires the most intense love on the mother's side, yet this very love must help the child grow away from the mother, and to become fully independent.
> —Erich Fromm, *The Sane Society*

There is a mother for whom separation is an unusually difficult key challenge: the woman who lost her mother during her childhood. It's a powerful life lesson: loss happens, and it can happen to you.

Daniella is just older than the age when she half expected to leave her own children motherless. Now thirty-nine, she's passed two profound personal milestones: being a mother at age thirty-six, and, at thirty-nine, having a twelve-year-old daughter. She was imprinted with this morbid imagining in the worst way: her mother died at age thirty-six, when Daniella was twelve. Her mother became ill when Daniella was five, and she has no memories of her being strong and healthy.

The actual medical facts are blurry—her father remains closemouthed about her mother's cancer, being "of the old school." She thinks her mother had ovarian cancer, and probably also breast cancer, because she remembers her mother returning from surgery looking very different—flat-chested with a swollen belly—which she now concludes was due to a double mastectomy and liver metastasis. Her father won't even discuss the fact that his sisters had a thyroid illness—it isn't just cancer he won't talk about.

Her mother was so ill during her childhood that Daniella often stepped in to care for her sister, younger by twenty-one months. She did the laundry as a child, got her sister ready for school. She doesn't remember any discussion of what was happening, with either parent. The word "cancer" was not used. After seven years of living with her ailing mother, she took her illness for granted, but never expected her mother to die. In fact, the family covered up the fact that her mother's condition was terminal. It came as an enormous shock when a doctor called and told her, "Your mom isn't going to make it through the night." Her memory of the final hospitalization is of her mother crying, in terrible pain, bloated, with drainage tubes and IV lines everywhere.

Daniella knows that she has suppressed most of her childhood memories of her mother. She has one especially vivid fond memory, of coming home after the first morning of first grade, not realizing that it wasn't like kindergarten. Her mother gently explained that she would be in school all day now, and took her back to school. She looks at photographs of family events and outings, and does not remember most of them. She consulted a therapist at one point to help her grieve, and solidify what memories she could. She remembers her mother's creativity, her paintings and the beautiful clothes that she made.

Daniella's memory picks up after her mother's death. Her father began dating a year later, and remarried after another year. Daniella was scared and furious. The kids at school teased her about having a "wicked stepmother." Her stepmother had no children of her own, and had not been married before. Daniella feels in retrospect that it must have been quite a challenge for her, a previously independent woman, to enter a family with two hurting girls. Daniella remembers saying to her father, "Fine, do whatever you want, but don't expect me to call her 'Mom.' " Her sister was more welcoming and did call her stepmother "Mom." At the time, Daniella scolded her enthusiasm: "We're not the Brady Bunch, not one big happy TV family." Her sister sees Daniella's willingness to be interviewed for this book as a betrayal of their stepmother, as if she believes that the lasting impact of losing their mother should continue to remain a family secret.

Daniella's father and stepmother made a choice that Daniella feels was a mistake: they stayed in the same house, kept her mother's paintings on the wall, took her mother's Christmas ornaments out every December. She feels they meant well, but should have made a clean start in a new home. She felt confused by the fact that nothing was different, as if her mother hadn't died, but had simply been replaced. No doubt the family environment of silence didn't help a confused, angry teenager adapt. Daniella recalls being a "hellacious" teenager, especially during the last years of high school.

Daniella was slow to attach to her stepmother. When she got married, she shopped for her dress alone, and the invitation made no reference to parents. In hindsight, she knows she hurt her stepmother's feelings. Her stepmother made a healing gesture she remembers well: she put Daniella's mother's wedding tiara in her bouquet of flowers, and Daniella remembers feeling "finally." Finally, the secret was out: Daniella's mother had died, Daniella's love for her remained alive, and it was okay. Her father, responding to the question of who gives the bride away, said, her mothers and I do, naming both. She was grateful for the public acknowledgment of her loss. Since then, Daniella and her stepmother have grown closer. A few years ago, Daniella caught herself introducing her as her mother, although she believes she will never call her, or her mother-in-law, by the special word "Mom."

It's no wonder that Daniella was hesitant to attach to her stepmother. Daniella has a big residual fear: she is terrified of being abandoned or betrayed by women. If a girlfriend hurts her feelings, she is so skittish that she can hardly stand to work through anything, however minor. She lost a lot of close women friends before she realized she needed to overcome her terror of being hurt. No doubt, the threatened loss of an important woman reactivates the pain of losing her mother, but the conspiracy of silence left her with significant trust issues. Her mother never prepared her for the inevitable. To be fair, times were different, and her mother may well have been advised to keep the illness secret, or may have been misled herself by her physicians. But perhaps in trying to spare her daughter pain, she left her with a significant wound.

Daniella believes that she and her sister were permanently affected as potential mothers. Her sister is childless, and Daniella considered not having kids, but her husband, whom she describes as "wonderful," agreed to her conditions for having children. They made a vow: if she got the cancer that runs in the family (an aunt also died of cancer at a young age, leaving her two daughters motherless, and Daniella began getting medically recommended mammograms at age nineteen), they agreed to tell the children together. It would never be a secret. Daniella saw a show on *Oprah* about a woman who wrote letters and made a video for her children before she died of cancer, and Daniella felt a huge relief: there could be another way; she could do that, too.

Daniella's maternal loss permeates her mothering, especially when it comes to separation. She had a high-powered career at the time her daughter was born. She and her peers believed "women were going to conquer the world," and she knew no full-time at-home mothers. She took her maternity leave, and went back to a management position within a few months. She remembers coming home from work one day seeing her baby holding a rattle for the first time. The caregiver casually said, "Oh, she's been doing that for a few days." Daniella was overpowered by the sense that time was short, that she couldn't waste the finite mothering opportunity away from her daughter. She quit her job the next day.

Financially, not bringing in an income was very difficult. Daniella also felt criticized by other working women for letting down the team. She didn't think of it in political or financial terms: she simply couldn't separate from her baby Emily. "I had to take every moment I could to be with her." Even being home, Daniella rarely left her daughter's side. "I wasn't quite as bad as Shirley MacLaine in *Terms of Endearment,* but I know I checked on her more than any other mom." When she had her second daughter, Elizabeth, now ten, she raised her the same way. The girls went everywhere with Daniella—even as squirmy toddlers, they accompanied their parents to a fine restaurant for an anniversary dinner, for example.

The first important psychological separation for a mother may be leaving her baby with a caregiver, or it may be having her baby sleep elsewhere. Daniella had difficulty with both. She kept Emily in a bassinet at her bedside at first. Her husband, Mark, has a very important role in parenting: he helps her separate appropriately. At four months, he pointed out that "the books" suggest that it's okay to put her in her crib, in her own room. She agreed, but Daniella (not Emily) cried for thirty minutes straight. He brought the baby back in, to her great relief. When Daniella was finally ready, she slept with the bedroom doors open.

Each step of separation has been tough for Daniella, although she finds it easier with Elizabeth, her second child. For example, she kept Emily home from preschool, partly due to cost but also to keep her close, but Elizabeth attended preschool. Daniella separated all at once, when she felt ready: Emily started kindergarten at the same time that Elizabeth began preschool. The hardest school separation for her was first grade, when Emily was gone all day. Daniella tried to hide her anxiety from Emily, hoping she didn't pick it up from her. Still, she'd sneak by the schoolyard to "eyeball her," her anxiety alleviated when she saw Emily at lunch recess. She'd think to herself, "There she is, she's okay."

A breakthrough moment came for Daniella in the fall when she saw Emily sitting at lunch reading a book while her friends played nearby. Daniella saw Emily's comfort with herself and her environment: "There she was being herself, reading." Daniella, who also loved to read as a child, would never have read during lunch as a first-grader—she was too insecure to stand out from the crowd. But Emily loves to read, and when Daniella saw her unaffected by peer pressure, she suddenly realized that Emily was her own person. Psychologically, in the flash of that moment, Daniella stopped over-identifying with her daughter. She realized that Emily was not the unhappy six-year-old Daniella had been, and therefore, she didn't need Daniella to keep her safe from the ghosts of Daniella's past.

Protecting Your Child from Your Separation Anxiety

Daniella considers it her duty to shield her daughters from her separation anxiety, and I agree. It's never gone from her, yet she is vigilant about the risk of holding on too tightly. Her husband, Mark, continues to play a key role in supporting her conscious mothering. He respects Daniella's fears while also encouraging and supporting progressive separation. For example, Emily, now a preadolescent, recently began rejecting the clothes her mother makes. Daniella's instinct is to fight her on this point, especially since one of the few ways she can consciously model herself after her mother is to provide beautiful clothing. Alas, preteens often have very different ideas of what constitutes beautiful clothing. Emily wants to wear what she likes, things Daniella thinks are ghastly. Mark gently encouraged Daniella to let go, to relax. She reminds herself that she was forced to be independent, lost her childhood overnight, and that it's her job to let her daughters go through the rough-and-tumble of pushing her back when they're supposed to do that.

When I interviewed Daniella in her home, she had returned

the previous day from her first trip away from her daughters. A giant "Welcome Home, Mom" sign that they had put up was still by the front door. Daniella went to visit her best friend for "five days and four nights." She had never left both girls before; neither has gone to overnight camp, for example. She felt "a little clingy"—calling at least twice a day. But she got to experience the flip side of separation: the joy of reunion. Her daughters told her they missed her, especially their good-night hugs.

Unlike the incident that caused her to leave her employment, she survived missing a first. Her daughter's first romantic encounter with a boy happened while Daniella was gone, and she wasn't there to review the details in person. When she had her first crush, her mother was in the hospital, so her comfort with missing this particular event is a huge step for her. Perhaps because she passed the subconscious milestone she had in her mind when she feared dying, she's a different mother than she was a decade ago. Her daughter's first crush brought her pleasure rather than anxiety about a missed milestone. Sometimes she still has to think her way to being the kind of mother she wants to be, but this time, her emotional reaction was uncomplicated.

Daniella knows that she has some tough times ahead of her. Letting go of adolescents is likely to be especially hard for her, and college isn't all that far away. She does as well as I imagine any mother can who has a similar history, but there's no doubt that releasing a daughter into adulthood will be painful for her. While her husband deserves credit for helping her navigate the progressive separation that characterizes parenthood, *she* deserves credit for letting him help her. Some highly anxious mothers can't tolerate input even from their husbands, can't relinquish the reins for a moment. She knows her blind spot, and lets him help her be the best mother she can be. Mothers in therapy often want to be changed, want to have their vulnerabilities surgically removed. Daniella accepts that she is the way she is, but she also refuses to surrender to her past. She's a mother with a gaping wound who's damned if she'll bleed on her kids.

My bias is that mothers who spend a good deal of time thinking about how the past influences their mothering often do better than they give themselves credit for. When I ask Daniella if she also uses the pain she experienced to enrich her mothering, she is slow to sing her own praises. She finds it easier to talk about her fears, but eventually she confesses to something. "I have a sense of priorities. Big deal if it's cleaning day—let's make memories, let's go for a ride on our bikes if it's a beautiful day. If we feel like it, let's drop everything and go get ice cream." She gives her daughters something that she was denied by her family's secrecy: the lesson that life, in its brevity, is worth savoring.

Day Care and Preschool Separation

Lakeisha, a twenty-six-year-old single African-American mother of four-year-old Jevon and almost one-year-old Chevonne, has no choice about leaving her children. Half of mothers of infants work outside the home for a variety of personal and professional reasons. For Lakeisha, separation isn't optional because of so-called welfare-to-work programs that require low-income mothers to participate in the labor force. She is working toward her GED (high school equivalency diploma) while cashiering at a neighborhood restaurant. Recently, she's enrolled her son in a federally subsidized Head Start/day-care program for children of low-income parents.

Good day care has been an issue since Jevon was born. The first affordable home-based day care she found gave him baby milk even though Lakeisha repeatedly told them he was lactose intolerant. Matters got worse when they gave Jevon soda pop in his bottle instead of juice. She hated leaving him there, and finally ended up taking him out. Unable to afford better, she pieced together a patchwork of extended family care: her baby's father, her own mother, his paternal grandmother, and other relatives pitched in to cover her work schedule. Somehow, they all managed.

The care he got with family and friends (the care her daughter still receives) was warm and loving but a logistical nightmare. If you think your boss doesn't appreciate the problems of working moms, imagine that you work for minimum wage, and you need to tell your boss you can't come to work because your babysitting fell through. Picture yourself with a schedule that changes week to week, needing to find a friend or relative to care for your child, for free, every single shift. You can't afford backup day care on your salary, and if your aunt is supposed to cover on Tuesday and she gets sick, your choices are to skip work and risk losing your job, or beg another relative to babysit for free—right now!

In theory, welfare-to-work programs are supposed to help mothers access subsidized child care, but openings at quality sliding-fee programs are few and far between. Lakeisha was thrilled when Jevon finally made it off the waiting list for a Head Start preschool that also had day care, so that he could have the advantages of early childhood education prior to kindergarten. Despite the limited choices caused by economic hardship, she approached the impending separation with a mother's need for reassurance that her child would be in good hands. She took her mother along for a second opinion, and they agreed: it was a great place. The staff was friendly, the center spotless. They were organized, with a routine of activities, nutritious food, and scheduled naps. Most of all, she liked what she saw the children learning: letters, days of the week, beginning writing.

It was a good thing that she loved the program, because when Jevon started, it was a big change for mother and child. He was accustomed to being home or with friends and family caretakers, where good-byes were easy. Like most children at preschool, he cried when she first dropped him off. In fact, he started crying as soon as they walked in the door, as if he instinctively knew what lay ahead. She felt "terrible." Her distress must have shown: a kind teacher promised her that he would be okay. Emotionally, though, she just couldn't turn and go, and she promised him that she'd stay for a while. The first day, she stayed for an hour. She sat in a chair off to the side, while he slowly got involved in the activities. She remembers that he checked on her frequently. After about an hour, when she was convinced that he was fully engaged in play because he stopped looking for her, she crept out unnoticed.

At pickup, she was relieved when a teacher promised her that he was fine after she left. But the next morning, he cried once more, this time from the moment they left for school. He knew exactly what was in store. He stopped crying when she again promised to stay for a while. Once he got settled into his activities, she again sneaked away.

From the start, Lakeisha frequently reassured Jevon that she'd be there to pick him up at the end of the day. She feels that it took three days for him to believe it, because by the fourth day, he seemed much less anxious about being left. Still, it took two weeks for him to leave for school without crying. By then, he was happy to go to school, and now, five months later, he proudly marches off to school, saying that Mommy has work and Jevon has school.

Lakeisha was sensitive to and accepting of Jevon's anxiety about being left. She knew that it was normal for him to fear abandonment, and she was not irritated or annoyed with his crying and clinging. She helped him transition a successful separation along a timeline that experts consider typical: two to four weeks.

Lakeisha went to the heart of Jevon's worry: I'll be back. But she did not follow the classic advice about how to separate from a preschooler. She violated two of the "rules" mothers are given about preschool separation: (1) never linger at good-bye, and (2) never, ever, sneak away. I'm one of those parenting experts who believe there's a right way to leave your child at preschool, and I've practiced as well as preached this approach. Say good-bye for no more than five minutes, be firm, reassuring, and optimistic, and rely on your child's teacher to let you know if things are disastrous. But Lakeisha practiced another rule I preach: trust your maternal intuition. It's hard to argue with success, to tell a mother who did just fine that she should have done it differently.

As is often the case for mothering rules—and a Google search for "preschool separation" results in 56,000 hits, the majority with nearly identical advice—most of them exist for the occasions where our instincts are very contrary. We need to be told to leave our crying child at the nursery school door *because* it's so very painful for mothers to do exactly that. It's easier to linger. You feel much less guilty if you sneak out. The look in your child's eye as you pull her off your leg and push her back in the door is agonizing. Every September, in preschools across the country, some mothers follow these rules and some do not, and yet, by mid-fall, kids and their moms almost all work it out.

Lakeisha has a very good rationale for her approach. She is desperate to minimize Jevon's crying because he has severe childhood asthma, and crying itself can trigger a respiratory attack. She's seen it any number of times: he starts crying, and the next thing you know he needs a medical breathing treatment in order to get enough oxygen in his lungs. Her gut told her that he'd cry less if she lingered, less if he didn't see her departure. She was correct: he never had an asthma attack triggered by separation at preschool. Of course, she had given the school careful instructions on how to manage his asthma, provided medical information and supplies, a doctor's note, and a reminder to call 911 if they couldn't reach her. But she was understandably terrified about whether they would do it exactly right if he did get an attack, and became comfortable only when she got to know them better.

Because she believes that preschool is good for children, Lakeisha did not doubt her decision to send Jevon. At his age, she felt this would be superior to her previous child-care arrangement due to the cognitive and social stimulation he'd get. Once she was satisfied with the quality of the surrogate care, the decision to force this separation on him was easier for her because it was in his best interests. She lingered, and she sneaked out in order to feel less guilty, but she never for a moment considered relinquishing his position in the program. He was going, period. She knew she'd have to overcome her fear about his illness when he entered kindergarten, and she didn't want her fear to hold him back now.

Emotional Ambivalence About Separation

Fear and guilt accompany the separation process for many mothers. The fear makes sense: it's scary to trust others with the child you know and love so well, even if he is perfectly healthy. It's easy to picture an endless series of disasters: what if the teacher turns her back and your child wanders off down the street, what if they accidentally give him peanut butter when he's allergic, what if she never stops crying and they don't call you?

The guilt is more complex. You feel guilt in part because your child is protesting, making it very clear that she doesn't see the long-term advantages of being left in a roomful of strangers. Leaving a protesting child at preschool is exactly like holding a crying infant for a shot: the child doesn't understand the big picture, only sees you as aiding and abetting something painful. And that feels terrible to mothers.

But separation guilt is often more complex than an immunization, because not only is it good for kids, it's good for moms, too, and that makes us feel bad. It violates the romantic notion that good mothers wish to spend every second with their children, the Perfect Mother myth. The relief about having two hours to grocery shop alone, to finally have a day-care program that isn't more complicated than poorly translated bicycle assembly instructions, or to have a few hours with the new baby while a sibling is at preschool, is unwelcome, guilt-inducing. Often, the harder it is for a mother to accept her relief at a bit of time to herself, the more her angst about preschool separation. When school starts every fall, guilt makes many mothers frame their relief in terms of the benefit to children, not themselves. "Jessie will be so much happier once she isn't bored being home all day," not "Thank God." This guilt is not, apparently, something our mothers experienced when they were culturally permitted to acknowledge mothering stress, allowed to remain good mothers yet say, "Go play outside and don't come back for two hours."

The poorly mothered woman is especially eager to push down awareness of the pleasure of a break from entertaining a three-year-old or sending her teen off to camp. If her mother was explicit about feeling burdened by her presence (for example, my patient who was told by her mother that it was a darned shame *Roe v. Wade* didn't happen sooner), she may not be able to distinguish between the healthy pleasure in having time for herself and callous narcissism. If in her quest to undo her own deprivation by being all-giving, the unmothered mother becomes aware of relief about her child's diminishing dependency, she may feel shame as well as guilt.

Banishing the Audience

Every spring, one or two of my patients consult me about the preschool decision, wanting reassurance about what good mothers do. Amy has been taking her son Jeffrey to a weekly mommy-and-me toddler class at her local church, and some of the children in the class will be entering their two-day-a-week program for three-year-olds in the fall. A Montessori school in her community has a three-year-old program that meets five mornings a week, and Jeffrey seemed very happy in the classroom when they visited recently. But she feels ashamed of even considering it: the moms at the church program keep saying how much they're going to hate it when their children are gone two mornings a week. Amy is pregnant and due in late July, so having Jeffrey, who loves being with other kids his age, occupied after the new baby arrives is especially appealing.

"You must think I'm terrible for even thinking about it," she says, although since Amy had been asking for reassurance for a year before she even got pregnant, I think she must know that's not how we usually review her mothering decisions. She is cursed with the pernicious combination of high anxiety and perfectionism, causing her to doubt herself at every step of the way while often failing—humanly—to meet her own impossible expectations. She would never consider asking her self-centered mother for advice, and she can spend hours obsessing on which of the five-star-rated *Consumer Report* strollers she didn't but should have purchased. Our therapy began with her insecurity that she could ever be a competent mother, given how poorly she was raised, and her belief that perfection is an achievable goal.

When she gets stuck, she typically presents her dilemma to me with predetermined harsh self-judgment, and this is no exception. There is a pattern to how Amy finds fault with herself. She has an idealized image of what a "good mother" feels, and then she finds someone who espouses those views, comparing her insides with other mothers' outsides. I remind her, as I've done countless times, that what mothers say about mothering is often what they think they should say, or what they hear others saying. They may be as terrified of disapproval as she is, and as soon as one mother in a group verbalizes the Authorized Maternal Message, others chime in. I remind her that mothers' feelings about mothering are usually complex: yes, they may feel pangs of sadness about their children growing up, and that's the part they share. They almost certainly also feel relief, and that's the part they *don't* share. It isn't her responsibility to be the bullshit detector in the crowd, but it isn't fair for her to swallow it, either. I point out that it's unlikely that the Montessori program is tailored only for children of selfish mothers—many kids at this age thrive on socialization, and it sounds to me as if Jeffrey is ready for the stimulation.

If she listens to her own instinct, she thinks he'd like to go seven days a week if he could. He loves being with other children. Do you want your mothering decision to be based on what you know about your son, or what you think the mothering audience endorses? Amy gets what she needs from me to make the decision: validation, and a different way to think about her decision. The fact that she's even looked at the Montessori program in the first place is progress for her, because she had to force the I'm-a-bad-mom voice to be quiet long enough to go. Eventually, I hope, she'll mother with more self-confidence and beat up on herself less when she lands in the normal ambivalence of mothering emotions. Perhaps someday she'll even notice when the other mothers protest too much.

Context Matters

Because it is perfectly normal to feel somewhat bad about separation, it can be difficult to know when you're doing just fine. One sign of satisfactory adaptation to appropriate mother-child separation is that your emotions are context-specific. Bona fide selfish mothers don't concern themselves with whether separation is in their children's best interests. Any port, any child-receptacle, will do, and the child has to deal. On the opposite end of the spectrum is the mother who feels *too* guilty, who is clinging, struggles with separation in any and all situations, even if she feels the separation is something kids ordinarily experience, or is in their best interest. It wouldn't surprise me, for example, if Denise (see Chapter 1), ends up home-schooling Noah because the separation, while ordinary for American children, is too hard on them both. Lakeisha demonstrates excellent psychological adaptation when she carefully distinguishes between what is good for her from what is good for her son. It's easier for her when she knows it's good for him, even though it's scarier for her because of his asthma.

Lakeisha displays another aspect of context-specific separation from her child. She differentiates the "ordinary" from the unusual. She won't let him experience separation she doesn't feel a child should have to endure: being at the hospital alone. Because of his asthma, Jevon has been hospitalized a few times a year since infancy. Since even bad attacks of asthma can often be managed in the emergency room, when he *is* admitted, he's usually desperately ill and in the intensive care unit. He's hooked up to breathing machines, intravenous lines, immobilized by tubes and equipment. He's entitled, she says, to have the reassuring presence of a loving adult under those circumstances. She schedules shifts with her mother and with Jevon's father, although she moves mountains to be there personally even when they are "on duty." It's not because she fears mistreatment: he has never had a bad or uncaring nurse, and she knows that the children's hospital is nationally renowned. It's just a fact that he wants her there when he's sick and vulnerable, and she can't stand to be apart from him. In the context of illness, her expectations for separation for both of them are completely different from when it comes to preschool.

Separation in Divorced Families

There is a type of separation that used to be extraordinary that is now ordinary for many modern children: maternal separation due to divorce and blended families.

Cheryl, thirty-five, is a middle-class, married, African-American mother of three. Her oldest child, twelve, lives mostly with his father and stepmother in a racially integrated suburb, visiting her on the weekends. Her younger two children, ages four and five, live with Cheryl and her husband, Dennis, their father, in one of

Chicago's most troubled neighborhoods. Over half of the residents live in poverty; one third of the neighborhood children are born to teen mothers. A 1995 Harvard University study found that one in ten children under the age of six in this neighborhood had been present when someone was shot; three quarters have heard gunshots by first grade. Cheryl and her husband purchased his grandmother's home to help her out, with the intent of temporarily rehabbing and selling it. It's taken longer than they thought, and they hope to move within a year.

Cheryl's husband and her mother are both teachers. She did not complete college herself, but had a successful career working for a major downtown accounting firm. Now mostly an at-home mother, she has a small business of her own that provides bookkeeping and financial services. She rose quickly in the ranks at a company she says you'll see listed among the top places for working mothers, although that wasn't her experience. She got sick of coworkers commenting about her kids—"How many kids are you planning on having?" "Why don't you give them zinc so they don't catch colds?"—and she came back from her last maternity leave to find that someone had been moved into her job. When her request to telecommute was denied, her husband had just been promoted, so she decided to stay home with the kids.

Cheryl did not marry her older son's father, Charles, but their relationship mirrors a first marriage. They dated for four years, and thought they would be together forever, even though they actually split up when she was pregnant. When their son was a baby, they shared babysitting, alternating shifts so that Charles Jr. was always with a parent. Charles Jr. lived with her from birth until he was nine, staying with his father on weekends. They had a friendly shared-custody relationship, flexible and respectful. Their extended families are close, and she points out that her "ex's" aunt threw her bridal shower when she and Dennis got married.

Cheryl's mother is an unusual woman: educated in England and France, she is a bilingual teacher with two graduate degrees.

She's on her fourth marriage, to a ballroom dance instructor considerably younger than herself. She lives on tofu and vegetables, and doesn't fit anyone's stereotype of an African-American grandmother. Cheryl's younger two children know her mostly from her photographs, although she lives in their town. She has an e-mail correspondence with Charles Jr. An absentee maternal grandmother is unusual in most families, but especially so in an African-American one. Cheryl's childhood was marked by a mix of middle-class luxuries—ceramics classes, gymnastics, voice lessons—and harsh deprivation. She recalls being shown how to use a gun before she was ten, so that her mother could teach at night while Cheryl babysat her siblings. She was whipped more than once, and shrugs when I ask if she considers that child abuse. Of course, she says, but everyone I know was raised that way. Ironically, things got better when her twelve-year-old brother made a suicide attempt, as if the family woke up to the needs of the children, or perhaps got outside help. Cheryl shares a history I've seen in numerous unmothered mothers: she moved out the day she turned eighteen.

Cheryl's mother did something Cheryl gives her credit for: she married a "great guy." Cheryl's stepfather raised her since infancy, and Cheryl considers him her father. Unlike her mother, her stepfather is an active grandparent, and she talks to him almost daily. She has forgiven him for his role in her painful childhood, perhaps because she always felt he treated her as if she were his own child, never put her second to his biological children.

Cheryl hoped that things would go smoothly when she married Dennis, but it wasn't the case. Dennis, who had no children before the marriage, got off on the wrong foot when he'd introduce Charles Jr., then six, as "my wife's son." She tried to correct him, sometimes writing down what he should have said in order to help him find better ways to transition into being a stepfather. Rocky relationships, especially at the beginning, are common in blended families, much more so than the seamless transition Cheryl herself recalls. Cheryl often felt torn between her son and her husband. At times, she wanted to take her son's side, saw Dennis as overly tough, but felt that it was important to stand with Dennis in a united front.

Cheryl has identified some factors that made it more difficult. She thinks her own stepfather learned a lot from being a father before he married her mom, and the fact that she was so young may have helped them bond. She had no competing biological dad, but Charles Jr. had never been without an involved father, and wasn't about to view his stepfather as "Dad." Since his parents separated when she was pregnant, he had never lived with two adults, never had to negotiate as a member of a threesome. Finally, Dennis is a teacher, accustomed to having children respect him just because he is an authority figure.

Shortly after she and Dennis married, Charles did, too. Cheryl knew Charles's new wife, Barbara: she was their son's Sunday school teacher. Church is extremely important to Cheryl, who attends weekly and volunteers as the church treasurer. Perhaps because of their religious affinity, Cheryl has the most positive feelings about her child's stepmother that I've ever seen, describing her as a "wonderful person," "very sweet." When Cheryl had a scare during her third pregnancy, she experienced Barbara's kindness to her as consistent with being a good Christian. Barbara stepped in to help with both of Cheryl's kids, took them to visit her in the hospital, prayed for her. Most important, Barbara has done what Cheryl had hoped for: she treats Charles Jr. as her own son. Cheryl knows that he also calls her "Mom," although she appreciates that he refers to her as "Barbara" when Cheryl is around. Cheryl doesn't want to hear Charles Jr. call Barbara "Mom," but it is extremely rare for a mother to tolerate knowing that it happens at all.

After both of his parents married, Charles Jr. continued to spend most weekends with his father. At age nine, he developed headaches and stomachaches. Cheryl took him to the doctor, "over and over," and they couldn't find a medical cause. When they told her it was "stress," she was upset but not shocked, since he'd always been a sensitive child. She thought it must be school-related, and she kept trying to get him to talk about what was bothering him. Finally he did: he wanted to live with his father. He was afraid to speak up, worried about hurting her feelings. She understood two of his reasons: conflict with his stepfather, and worry about how sad his father had become following a stillbirth he and Barbara suffered.

When Charles Jr. told her that he wanted to live with Charles, Cheryl was heartbroken, but she also believed he had the right to make that decision. They reversed the custody arrangement: now Charles Jr. comes to visit her on weekends. She used to cry when he left, and worried about him when he was away. She's adjusted now, and three years later, she can admit her secret: she also felt a little relief, which made her feel very guilty at first. The house became more peaceful without the disciplinary struggles, and her son's stomachaches went away.

Cheryl says, "We have two families but we're also one." Still, she needed to see that they would remain connected as mother and son, and indeed, they continue to have a strong relationship. She remains special to him as the one he confides in, telling her things he doesn't bring up with his father, such as the fact that some kids at school were making fun of his appearance (his teeth were damaged in a baseball accident and he wears glasses). This isn't different from any other family in which boys are more likely to show their tender side to their mothers. She maintains another special mothering role: helping her son become increasingly competent in his relationships. For example, she coaches him on how to get along with Barbara and Charles's daughter, as well as his half siblings at her house.

She worries about the signs of adolescence: his love of Starbuck's coffee, the fact that he wants to wear his pants low to his hips, letting his boxers show above the waistline. Cheryl raises her children with a conscious resistance to permissive popular culture: no more than one hour of television per day, and no secular music, for example. She does crafts projects with the kids, they read the Bible together, and they play Boggle, Upwords, Monopoly, and other family games for entertainment. Things are more lenient at his father's house, so it has become hard for Cheryl to be the heavy who says he can't listen to rap, can't watch MTV or Ricki Lake, especially since she was used to being the one setting the rules. Sometimes she hears him mutter "I'm ready to go back," and that hurts. But she also knows that griping is normal early adolescent behavior.

Recently, after a spat with his father, Charles Jr. wanted to live with her again, and as much as that appealed to her emotionally, she knew that they couldn't allow him to pop back and forth during his teenage years, pitting one household against the other. She said no. Saying no was made easier by the fact that Charles Jr. lives with his dad in a racially integrated Chicago suburb where 98 percent of the high school students go to college, a world apart from her neighborhood.

Thinking Your Way to Contentment with Separation

Cheryl has made a remarkably peaceful adjustment to the psychological challenge of this separation. She resisted key emotional traps called "cognitive distortions" that might have left her feeling depressed, angry, or guilty. Cognitive distortions are habitual irrational thinking traps that contribute to feeling blue. For example, pessimistic, automatic negative thoughts contribute greatly to how we emotionally process challenging events. Our beliefs about our circumstances often dictate how we feel about them.

If Cheryl had used emotional reasoning, one type of cognitive distortion, she might have concluded that because she *felt* rejected, Charles Jr. was indeed rejecting her, when clearly he was not. She didn't personalize his decision, or blame herself or her husband. She also did not catastrophize or use all-or-nothing thinking, never telling herself that their relationship would be irreparably damaged, that he wouldn't love her anymore, that the best days were over. Instead, she remained objective: Charles Jr. had two loving parents, two welcoming households, and he chose one as his primary residence. By remaining coolheaded about her son's decision, she avoids taking it as a painful personal rejection.

She also uses altruism to guide her, believing that it was more important to figure out what was best for him than what was best for her emotionally. She considered the stress he was experiencing with her new husband, her son's wish to be able to look after his father, and the comparative advantages of the academic and social milieu in the other school system, and she let go. She heard what her son said about loving her, not wanting to hurt her feelings, and she assumed that just as he loved his father when he saw him weekends, he would love her when he saw her only on weekends, too. She selectively attends to the positive, noticing, for example, the ways in which Charles Jr. shows her how special she is to him.

Conclusion

Separation is an emotional challenge that no mother escapes. The pangs of letting go may begin when the baby is first taken to the hospital nursery, and will extend into the child's adulthood. The issue of letting go of adult children is so emotionally significant that the final chapter in this book discusses it as a separate developmental challenge for mothers.

The key challenge is to master the ambivalence of separation. It isn't supposed to be easy to let go, and wanting to hang on tight isn't abnormal. Yet it isn't supposed to be horrific, either, and hanging on too tight is problematic. It's normal to want to freeze time, to imagine keeping a young child cocooned in your protective embrace forever, to wish that you could halt the march that accompanies a child's growth and development. Yet we know, as Dr. Erich Fromm points out, it's our job to raise children to be independent, to function without us. The duty of a mother is to help her child not need her, and there's the rub. When a mother can take pride in her child's ever-expanding self-sufficiency, understand that a child's love is not the same as dependency, and can allow herself to experience with pleasure those moments in which her child's freedom gives her freedom, too, she has made peace with the challenge.

Signs of Poor Adaptation to Separation

1. Belief that you are the only person who can keep your child safe from danger, often despite evidence that others are capable caretakers.

2. Inability to distinguish your emotional experiences, past or present, with separation issues from your child's emotional reaction to separation—for example, if you were afraid to go to summer camp, assuming that your daughter is, too.

3. Hovering and clinging, or other behaviors directed at minimizing your own anxiety. For example, not allowing a child to participate in school field trips unless you are also on the bus, or insisting that a child who would rather stay at school come home for lunch.

4. Refusing to allow your child to participate in separate activities that are customary in your community may be a sign of poor adaptation, just as pushing an unwilling child into independence may also suggest problems. Be neither

the first nor the last parent to let your child walk to school alone, participate in overnight sleepovers at a friend's house, or fly unaccompanied to spend a weekend at his grandparents'.

Strategies for Successful Adaptation

1. Consider the alternative. Stay focused on the goal: a happy, independent, confident child who flourishes as an adult.

2. Allow yourself to experience anxiety and sadness and relief about the normal separation that marks a child's maturation, while keeping your anxiety as invisible to your child as humanly possible. Give your son or daughter permission to take pride in autonomy without experiencing it as a rejection of your mothering.

3. Allow other adults (spouse, girlfriends, teachers) to validate and support you. Let others give opinions or advice about age-appropriate independence. Absorb praise for letting go, and take comfort in knowing that mixed feelings are normal.

4. Remember that need is not synonymous with love. Do not mistake a child's diminishing dependency on you for diminishing connectedness.

5

Setting Limits
The Fifth Key Challenge

> There are also many.... parents who simply do not say no to
> their kids, because, well, they get such a negative reaction.
> Kids really, really don't like it when you say no to them....
> To what depths have we sunk as parents? We have become
> ineffectual lapdogs to our children, with all the power
> and authority of retired security guards.
> —Christie Mellor, *The Three-Martini Playdate:
> A Practical Guide to Happy Parenting*

Although the first go-round with limit-setting is often during the toddler years, the need to modify, establish, and enforce limits ever lurks. At some point, parents and children will disagree about bedtimes, chores, clothing and/or body piercing, curfews, safety measures, table manners, participation at religious institutions, and homework. Any of these conflicts can trigger discomfort when a child expresses anger or feels unfairly treated.

Christina is losing the battle.

Christina's two girls are, simply put, brats. They are chronically disrespectful and disobedient at home as well as at school, where she has regular contact with their teachers, the principal, and the school social worker. They're the kids no mother wants assigned to her on a school field trip, the children who aren't invited back for playdates a second time.

Christina's inconsistency with setting limits with her children is among the worst I've seen. No surprise, then, that her problem has roots that go way back. She was raised in California by a chemically dependent mother, who, addicted to prescription painkillers, was generally too buzzed to create any family structure. Reared mostly by the housekeeper, Christina grew up with no boundaries at home. Christina looks to her children for the unconditional love she missed in her childhood, and she mistakes their pleasure in being overindulged for being loved by them. They constantly manipulate her vulnerability, telling her "I hate you" when they are denied McDonald's three nights in a row. It works every time; McDonald's it is.

Her self-esteem is so fragile that she throws in the towel whenever she feels resistance from her children. Since she cannot bear for them to be angry with her, limit-setting is an impossibility. In order to see herself as a good mom, she blames the children: no one could be consistent in the face of their whining.

It spills into her marriage, of course. Christina's husband wants to make dinnertime a no-television period, and she is furious at his suggestion that her rules could be improved. When I ask her what he thinks might be nicer about dinner if the TV was turned off, she erupts defensively: "You sound just like him. Try being with my kids for a whole day, and see how you react when they start screaming about not seeing *Rugrats* at dinner. It's a nightmare." Christina is miles away from understanding that her children don't respect her limits because they don't have to, and she isn't open to any other perspective.

By trying to compensate for the sense of deprivation she experienced growing up, she has created children who cannot tolerate ordinary limits. Christina needs intensive support, and I recommend a child psychotherapist to help her strengthen her parenting skills with her daughters. Couples counseling might help both parents be internally consistent, reducing the ability of the girls to play one of them against the other. But Christina probably needs years of individual psychotherapy, because the primary reason she is failing the developmental challenge of setting limits is that she hungers too much for her children's approval.

How do I distinguish whether a mother's problem with limit-setting is significant? The first question I always ask is whether that child shows an inability to conform to expectations at school. Christina's daughters are awful at school and that's a very worrisome sign. Renee, the mother in Chapter 2 whose son, Michael, refused to leave playdates, had difficulty getting Michael to follow her expectations and ended up swatting him in frustration. When we explored his behavior at school, she told me something I hear often: the preschool and kindergarten teachers always seemed to be describing someone else's child. He was never a discipline problem at school, never refused to follow the rules there. This is a relief to me: Michael is perfectly capable of adapting his behavior to a particular set of social expectations. His mother has a problem enforcing her own rules, and needs to overhaul her system of conveying and following through expectations at home. Michael has learned the bad habit of ignoring his mother's limits, but he isn't hopeless. He doesn't have a major behavior problem if he can get along just fine in other situations—she's the one who needs to change. Renee needs support and guidance for setting limits, but she can see that if she changes, so will Michael. Alas, Christina's children are so wild that even the pros can't rein them in.

Why Is It So Hard to Say No to Your Child?

No one wants to raise bratty kids. We all want our children to behave well, get along socially, and be good citizens. We all want our kids to listen to us, whether we're asking them to brush their teeth or be polite to the boss when she comes for dinner. But something is seriously wrong in mothering today, even when things aren't as out of control as they are in Christina's family. As author Christie Mellor notes, today's mothers *are* all too often "lapdogs" to their children. We have an epidemic of mothers who are regularly disrespected and disobeyed by their children.

Judith Warner attributes the loss of parental authority to "Sacrificial Motherhood." She notes that by the 1960s, parenting expert Dr. Benjamin Spock was already lamenting the " 'considerable misinterpretation and misapplication' of Freudian parenting practices [that] had allowed American children to start to run amok." She describes "how atrocious efforts to 'empathize' [have] become, at the turn of the millennium, as children tromped around on furniture or threw sand in each other's eyes, and their mothers . . . asked them if they had 'something to say.' " She's not blaming the victim, but rather noting that the "new message about motherhood: to do it well, you had not only to take care of your children but to be mindful of your children's *inner children,*" makes it almost impossible to be anything *other* than a lapdog.

No mother who fails at setting limits with her child wants it that way, or somehow missed understanding how it is supposed to go. There isn't a parenting magazine at the doctor's office that doesn't lead with a cover story about discipline, for example. Warner and Mellor are among the legions of parenting experts who regularly preach what I call "Limits 101," a core set of basic principles: be firm, be consistent, stay calm, and let consequences flow naturally from misbehavior. Readers of this book have without question encountered numerous articles, lists, television shows, and books on discipline and setting limits, all of which include Limits 101.

Warner makes an excellent point linking the culture of Perfect Motherhood to the growing loss of parenting authority. This challenge is tough for collective and individual reasons, and I believe Mellor hits the nail on the head when she says the problem for today's mothers is the "negative reaction." It is hard to have your child rip-roaring mad at you, and for many mothers this is the single most difficult challenge of motherhood. In previous generations, mothers were supported by the culture that placed a far greater emphasis on good behavior—yes, it sucks to say no to your kid, but you do it for their own good. And, as Werner notes, parents used to be far less culturally paranoid about the risk of bruising their children's self-esteem. If your kids don't respect your authority, you're floundering in the face of this key challenge, and it's time to change.

The Goal: High Warmth and High Expectations

It takes tremendous psychological strength to master setting limits these days, and that's because it requires a woman to fight the romantic notion that the well-loved children of good mothers behave perfectly. Alas, you cannot always please and soothe your child *and* set limits. One or the other goes. In fact, family psychologists note that behavioral control and parental warmth are entirely separate domains. Studies that classify parenting styles based on how families combine emotional responsiveness (affection, rapport, empathy) with control consistently document that children do best with a combination of love *and* limits. These studies confirm the obvious: the most important thing parents do is demonstrate that they love their children. You can't do it too much. But you *can* expect too little, can fall short if you don't have standards.

Parenting Domains of Limits, Warmth*

Responsiveness/Warmth	+ Rules and Limits	= Parenting Style
Low	+ Low =	Uninvolved

"Absentee landlords"; children are at highest risk for depression, school problems

Low	+ High =	Authoritarian

"Military style"; children at increased risk for depression but not problem behaviors

High	+ Low =	Indulgent

"Flower-child parenting"; children show high self-esteem but have higher risk for school and problem behaviors

High	+ High =	Authoritative

The Huxtables on the Cosby Show; *this is the parenting style best correlated with child well-being in all domains*

---

* Originated by Diana Baumrind, Ph.D., at the Institute of Human Development, University of California, Berkeley

Limit-Setting Can Be Learned

Lakeisha (see Chapter 4), whose son, Jevon, has severe childhood asthma, has an especially difficult problem with setting limits because his crying may trigger an asthma attack. After undergoing the trauma of numerous intensive care unit admissions, denying him candy for breakfast, therefore, is harder than it might seem at first glance. To make matters worse, some of the medications for asthma can cause excessive energy, overstimulation, and/or insomnia. Lakeisha says Jevon's medicines leave him "hyper" and "hungry all the time." She notes that Jevon's medicines sometimes make him unable to "sit and do one thing." He'll "bother his sister, keep asking for water, beg for candy, and go back and forth from TV to Game Boy to coloring. He's very busy."

But as much as she fears an asthma attack, she isn't going to let him get away with murder. Jevon sometimes has temper tantrums when she won't give him dessert if he didn't eat dinner, for example. He may kick and stomp his feet in protest, or he may cry. She started using time-outs as soon as he could understand it, age one and a half or two, she recalls. Currently, he'll average about ten minutes in his room on time-out, with the first five minutes kicking the door. "I tell him, 'the longer you do that, the longer you'll be in there.'"

Lakeisha gives her mother credit for helping her learn to manage his tantrums, which were very difficult at first. She felt helpless and frustrated when she couldn't get Jevon to listen, and she'd find herself screaming at him, which didn't help. She noticed that Jevon was far more likely to respond to his grandmother's limits than her own. When Lakeisha asked for advice, she asked her "What are you doing differently than me?" Lakeisha owned up to yelling, and her mother suggested, "Try to talk to him calmly, maybe that's the reason." Over time, Lakeisha worked hard to keep her voice calm, and she feels it made a huge difference. She doesn't bristle when her mother, with whom she lives, reminds her not to raise her voice, and it's become much easier to get his cooperation.

I asked if perhaps Jevon differentiates mom as "business" and grandma as "play." She agrees, and notes that her mother said the same thing. A mother is usually going to be the heavy more often than anyone else, and that means she has to live with the fact that her child will struggle and resist *her* most of all. One of the key developmental challenges that setting limits creates for mothers is that they must bear the discomfort of their children's anger. In babyhood, children cry out of distress. But when a child begins to need limits for safety and socialization, the mother must be able to sustain a sense of being a capable, loving, and loved mother, despite the fact that her child, who until now loved her without reservation, is furious with her.

Lakeisha accepts input on her mothering. She has a firm set of values about how to discipline: no spanking, for example, even though some members of her family believe physical punishment the correct way to change unwanted behavior. Yet there are many things she isn't so sure about. The ability to consider multiple perspectives is a trait associated with the concept of "emotional intelligence." When Lakeisha accepts her mother's advice about how to verbally correct Jevon, she demonstrates appropriate emotional flexibility. She isn't wishy-washy, but rather assumes that since mothering is learned, others' viewpoints are worth considering. When she tried using a softer voice with her son, it worked, and she felt pleased with her new competence, not defensive or ashamed that this was something she needed help with.

Defining "Consistency"

Lakeisha is currently working on something that she finds difficult: perfect consistency. Her mother encourages her to be ruthlessly consistent, helping her see that it would be easier in the long run if Jevon got a crystal-clear message about the rules. She struggles with being consistent, and sometimes gives in to a request that she's already denied. Now that he's four, Jevon understands that crying can trigger his asthma, and tends to listen when she advises him to "Calm down or you'll get sick." But sometimes she gives in, especially when she's tired, because she's worried about his breathing or afraid that she's on the verge of blowing up. "Sometimes I think it's better to give in than to take out my frustrations on him."

You won't find parenting advice that doesn't advocate consistency. A quick trip to the major online parenting Web sites shows that "consistency" is on every list on how to discipline. But I'm going to be a heretic here: perfect consistency is another parenting myth. All mothers are inconsistent, even those who are parenting experts. Pediatrician and author Perri Klass, M.D., for example, notes: "Is there a reason you have to win the you-can't-go-barefoot-in-the-snow battle? Probably yes. But do you also have to win the you-can't-wear-the-same-shirt-two-days-in-a-row battle? Maybe not."

If you study excellent classroom teachers you'll find the same phenomenon: "rubber rules." Hard rules are enforced in every responsible home and classroom: you cannot hurt other children, for example. But rubber rules in the classroom mean that sometimes a teacher overlooks it when a shy child blurts out the answer without raising his hand first, or ignores behavior in some children that she doesn't overlook for a bully. If she's having a bad day, her rules might slide a bit. Rubber rules exist in perfectly good homes. You can't have soda at age three, unless you have a fever and need fluids and ginger ale is the only way to get them in you. You can't watch TV all day, unless Mom just came home with a new baby and she's too exhausted to play Chutes and Ladders. You can't sleep in her bed unless you had a terrible nightmare. Mothers change the rules and/or overlook misbehavior regularly when their children are tired, hungry, or sick.

The myth of perfect consistency makes setting limits a no-win situation for some. Kids are natural bargainers. A three-year-old who is determined to wear a lavender-flowered shirt with kelly green plaid pants is negotiating her own sense of style, just as a sixteen-year-old who prepares a spreadsheet indicating that other parents allow a later car curfew than ten p.m. on weekends is negotiating independence. Authoritarian mothers may use consistency to justify rigidity, never allowing a child to participate in setting family rules. The mother who is afraid that any compromise could lead to chaos is just as insecure as the woman who never says no.

The myth of perfect consistency can also create a sense of futility in mothers, especially those with low self-esteem. It's yet another impossible expectation. Lakeisha is a very capable mother with a highly challenging disciplinary issue (the risk that being thwarted can trigger an asthma attack), and yet she feels a sense of inadequacy for her occasional lapses. Aim for consistency, I suggest, but give yourself a break when you're only human. When you are inconsistent, try to explain why you've made the exception: I'm letting you have cookies before dinner because I got out of work late and I won't be able to make dinner at the usual time. A little wiggle room isn't the same thing as anarchy.

Learning to Bear the Discomfort

While most mothers find it painful to be the object of their child's anger, some women feel devastated by it. The first disciplinary struggles are usually associated with the "terrible twos," when children respond to limits with anger, tantrums, and perhaps hitting or biting. Young children are novices at anger, and have not yet learned how to cope with frustration without anger or emotional disintegration. The poorly mothered mother may see her child's anger as being identical to the anger she herself felt growing up, overidentifying with her child's emotional distress. She may be unable to differentiate the feelings of a child who is furious about not being allowed to take another toddler's toy during playgroup with the rage she felt when her mother mocked her as she left for her first date. Many poorly mothered mothers have unrealistic expectations about mother-child relations, and have the belief that good mothers magically discipline children, without tears or tantrums. Some are able to modify their unrealistic expectations for themselves by observing other mothers: they find comfort at the park when other mothers have to drag their screaming toddlers away from the sandbox at nap time.

Some women learn to bear the discomfort simply by reminding themselves that it is in their children's best interest to learn to get along socially, to learn to behave. This works for Renee and Lakeisha: they use the defense mechanism of altruism to cope with their children's angry responses to limits. Defense mechanisms are ways in which we handle emotional conflict. They fall along a spectrum of narcissistic to mature, and altruism is considered by psychologists to be a mature (highly adaptive) defense. When faced with a conflict ("I need to set limits on my child but I hate when she's mad at me"), individuals who use altruism are emotionally gratified by knowing that they are serving a higher purpose ("Even though I prefer my child to adore me at all times, I know it's in her best interest to learn to play nicely").

Another healthy defense mechanism is affiliation, turning to others for support and advice, while not expecting that others solve the problem for you. When a mother turns to another mother at the playground for support and validation ("Don't you hate being Bad Mommy?"), she is using a high-level defense mechanism. Less healthy defenses against a child's anger at limits include displacement (erupting in anger at a nanny who fails to control the very behavior she herself cannot control), denial ("the teachers say bad things about my children because they can't manage gifted children"), somatization (mom gets a headache to guilt-trip her children into stopping a fight), and help rejecting complaining ("my children are poorly behaved but there's nothing anyone can do about it").

In addition, most mothers will need to learn specifically to bear the discomfort of embarrassment. Children will try to get away with more when there is an audience. When Libby was driving to a soccer game with her friend Jill and their kids, Libby's fourteen-year-old daughter said something specifically designed to embarrass her mom. Libby ignored it because she was "horrified that Ariel talked to me that way in front of Jill." I point out that Libby's daughter has earned the right to be embarrassed, not Libby. Both of my teenagers have tried it, and yours probably have or will, too: flexing their muscles by reporting something you'd rather not make public.* This one I know for sure: if you bring it out in the open, they will stop trying to embarrass you. I encourage Libby to be ready next time: "Ariel, it really hurts my feelings that you are obviously trying to make me uncomfortable in front of my friend Jill. I think that's mean, and I know that you know how to be a kind person." Learning to bear the discomfort in public means banishing the audience. Chances are good that when you're mortified because you've taken an angry/crying/protesting child out of a restaurant, playground, theater, or other public place, for the one mom who thinks you must be a bad mom or your child would behave, there are ten others thinking "You go, girl."

Bearing the discomfort in public may also mean that you, with grace if not joy, let other authority figures correct unacceptable behavior. Muffy Mead-Ferro tells of the time her son refused to obey a lifeguard's order to clear the pool. "She got down from her perch to crouch in the shallow end of the pool, nose to nose with Joe, and told him if he didn't obey the rules. . . . he wouldn't be allowed to come back to the pool ever again. So, out, now." Many mothers would find this embarrassing, might look around hoping no one they know saw the incident. But Muffy is clear that Joe *made a choice* to ignore the lifeguard. "Ride 'em, cowgirl. I hope this lifeguard becomes a mom someday. . . . Or takes over inane parenting class."

Confident, thriving mothers let others share the burden of so-

---

* A short list of the things teens can purposely embarrass you by observing and mentioning in public: your gray roots, your age, the fight you and your husband had last night, your addiction to *American Idol,* the mean thing you said about a neighbor, and the weight you listed on your driver's license.

cializing children. The other mom who reflexively takes a sharp stick out of your three-year-old's hand at the sandbox, the waitress who tells your child that he shouldn't have dessert when he didn't eat a bite of dinner, the museum guard who reprimands your ten-year-old for ignoring the signs about standing back from the painting, the school administrator who sends your senior home because she ignored the no-strapless-dress-at-the-prom rule, can be part of a mother's village.

Tailoring Consequences to Fit the Crime

The lifeguard's threatened consequences were perfectly tailored to the crime: if you don't follow the rules at the public pool, you don't get to use it. Angela's having problems establishing contingencies with her three kids, ages five, eleven, and fifteen, although what she first tells me is that her dog is driving her crazy. Her children rarely walk the dog, a puppy that needs lots of exercise. It is summer, and it isn't like the kids are too busy. They don't even feed the dog, despite the fact that she's put the food bowl on top of a bin of dog food, requiring about ten seconds' labor to open the bin and scoop the food directly into the bowl. When she instructs a child to feed the dog, the most likely response she gets is, "I did it yesterday." I have raised my concerns now and then about the kids' behavior, and she knows what's coming. "Sounds like there isn't any respect for your authority," I say.

Although for several years I've been encouraging her to face her difficulty setting limits, she's been ignoring the problem. She hopes that if she waits it out, her kids will mature and begin taking responsibility for themselves, or become more sensitive to her workload. In fact, their problems are getting worse, and they are clearly spoiled. For the first time in therapy, she's more open, less defensive about discussing their behavior: "Yesterday one of my fifteen-year-old daughter's friends was over, and she said, 'My mom would kill me if I did that.' " In a slip of the tongue, she says, "Lauren has photographs she'd developed in the school darkroom all over her living room—every inch was covered." I raise my eyebrows, and she says, "Oops, I mean our living room. It's not *her* living room." But her slip is revealing: the kids are in charge. Last week, she asked the kids to do the dishes while she ran to pick up a video they had requested, and sure enough, not a dish was so much as moved off the table. Not one of them folds a piece of their own laundry, let alone pitch in with towels and sheets. Her older daughter likes to cook dinner, but regularly leaves the kitchen resembling a disaster area.

Angela's kids are very bright, adept with the weapons that kids use: protest, minimization, bargaining, distraction. When she wants them to feed the dog, they accuse her of being lazy. If she asks them to do the dishes, they promise to do it later, and never get to it. The older ones make the younger one do the chores they can't evade. They tune her out, and sometimes refuse to speak to her when she attempts to set limits. These weapons are nuclear powered when used against Angela. Another mother might laugh when a teenager who got out of bed at noon accuses her of being lazy, but Angela is devastated. A physically abused child, she was always angry and upset with her own mother. She told herself thousands of times that she'd have a good relationship with her kids, that she'd be the kind of mother who was truly loved by her children. She is unable to see that normal children stall, protest, whine, or criticize when made to be responsible, and she cannot tolerate their accusations.

Angela later reports a small victory: Lauren wanted a new outfit to wear for the first day of school. Angela refused to take her to the store until she cleaned the kitchen after making a huge mess. Within minutes, it sparkled. While they were shopping, Angela thanked Lauren for cleaning up; Lauren rolled her eyes and jokingly said, "Oh no, what have I done now?" I couch my own feedback gently: it's always a good idea to praise good behavior, but I'm not sure "thank you" fits the bill when a teen cleans up after herself. She gets it: "Yeah, like I'm supposed to be grateful because it's optional." She asks for help phrasing it—I suggest, "You did a good job cleaning up after yourself."

I see Angela's openness as an opportunity, and I'm not letting up. I tell her that praise alone won't turn this situation around. She needs a complete overhaul: more consequences, more contingencies. Her daughter has demonstrated that Limits 101—no privileges without meeting your responsibilities—works. Start by taking them to the video store *after* the dishes are done, or go right back to the video store and drop the unwatched movie off if the kids don't hold up their end of the bargain. Put the photographs in a bag, unsorted, and when she throws a fit, suggest that she take responsibility for her stuff next time. Advise eleven-year-old Jonathon that the four or five harried attempts to get him out of bed on a school day are over—he gets one wake-up call, and then he'll have to deal with the consequences of an unexcused absence when he misses the bus. Serve breakfast only after the dog has been fed.

Part of what makes it hard for Angela to establish natural consequences is that she is overcompensating. She has created a false dichotomy: if my mother was abusive, in order not to be like her I must never let my children suffer. The opposite of abuse isn't overindulgence, however. I point out that when her mother beat her with a hairbrush because she didn't empty her ashtray, the punishment didn't fit any crime Angela had committed. There isn't a rule that you have to clean your mom's ashtray. If you want to be different from your mother, make the consequences flow naturally from failing to adhere to reasonable limits.

Natural Consequences

Note: In every instance, the child protests, cries, complains, or whines. In every instance, the mother wishes her child wasn't upset, but she allows the consequences to flow naturally.

1. Four-year-old Malcolm breaks his brand-new toy by throwing it down the stairs. He is not given a new one.

2. Three-year-old Belle throws sand at a child. Her mother makes her apologize, and then whisks her home.

3. At the amusement park, seven-year-old Colin and nine-year-old Erin pitch a fit about not being allowed cotton candy. Their parents decide the outing is over.

4. Visiting friends from out of town, Tracy's family is invited out to dinner. Tracy's eight-year-old interrupts repeatedly, despite being entertained with games on his mother's BlackBerry. Tracy takes him outside the restaurant, scolds him, and stands with him for a quiet, boring time-out. When they return, he amuses himself appropriately, recognizing that his mom will not give in to his demands for attention.

5. After an argument about what time she needed to come home from the mall, fourteen-year-old Bertie ignores three calls from her mother on her cell phone. Bertie claims that the calls didn't go through. After she sees her calls on the missed-call log, Bertie's mother repossesses the cell phone for two weeks. Without a cell phone, Bertie's activities are limited to places she can be reached by a landline.

6. Seventeen-year-old Scott gets a special weekday midnight curfew for a party for the (mostly older) counselors at the camp he's worked at for the summer. At ten p.m.,

> ready for bed, his mother finds his house key sitting on the kitchen counter. She calls Scott and tells him that since she's unwilling to stay up to let him in, he needs to come home early. When he says his ride won't take him home early, she offers to call a cab, which he can pay for with his camp earnings. He arranges to have his older brother stay up until eleven p.m. to let him in, and Scott's mother goes to sleep.

I Think I Can: Locus of Control

Like Christina, Angela lacks authority at home because her children know how to manipulate her fear of their anger or disapproval. She can't bear the discomfort, and they know it. When she comes to see that linking consequences to unmet expectations means that she is *not* like her mother, she realizes that having your children's approval isn't a good mothering report card. Angela is ready to tackle the next goal: being effective. Angela lacks an essential ingredient that mothers must have in order to overcome the challenge of setting limits: the belief that it is within your power to modify your children's behavior. She tells me, "It's too hard to make them listen. I can't do it." Angela is a highly capable woman—she is asked to be on every committee and volunteer fund-raiser under the sun because she's a great addition to any project. But when it comes to her children, she lacks what sociologists call an "internal locus of control."

Psychologist Julian Rotter developed the concept of "locus of control" in 1966. Rotter characterized individuals as having an internal locus of control if they usually feel in charge of their own destiny. Individuals with an external locus of control, in contrast, believe that most things that happen in life are determined by outside forces, such as fate, luck, or the influence of other people. For example, an individual with an internal locus of control is likely to agree with the statement "If you set realistic goals, you can succeed no matter what," while a person with an external locus of control is likely to agree that "Bad or good luck can really follow you around." Rotter's concept is succinctly defined by author Steven Covey in his bestselling *The Seven Habits of Highly Effective People*. His first lesson, "Be proactive," notes that one can "act or be acted upon." A proactive individual has an internal locus of control, where the passive person, who is "acted upon," has an external locus of control.

A parenting locus of control scale has been developed, composed of statements that are typically made by active versus passive parents. A mother who lacks an internal locus of control when it comes to parenting is likely to agree with statements such as "I feel that I do not have enough control over the direction my child's life is taking," and "I find that sometimes my child can get me to do things that I really did not want to do." A mom who has an internal locus of control does not characterize her authority in a docile way.

Christina and Angela both claim that their children's behavior is not under their control. Mothers who lack an internal locus of control are far more likely to have unmothering and addiction in their backgrounds—parental consistency and predictability in childhood promote the development of an internal locus of control in later adulthood. Others have specific events that diminished their belief in control over destiny, such as sexual abuse, rape, death of a sibling or parent, or severe illness in their own childhood. In other words, the mother who lacks an internal sense of control often either has no model of effective parenting, or has experienced a traumatic loss of control.* Because they *feel* ineffective when it comes

---

* However, some poorly mothered women emerge with a highly developed internal locus of control, especially when they functioned as caretakers prematurely. Hilary, who I'll describe in Chapter 8, for example, "raised" her siblings, and entered motherhood with a strong sense of being able to establish guidelines and structure.

to unwanted behaviors, they *are* ineffective. They bribe, cajole, cave in, and plead in the face of opposition. And there is a natural feedback loop: a mother's sense of efficacy is enhanced by success and diminished by failure. Humans generalize from the particular, and when a mother doesn't manage to tame an angry toddler's outbursts, her perception that she *can't* do so is reinforced, just as a mother's success in setting limits reinforces her sense of self-efficacy.

Modifying an external locus of control usually takes help, be that in the form of parenting coaching, classes, psychotherapy, or practical parenting books. It also takes time, as a mother first strings together small successes. Think baby steps. The woman who knows what she wants to do but nonetheless can't do it—whichever parenting model or advice she chooses to follow—usually has an emotional obstacle to limit-setting, often one of perceived inadequacy.

Conclusion

Fortunately, it's never too late to establish high expectations, or to challenge your own mistaken beliefs about perfect mothering. Angela's victory with Lauren, when she cleaned the kitchen as asked, helped her feel empowered: she did something that caused Lauren to modify her unacceptable behavior, and it felt great. Parenting seminars, books, magazines, and Web sites often provide hands-on practical advice that help mothers become more self-confident in their ability to positively influence behaviors, and many women will find that continuing to seek out information to strengthen their own sense of effectiveness is well worth the effort. Mastering appropriately responsive discipline is an opportunity to help her own children acquire an internal locus of control, even if hers is rusty at times.

Regardless of the child's age, a useful sign that a mother is coping well with setting limits is that the consequences of behavior flow naturally from the misbehavior. When kids are fighting in the backseat of the minivan, a woman who is comfortable with setting limits pulls over, explaining that she can't drive safely when she's distracted by the noise. If a child treats his mother as a servant, she ignores the demands until the request is stated politely. The mother who is thriving in the face of this critical challenge views limits as an uncomfortable but important learning opportunity: your behavior affects what happens to you.

Signs of Poor Adaptation to Setting Limits

1. Belief that you are powerless when it comes to effecting positive changes in your child's behavior.

2. Defensiveness or defeatism when trusted others attempt to make suggestions.

3. Inability to tolerate the discomfort of your child's expressed negative emotions when you apply limits.

4. Regularly covering up, excusing, rationalizing, apologizing on behalf of, or being ashamed of your children's bad behavior, or regularly telling yourself "Just this one time."

Strategies for Successful Adaptation

1. Start with the basics of Limits 101: be firm, be consistent, stay calm, and let consequences flow naturally from misbehavior. Clarify the difference between entitlements and privileges.

2. Notice and give yourself credit for successful steps, however small. If you have an external locus of control, con-

sider seminars or hands-on parenting classes to help you become more effective. Start a journal with a daily entry that begins, "Today, I was an effective mother when . . ."

3. Take pride in having the fortitude to bear your children's anger, knowing that good mothers bear the brunt and are loved anyway.

4. Keep the big picture in view. Remind yourself regularly that it's in your children's best interest to acquire socially appropriate behaviors and internal self-control.

6

Imperfect Institutions
The Sixth Key Challenge

>What makes watching a child trot off to school so tough for a parent is that there is perhaps no setting that drives home a parent's sense of helplessness as acutely.... Having a child in school hammers home the discrepancies between a parent's dreams and the sometimes ruthless reality....
>—Michael Thompson and Teresa Barker, *The Pressured Child*

It's good to be queen, and until your child starts formal school, chances are, you're the one and only queen. Enrolling your child in kindergarten drastically changes the primary role a middle-class mother plays in her child's day-to-day life. Even if you used day care, you were a paying customer or an individual's employer, and that carried weight. At preschool, the classroom child-to-adult ratio was at least half that of kindergarten, and you were likely welcome to help out as often as you liked.

But suddenly you're an outsider, and you can't drop in unannounced. You can't tell the professionally trained and certified teacher how to care for your child; her boss is the principal, not you. She may have a couple of very draining students who corner the market on her time and energy, and that's just tough luck for your kid. This lack of control combined with a built-in reduction of individualized attention makes sharing your child with the school so challenging. You're not queen, and your child isn't royalty, either. Oh, and it's a colossal separation, the likes of which you may not have ever previously experienced.

One might have predicted that Kathleen would find it hard to hand over her daughters to school. Her nonconformist family tree includes many noted Chicago artists and social activists. Her grandparents and great-aunts and -uncles lived the Bohemian lifestyle, founding labor unions by day, passionately reciting Yeats over jugs of cheap wine at night. Third-generation Irish Catholic, she acknowledges the stereotypical alcoholism, noting the combination left the family "troubled and poor, but intellectually rich." To help make ends meet when she was a child, Kathleen's family moved out to the country, where her mother, a former actress, gave performances at the local Catholic school in exchange for tuition for her children.

In the small-town environment, the family stood out: "You could hear the fights at home around the neighborhood. We were odd, but also beloved in the community." Periodically, a neighbor would "turn us in," prompting a visit from the government social workers. The family was so different, and so chaotic at times, that outsiders worried for the health and safety of the children, although the visiting social workers considered neglect to be unfounded.

Kathleen did not consider providing her own children a Catholic education, which she experienced as being "guilt- and shame-based." She and her then-husband, also raised in an Irish-Catholic family, decided that if a label was necessary, the girls would be considered Unitarian, although she is quick to reject lines that divide people. To some extent, she draws on Buddhism for spirituality, and describes herself as having an active spiritual life that is peace-oriented and sensitive to karmic energy to become aware of the higher purpose of life. Some would label her "New

Age." In the family tradition, she has made a career as an artist and performer to promote social justice.

When her oldest daughter, Ciara, was ready for kindergarten, she had rarely been cared for by anyone who wasn't related to her. Kathleen and her husband had flexible schedules that allowed them to have a parent around, with backup provided by the extended family at times. A bright girl, Ciara tested into one of Chicago's most-sought-after public magnet schools, a multicultural elementary school that offers gifted education along with bilingual sign language education. Given its stellar reputation, Kathleen was optimistic.

Quickly, however, it became clear that Kathleen's values clashed with those of the school. From her viewpoint, the school offered rules and more rules. Bathroom privileges were scheduled, there would be no talking in line, girls in one row, boys in another. Most shocking to Ciara: children were not permitted to question the rules—you got in worse trouble if you challenged *why* you were in trouble. In their family, the expectations were that the kids self-monitored their behavior based on reasoning—if Kathleen had a rule, the children were not only permitted, they were *expected* to question it. Her parenting philosophy was grounded in the idea that children followed rules they understand. To Ciara, asking questions of adults was both natural and comfortable, but to her teachers, it was a challenge to their authority, anarchy waiting to happen, or simply too time-consuming. It's easy to see both sides—the teacher has twenty-four children to get to the bathroom, yet why wouldn't six-year-old Ciara wonder why you couldn't talk quietly, as long as you weren't disruptive?

Kathleen grew up with a family that questioned authority. She saw power misused at times, such as when the state social workers would repeatedly investigate a socially nonconforming family based on neighbors' discomfort with their lifestyle. Her entire extended family were peace activists during the Vietnam war, and she and her husband were uncomfortable with organized religion. She is not a mother who hands her daughters to a school system assuming that institutions always act benevolently.

At the same time, she honors education in her roots and in her daily life (seven of her nine siblings are schoolteachers, and she herself teaches painting to adults). She says, "We question *and* we respect. Represent your viewpoint, but don't just be rude or manipulative." She understands the enormous pressures placed on teachers these days, and yet she also questions the slippery-slope argument applied to conformity: If we allow your child to be different, what next? At its worst, she feels school as an institution values conformity of behavior in order to maintain order and attend to the reams of paperwork, and uses shame to control unwanted behavior.

Whether conscious or not, most mothers have fantasies and expectations about what an ideal teacher and school will provide for their children. Kathleen came into school as a parent who especially valued creativity and innovation, and lots of rules are often mutually exclusive. Those who are truly creative often have very different ideas about how to foster creativity in children than the rest of us do. For example, many parents feel that the best way to nurture the arts is to expose children to a wide variety of lessons, and may emphasize the discipline of lessons and repetition. Kathleen feels that the best way to nurture creativity in children is to leave them alone, to allow them sufficient artistic license to tap into their own natural imagination, perhaps insist that they reach inside their mind's eye for inspiration when bored. She remembers noticing that Fred Rogers always waited patiently for the child to answer, and thought, "Aha, that's the way to foster imagination." She saw lost opportunity time and again: while the school showed Disney movies during recess on snow days, *she* would have encouraged creative play. The school recitals at which children lip-synched made her blood boil. She views the emphasis on standardized tests as woefully misplaced.

The magnet school Ciara attended offered no automatic enrollment for siblings. When her younger daughter, Maura, was ready for school, Kathleen was just as glad they didn't. She enrolled Maura in an experimental alternative public school, with open walls between multiple classrooms. This was a case of throwing the baby out with the bathwater: "insanity" ruled. There was so little structure and order that chaos dominated the classroom—the noise alone made it impossible to think, let alone meet her ideal of "providing the opportunity for the child to sit still in her imagination."

When Kathleen's husband hit a period of artistic prosperity, she had the opportunity to get the girls enrolled together by switching them to a private school. Her marriage was breaking up, and she knew that others felt the girls should remain in a familiar school setting during the transition. But after too many parent-teacher meetings, where she felt parents were disenfranchised, even treated with condescension when they made suggestions, she did not believe that either school would ever be the best place for her children. She felt that they'd weather the family change better if they were happier at school.

And she wanted to model a value she prizes: don't just complain, *do*. She asked around the artistic community for suggestions, and was referred to a Montessori school in Chicago. She knew she was in the right place when her third grader was invited to interview the principal. The girls sat in on classes, and both were eager to attend. The teachers felt that both girls were a great fit, and, indeed, that's how it turned out.

Kathleen says the Montessori approach "changed their lives." They'd found a school that held creativity in the same regard she did, and saw the same pathway to nurturing it. Kathleen felt respected as a parent. For example, when the school remained silent after the Columbine tragedy, she initiated a panel discussion about peace and nonviolence, which the school welcomed as a good idea put forth by an involved parent. The girls went on to different high schools—one with a highly alternative orientation, the other a standard college preparatory high school, and both flourished. They remained intellectually curious, artistic, and confident in their ability to be independent thinkers.

Each of Kathleen's daughters internalized the philosophy of "question and respect" in their own education. Since Ciara's alternative high school was graded on a pass-fail system, her first-choice university rejected her admission after they assigned a grade value of "C" to each of her classes. Ciara, who grew up believing it was permitted to challenge educational institutions, successfully appealed the admissions decision and is now enrolled at this very fine university. Likewise, Maura, enrolled in a highly conventional school, resisted the high school's pressure to substitute advanced placement chemistry for a painting class in order to "look better" to prospective universities.

Kathleen was fortunate that she had the resources to eventually find a school that nurtured her children in the way she herself would. Until then, she had to swallow the pain of a school setting that she experienced as pushing mindless conformity. A dozen years later, she can hear the language the school used to justify their insistence on particular rules: "If you want to get along in the world, you have to do it this way." And she beautifully articulates the shock of the culture clash: "The sweet loveliness of your child is allowed for, then—*clap!*—it's time to Get Real. Buck up and be part of the system."

Trust Is the First Requirement

Successfully putting your child in the hands of an organization, be it school, camp, a summer theater program, after-school child care, or religious instruction, is by definition an act of faith. Since she cannot be there, a mother must believe that the organization will adequately care for her child. Kathleen did not trust her children's first schools. She had positive experiences with some of the teachers at both places, but enough negative ones that she could not fully relax in the knowledge that her children were in consistently nurturing hands.

Stephanie is an elementary school teacher and a mother, so she knows both sides of the fence. She articulates Kathleen's struggle: "The extent to which you can hand your child over comfortably is the amount you can trust the teacher, even if [her educational philosophy] is a value you don't share at home." As any mother has, Stephanie has had moments where she's questioned what's happening in her own children's classroom, even though as a teacher she is also aware that "my child may have left something out that may have made the situation make sense." But she also understands mistrust: "If it keeps happening, it's a different matter. You call." She had one particularly bad experience with a permanent substitute teacher filling in for a maternity leave. The substitute kept calling lavish attention to her daughter's exceptional academic talent ("everyone in the class—look at how well Hannah is reading") and ignored Stephanie's request that she cut it out. With two months left in the school year, Stephanie opted to let it slide, considering it annoying but not harmful.

Stephanie teaches in a suburban public school near St. Louis, Missouri, where parents have very high expectations. As a second-grade teacher, her most troubling encounters with parents are generally about her perception that a child may have a learning disability. She says that trust is especially important between parents and the teacher when they have a different picture of who this kid is. The parent says this teacher doesn't understand my child; the teacher says this parent doesn't know this child in this setting. The mother wants you to "get" their kid in the way she does.*

---

* Since I was interviewing Stephanie about a book on mothering, we spoke about the mother-teacher relationship. At the end of the interview, I asked her to compare her experience of mothers versus fathers. Her community is like any upper-middle-class community: some mothers work part-time, some full-time, some are full-time at-home. The majority of fathers work full-time.

Unfortunately, Stephanie may be one of the first people to raise concerns about a child's learning difficulties. She's sensitive to the pain: if she suspects that a child may have a learning disability, or attention deficit disorder, "It's a little death for that parent. We all hold a picture of our own children—what competent enough means, what smart enough is. I'm asking a parent to put her vision of her child on the line—it's a lot to ask." I ask her what are the common ways in which some mothers resist her suggestion that a child be formally tested for a learning disability (the testing and subsequent special services cannot be initiated without parental consent). She describes the most heartbreaking response: "My child is just lazy." She believes that some parents prefer the idea that a child is lazy in part because they don't understand what a learning disability is. ("They hear you say their child is stupid, or they have an ancient picture of a special education room as a closet in the back of the school where the labeled kids are warehoused.") And she believes that mothers see laziness as something with a maternal solution: I'll give her extra help at home, make sure she does her homework before television, shape his character, control his problem for him.

One thing she knows is that mothers are concerned about the stigma of a learning disability. They worry that their child will be socially ostracized when they get pulled out of the regular classroom for learning assistance. She notes, "The irony is that kids are extremely aware of who's on top of the material. The child who isn't getting needed services is the least prepared to show mastery, and the other kids see it in a heartbeat."

Off the topic of learning disabilities, I asked Stephanie to describe what she observes about mothers who might be having a

---

"Mothers are around a lot more. But also, if there is an issue, the mother is quicker to excuse the behavior, find a reason for the child's issue. Fathers are generally quicker to be critical of the child, and much quicker to say to me, 'Whatever you think is best.' "

hard time with trust more generally. At her school, most mothers drop off and pick up their children at the school entrance. But every year, one or two mothers come into the classroom at the beginning and end of every day. The overanxious mother helps the child hang up her coat, assists the child with packing up even if the child doesn't need it. This mother also advocates for her child when the child could stick up for himself. I ask for an example, since for many of us, finding the line between being supportive and being overprotective can be tough. Her answer makes it clear that there is an extreme: "When a mother calls to say her child doesn't like the girl she was assigned to make a social studies poster with and can I please switch." I ask her to articulate a better approach: "I'd like to see the mother coach the child about how to approach me, how to advocate for herself." She also implies that she'd like parents to stop sweating the little stuff.

Finding the Right Fit

Yvonne is a middle-class thirty-six-year-old African-American married mother of two boys, ages eleven and thirteen. She, too, had issues with her children's school, but she reversed the path taken by Kathleen. She started her children in private parochial schools, and subsequently found a better fit for them in the public schools. She had been a full scholarship student at Chicago's most academically rigorous Catholic high school, and her experience had been very positive. She loved the Catholic preschool her sons attended, and assumed that a Catholic education was best for them.

Unfortunately, she tried three different schools before throwing in the towel. She felt attacked by the principal of the first school when he raised issues about her son's behavior. She immediately switched schools, in part due to an admittedly exaggerated vague fear of being reported, somewhere, as being a bad parent. She is married to a man born in Africa, where parental authority is high.

He didn't understand her anxiety about being singled out by the principal. "I was terrified—schools have so much power. They have the authority of the government, and they can abuse it." She grew up in a public housing project, and saw countless examples of government intrusion into family life. She acknowledges that she is highly emotional, and perhaps she overreacted.

However, she has a child who needs special handling by the schools. Her older son is, in her words, "near genius," yet gets C's and D's in school. "He doesn't turn his homework in; he's the classic underachiever." She feels that part of the problem is that he's bored by material that isn't challenging enough for him. She blames him for being "a slacker," a student who lacks the internal discipline to get his homework turned in. Her younger son "was in the principal's office every week," usually for boisterous behavior. Neither has been in any serious trouble, but they are spirited boys who will push the limits to the maximum.

She constantly thinks about her mothering, and she's the classic unmothered mother. Her father spent most of his adult life in prison, and she says that her mother "always" had one or another drug-addicted boyfriend who she put before her only child, Yvonne. "I was at the bottom of my mother's totem pole: my grandmother, her job, her boyfriend came first. Then me." She's grateful for her mother's devotion to getting her a great education, but that's about it. Yvonne describes parent-child role reversal: she was her mother's "shoulder to cry on—I never had one for me." Her mother was brutally raped when Yvonne was a teenager (she remembers vividly her mother's facial mutilation), and she's appalled to remember that her mother invited her to make a suicide pact after the rape. Yvonne acted on it, taking an overdose, which she survived.* She's had enough therapy in her life to realize that a mother who would

---

* Needless to say, this is one of the worse examples of mothering I've heard, and Yvonne describes some characteristics that suggest that her mother was seriously mentally ill if not also drug-addicted.

invite her teenage daughter to make a suicide pact after the mother's rape has "no boundaries. None."

Yvonne grew up in an all-female family, raised mostly by her grandmother and aunts. Her mother's rape left an indelible impression about sexual violence, about men as dangerous. "Why did God give me boys?" she asks herself, and she knows that she struggles every day of her life with discipline. She "never" was punished as a child—if she was sent to her room, her mother relented within minutes. As an only child, she feels ill-equipped to handle sibling rivalry. When her boys are mildly aggressive with one another, she freezes. She took them to a family violence therapist for a while, who informed her that her boys' way of relating to each other was perfectly normal for brothers their age.

Her experiences with the next two Catholic schools were no more successful. Whenever her sons have difficulty in school, she immediately blames herself. "I always feel it's ultimately because of me. The environment shapes them, so it must be me. The hardest part of parenting [for me] is guilt." She came to believe that since guilt is her parenting blind spot, a parochial school is a poor fit for her. "Catholic schools try to make you feel guilty." When her boys "acted up," she felt the schools were more interested in making it out to be her fault than in offering practical advice that might have helped the situation.

When she and her husband decided to enroll the boys in a public school, they bought a house in an integrated community within Chicago. She clicked with the principal and assistant principal right away: "They're solution-oriented. They want to help, not blame, like the other schools. They start by talking about my sons' assets. Your ears are open because they see their great stuff. I know my kids really well, and they recognize that."

She describes the signs she sees of a collaborative approach. First, they meet with the parents, later bringing in the child. Then they talk about what to do, "counseling and stuff to help with the behaviors." She is an active volunteer at the school. "It helps the school to know that there is a parent who cares. If trouble arises, they know it's a good household." She helps in the classrooms, makes copies in the office, and works in the library. "I never go in my own children's classroom—I want them to have independence." Her advice to any mother having difficulties with the school administration: get involved. But like Kathleen, she also has seen the powerful impact of finding the best fit for your family. She echoes Kathleen's words, "The new school has made a world of difference for my sons." Her older son is pulling his grades up, and her younger son "is always in the school newsletter they send home" (for his achievements).

Kathleen and Yvonne share a number of similarities. Both are highly invested in the value of education, and both are well-educated, intellectually curious women. They also share a concern about the misuse of institutional authority, and yet have faith that the right school setting can be wonderfully enriching for their children. Each approached an imperfect school system with hopeful expectation, optimistic that they could make the school a better fit for their children by becoming advocates and activists on behalf of their kids.

They gave the school a chance before deciding that they were unable to get the responsiveness that they sought for their children. Yvonne tried different Catholic schools before deciding that the public system would be a better fit, and Kathleen tried different public magnet schools before switching to Montessori. Both demonstrate an indicator of successful psychological adaptation to sharing their children with the school system: they were delighted when they landed at the right place. They are not impossible-to-please mothers who would find fault with anything other than perfection. Neither had a sense of entitlement, or unrealistic expectations about the school's ability to cater to each and every family's whim. Rather, they needed to feel respected as authorities on their children, and welcomed as allies in their children's education.

It Won't Always Be What's Best for Your Child

Sharing one's child with a school is likely the parent's first encounter with a large institution that has influence over her child. By definition, schools are organizations with a mission that at best overlaps with a parent's mission; they are imperfect. In theory, the school's objective is the same as yours: to nurture your child's growth, provide a strong academic foundation, and create a passion for learning. The school my own children attend proclaims that children are "our number one priority." I'm delighted with the school system, and yet there is simply no possibility that my individual children are *their* number one priority in the way that they are *my* number one priority. The school has multiple organizational goals, including meeting the needs of special needs students, be they significantly academically talented or disabled, performing well on state examinations, meeting federal guidelines for "No Child Left Behind," satisfying the local taxpayers who vote for or against property tax referenda, maintaining discipline, balancing their budget, and providing a wide array of student activities in order to meet the spectrum of community interests, ranging from after-school sports to geography competitions.

And a teacher simply cannot meet each and every student's unique learning style, but rather must, as a practical matter, create a learning environment that meets most of the students' needs, operates smoothly, and, ideally, refrains from harming the outliers. As examples: most students will learn to turn in their homework on time if penalized for not doing so, but some (especially children with attentional or organizational deficits) will repeatedly be penalized and may feel helpless and unfairly punished by such a system; most students will put an extra effort into academic competitions, working to learn their words for a spelling bee, but some will feel humiliated by always being eliminated quickly; some children thrive when asked to perform in groups, others do best when learning is individual. Good teachers balance these competing styles, but it's unrealistic to hope that a teacher can always meet each child's needs.

It may even be harmful to ask for such individual attention in that one unwritten objective of schooling is to help individuals learn to function as members working within socially constructed organizations. The teacher who said to Kathleen, "If you want to get along in the world, you have to do it this way," was going overboard in insisting that there is only one way for six-year-olds to get a drink of water, and yet, in another sense, she's got a point. Chances are very high that your child will eventually need to learn to get along in a large socially constructed institution, be it college, the workplace, or the military. This will involve some degree of conforming, by definition.

Learning to tolerate imperfect institutions conflicts with the sense of maternal responsibility that is in the air. As Susan J. Douglas and Meredith W. Michaels note in *The Mommy Myth,* "The problem with the new momism is that it insists that there is one and only one way the children of America will get what they need: if mom provides it."* The mother who complains about her eight-year-old daughter's assigned poster project companion is obviously attempting to micromanage her daughter's environment, believing that she has the duty, or power, to make her child's school experience perfect. The adjustment to sharing her child with school would be easier for her if she could tell the difference between the trivial and the problematic ways in which imperfect institutions ask our children to go along with the system.

---

* Momism is defined as "a set of ideals, norms, and practices, most frequently and powerfully represented in the media, that seem on the surface to celebrate motherhood, but which in reality promulgate standards of perfection that are beyond your reach" (pages 4–5).

Coping with the Appraisal System

All institutions have one thing in common: they appraise performance. The school is usually the first time a mother has someone "rate" her child. It's the first time your child is directly compared to others by an authority. In kindergarten, the teacher will tell you if your child is a good listener or "makes a good effort." You'll know if your seven-year-old reads at grade level or not. He'll get a solo in the holiday chorus show, or someone else's child will. The standardized tests will disappoint you or make you proud. They'll tell you if he belongs in honors biology or requires tutoring.

It might not be so bad if it didn't matter to children, but often the parent has to help the child as he develops his self-image as evaluated by the school: "I'm not as good at math as Jenny," "They make fun of me by calling me 'dictionary,' " "I'm only in the middle-fourth-grade reading group," "They picked me last at basketball," "The guidance counselor thinks I can't get into the college Dad went to." And no mother escapes having her child appraised imperfectly. Your son's brilliant science poster will have points taken off because it's messy, the standardized tests will be administered on a day when your daughter had a cold, or the teacher will choose her pet students for the leads in the Thanksgiving play.

Mothers of children who compete in extracurricular school-based programs have to rise to the challenge quickly. Jackie's daughter loves to perform, attends theater camp, and by fifth grade must audition for the school musical in order to get a part. Jackie is a mess during the week between auditions and casting, obsessing about how her daughter is seen by the drama club teacher. One minute she's anxious that she won't get a lead role, the next that she won't get any part at all. She's certain that favoritism plays a role, and it might. Yet that's the world of performing—it's arbitrary, a matter of judgment—and if her daughter cannot take rejection, I tell her, it might be best to find that out now. But whose issue is it—yours, or your daughter's? Jackie's anxiety is based in the belief that her daughter must get what she reaches for in order to feel good about herself. By focusing on her fear of how her daughter will handle the possibility of disappointment, Jackie misses the opportunity to honor her child's courage and determination.

Jackie has to let go of the idea that she can, or should try to, protect her daughter from institutional assessment. She cannot keep her in the maternal cocoon in which she receives nothing but praise. We're our kids' biggest fans, but every mother eventually experiences her child's entry into a world less wildly enthusiastic about her baby than she is. Very few children, if any, emerge from schooling being the best—only roughly 10 percent of the valedictorians who apply to Harvard will be admitted, for example—and mothers have to accept and help their children tolerate being, at something, perhaps many things, average or below average.

Being judged is never easy, but unfair appraisal is especially hard to swallow. Organizations are imperfect, without exception, and bias is an unsolved problem in America's schools. Many children will receive an unmerited poor grade, get cut from the soccer team when another kid was clearly worse, be overlooked for a leadership role in a club, and get on a teacher's bad side.

Marcia's son was accused of cheating on an exam by a still-wet-behind-the-ears teacher. Her son was a messy kid, and had unknowingly left a study guide under his desk during an examination. The teacher found it halfway through the exam, and publicly accused the seventh grader of cheating. He finished the test, and came home almost in tears, hurt and humiliated. Marcia and her husband met with the teacher that week. Marcia was enraged, ready to call the superintendent, or the local newspaper to tell the story. Her first instinct was revenge, to retaliate against a teacher who had hurt her son.

At the meeting, she arrived fuming. In the meantime, the teacher graded her son's examination, and realized that since he performed equally well on the first and second half of the examination, she had jumped to the wrong conclusion. She apologized to Marcia and her husband, and promised to apologize to their son. Marcia didn't let the teacher off easily: what if he hadn't been such a good student and couldn't prove his honesty? Had she learned from the experience that an accusation of cheating should never be made lightly, let alone in public? Marcia's son got over it more quickly than she did: *he already knew* that school wasn't always perfectly fair, that teachers had the ability to hurt kids' feelings. Marcia coped by using the incident to talk to her son about what it feels like to be treated unfairly, to be on the wrong end of an institutional failure. She told him: maybe the most important thing you'll learn in this class is that you have to know who you are, have to know that you're an honest student even if the teacher doesn't recognize that. And you have to do your best to fix the situation if you can.

A woman's prior experience with institutions is likely to color how she trusts her child's school. Marcia was generally very pleased with her son's school, and saw this situation as the exception. Growing up the scholarship kid from the housing projects, Yvonne was an outsider in a mostly white, mostly affluent school. Yvonne's response—become an insider, help out, be visible at the school—had been modeled by her own mother, who was a PTA leader at the Jesuit high school Yvonne attended. She responded to her mistrust of the school by doing her part to encourage a personal relationship, be seen as a trustworthy parent.

Because schools are imperfect institutions, the challenge for all parents is to be satisfied with good enough. Marcia couldn't undo the false accusation, but an apology and correction of the facts was good enough. For Yvonne and Kathleen, good enough was not easy to find, but they eventually got there. Stephanie found herself very unhappy with how her academically talented child was being singled out, but knowing that the school year would end soon made it troubling but not unbearable. The mother who cannot shrug off the small insults and slights that the school as an institution will likely make will remain angry or anxious, and may not be able to recognize when it *is* necessary and appropriate to challenge the institution's mistakes. She loses her objectivity, or is tuned out by a school that sees her as a chronic complainer.

Alas, It Gets Worse

The challenge of adapting to how one's child is treated by the institution of school is hard at first because it's new. This challenge, however, actually accelerates over the course of mothering. The size of the institution progressively enlarges, so that a grade school with three hundred kids becomes a high school with three thousand, and the principal who knows a mother's first name is replaced by a principal who doesn't even know your child's name. Performance appraisal accelerates as report cards that once offered "meets, exceeds, falls below grade expectations" are typically replaced by a letter-grade system, perhaps with pluses and minuses, weighted grades for the honors track, and/or class rank. The elementary school gym teacher who rotated players equally is replaced by the high school coach who wants to take her girls' softball team to state again this year, and couldn't care less about the individual players' emotional well-being.

While the student and his family become ever more anonymous, less empowered, the teachers become more powerful, and children become more aware of the power imbalance. In high school, grades matter more, at the same time that kids become sensitive to the quirks and foibles of those doling out the performance marks. The child whose mother suffers from bipolar affective disorder is told by her health teacher that depression is "a lifestyle choice," and her daughter is afraid of getting a bad grade if she protests. The advanced placement political science teacher who is grading your politically conservative son's paper announces that "The country will suffer if the Supreme Court is ruined by the Republicans," and your son, wanting a good report card in the semester he's applying to college, decides to write a paper he thinks his liberal teacher will like. Your daughter says the driver's education teacher looks at the girls in creepy ways, but she'd die before she'd risk not getting her license by going with you to the department head to discuss the issue.

Conclusion

You don't have to be a perfectionist to suffer when the institution that educates your child is imperfect. Of course, mothers want the best teacher, the nicest principal, the most inspiring coach, and the fairest grading system. Unfortunately, you can't always have it. Good enough is the best you can hope for.

Side by side with their children, thriving mothers develop calluses, as they see a child survive having the third-grade teacher who should have retired a decade ago, watch a daughter bounce back from grades that disappoint her, or learn that all the boys ignore the obnoxious blowhard who coaches the swim team. And flourishing mothers become more experienced at identifying things they can change (insisting that a school maintain appropriately high expectations for a child with a learning disability, for example) from the things they cannot change (high school health education teachers expressing foolish opinions).

The good news is that even while the stakes get higher, mothers who are successfully adapting to the challenge of sharing their children with imperfect institutions find it easier to manage. They come to see their children as being more resilient than they realized.

Signs of Poor Adaptation to Imperfect Institutions

1. Global distrust of school so that your automatic stance is adversarial. Conversely, assuming that the organization always has your child's best interests at heart.

2. Preoccupation with or rumination about how your child is appraised. Providing monetary rewards for good grades or penalizing average grades should be considered a possible red flag for overconcern about the appraisal system.

3. Belief that your child requires unqualified approval from the organization in order to have good self-esteem or develop a love of learning. A related belief is that your child cannot survive failure, and is therefore better off not trying out for selective activities.

4. Belief that it is a mother's job, or even possible, to make her child's school experience perfect.

Strategies for Successful Adaptation

1. Pick your battles. Be realistic about how powerful you as a parent can be within the organization, and don't sweat the small stuff. Figure out whether the best response is to talk to the teacher or principal, or whether compassionate listening and/or problem solving with your child is more appropriate to the issue.

2. Lay the groundwork by developing a personal relationship with your child's teacher or principal if logistically possible. If you need to address a problem with a total

stranger, assume that the teacher or administrator will be helpful, until proven otherwise.

3. Turn to other mothers for advice and support, perhaps formally through a parent advocacy organization, or through the informal girlfriends' network. Find out if someone has experienced a similar situation, and be open to feedback.

4. Bear in mind that imperfections are inevitable, and that every mishap your child experiences is a teachable moment. Try to take the opportunity to talk about your values and attitudes toward self-acceptance, authority, and social change. Model those values, including doing your best to transform untenable situations.

7

Revised Dreams
The Seventh Key Challenge

> There are many, many paths to becoming an interesting, successful person; one of life's hardest but most useful lessons is that we don't always get to choose which one we take.
> —Massachusetts Institute of Technology Admissions Guide: "Parenting the College Applicant—Dealing with Disappointment"

Parents begin to have hopes and dreams for their children from the outset. Some of the nicknames parents use in utero show us the first stirring of parental aspirations: Rocky, Little Dancer, Lucky. A baby is the perfect blank projective screen: anything is possible before reality slowly but surely erodes the extravagant hopes parents hold for their child. It's perfectly normal to fantasize about your child's future and probably abnormal if you haven't.

Sometimes your dreams are your own: opportunities you didn't have, or those you wasted. If you're better off financially than you were growing up, you may shower your child with activities you couldn't afford as a child: music camp, private baseball coaching, dance classes. If you always wished you had traveled, you may find yourself at forty-eight obsessively cruising Web sites for college-study-abroad programs your child might enjoy. Financially strapped mothers may fantasize that their children will find instant wealth: get signed to a fabulous sports contract, become the next American Idol.

Or your dreams may be derived from your children's hopes. If your daughter is the goalie, chances are you're both praying for a game-winning save. Any competition your child enters becomes your wish, too: auditioning for the church play, trying out for a dance troupe at the middle school, entering a drawing for the school yearbook cover, hoping to be named to the "A" team. Once your child has his heart set on getting into a particular college, you're probably right there with him.

But since dreams can't and don't always come true, inevitably, as mothers, we will have to relinquish some of what we would want on behalf of our beloved children. Reality sets in. The baby magazine doesn't choose your child's photo for its modeling contest, your son is put last in the Little League batting lineup, your child doesn't win a ribbon at the piano competition. The process is usually gradual, sometimes invisible. The critical challenge requires a woman to relinquish unrealistic or unmet dreams, and to resist the urge to live vicariously through her child. As her children grow and their true talents, gifts, and interests unfold, she must take joy in their actual accomplishments, and let go of her nebulous fantasies. The baby not chosen for the magazine is still a cutie, she admires the guts it takes for her son to keep at something that doesn't come naturally, and *she* still thinks her budding musician was the best.

Katie is embarrassed that she is having a hard time dealing with her son's dreadful athletic performance. Like many eight-year-old boys, her son Chandler is clear about what he wants to be when he grows up: a professional basketball player. But he appears to have no talent whatsoever. He hasn't made a basket all season.

The coach puts him in the game only when they are surely losing, so it won't matter that Chandler can't make a basket. Chandler has no insight into the fact that he's not on track to becoming a professional basketball player. He proudly tells Katie that he goes in last because that's the most important time, not noticing that the other kids in the game at that point are only marginally less talented than he is.

Katie wonders whether she should discourage Chandler. She tried to convince him to skip basketball and take up tennis, a nonstarter. She is mortified by the fact that you can almost hear the other parents groan when he misses a basket. She thinks it would be easier if he understood that he wasn't the best player, because part of what is unnerving is the discrepancy between his ambitions and his actual prospects. She worries that when he figures it out, or, heaven forbid, overhears someone making fun of him, he'll be crushed.

Katie is aware of Chandler's strengths. He's got a sweet, outgoing personality, and adults and kids really like him. He excels in academics. She is disappointed because he stinks at the thing that's most important to him. If she could wave a magic wand and give him athletic grace, she'd do it in a flash, but there is nothing she can do to help him achieve this dream. He may mature physically and become a decent adult basketball league player someday, but even at eight, you can see who the natural athletes are, and he isn't one of them.

She wonders whether it's her job to let him know what she knows: his dream isn't realistic. Since disappointment is inevitable, she reasons, why not get it over with, and spare him the possibility that it's harder the longer he holds on to his dream? I discourage her from hastening his disillusionment. He's hardly the first child to overestimate his or her talents and prospects, and he will, eventually, understand that he'll have to pursue a different career goal. We can hope that he comes to a gradual, gentle understanding of his actual skill level, and expect that the older he is when he faces reality, the better equipped he'll be psychologically to cope with frustration—that's what maturity brings. And it's admirable but unrealistic on her part to imagine that the realization will be anything but painful, whenever he gets it. If she tries to speed up the inevitable, she risks having him confuse the message with the messenger, or concluding that she's critical or negative about *him*, rather than his basketball skills. Her job, I suggest, is to be ready to soothe him when he is disappointed, and vigilant in helping him chase the aspirations that make sense.

Wishing They Could Do as You Say, Not as You Did

It's common for parents to dream that their children will not make the mistakes they made, will avoid the traps that caught them. A recovering alcoholic hopes that her children will never drink, the too-good girl wants her children to experience healthy rebellion and play hooky once in a while, the divorced mother prays that her kids will marry for life. Mothers who had sex early, smoked dope before class started, never took school seriously until it was late in the game are especially likely to have these "don't let my child do that" dreams.

Maggie is a woman with a long list of mistakes she hoped her children wouldn't make. When you walk into her Milwaukee home, you immediately know that you're in the home of a devoted mother. Photographs of the same three subjects cover the bookshelves and walls, sit on end tables. Some show two girls and a boy at a backyard cookout, others are groupings of high school yearbook photos. The most recent photos show three adults. There is framed kids' artwork from days gone by, and she shows me a recent watercolor made by her daughter Sarah.

Her home is located in one of Milwaukee's older neighborhoods, with gorgeous paneling, leaded glass, and hardwood floors. It's warm and a bit quirky, brimming with African art, Haitian prints, vintage furniture, plants, flowers, and a semi-finished bathroom with walls featuring handwritten quips that make you smile.

Maggie's had an extraordinary journey from youth to being the owner of this lovely house. The day after her eighteenth birthday, she left a home marked by depression, alcoholism, drug abuse, and disorder. One sister committed suicide, and another sibling died in a car accident.

The oldest girl of seven children, she was pressed into duty as a surrogate mother as far back as she can remember. She says her mother "sugar-coated it," telling Maggie that it was a privilege. Maggie helped her father ready her five younger siblings for school each morning. She remembers her mother taking frequent weekend trips to give herself a "break," when Maggie became the "little mom," helping her father with the children. At age ten, she took over all of her mother's duties when she was hospitalized following an emergency surgery that "almost killed her."

She hesitates to criticize her mother, softening her words with compassion. In her Catholic community, large families were the rule, and the oldest daughter simply stepped up to the plate. She hasn't really thought about why her mother always slept late, delegating the morning chores to Maggie and her father, or why she needed a break most weekends, a privilege Maggie did not receive despite her young age. Perhaps she was depressed, she says, or wanted to get away from the pressure. She believes that her mother struggled being "a frustrated, overeducated housewife" in the sixties. She also knows that her mother lived in the shadow of her husband, a successful businessman who ruled the house with an iron fist, because she confided in Maggie, and privately encouraged criticism of her father.

Maggie felt her mother was "totally unprepared for a house full of adolescents." She found an escape through community activism, as an avid participant in the civil rights movement of the sixties. When her mother was home, she was a "laissez-faire" mom, never snooping, or even noticing, the chaos around her. "You could be on acid talking to her and she wouldn't say anything about it," Maggie recalls. During Maggie's adolescence her mother was always gone, either out working for social justice, or completely detached from the situation at home.

Drugs played a role in Maggie's adolescence. When she says her mother wouldn't notice if you were on acid, she isn't just speculating. Maggie and her older brother were hippies in high school, which she sees as a response to the isolation they felt during a time when her community "dissolved" almost overnight. Her activist mother resisted the panic that overtook her white neighbors when integration was quickly followed by white flight, and the community resegregated. Suddenly, they were the only white family in a black neighborhood, and Maggie felt like an outsider at her high school. Teens are typically peer-hungry, and Maggie says she and her brother found their group in the larger Wisconsin drug-using hippie community.

When she turned eighteen, the two of them hitchhiked to a hippie community in a neighboring state, where they "found total liberation after eighteen years of being cooped up with conservative Catholic parents." They swam naked in the woods, smoked pot, and took part in the sexual revolution. "We went wild."

At nineteen, she drifted for a while, ending up in what she calls a "spiritual community," or a "commune." She's not prepared to call it a cult, but she will admit that it was "cult-ish." The group's leader was a charismatic professor of philosophy who directed the group's study of the gnostic texts. At first he seemed to be a loving, highly educated, dynamic spiritual leader. But he went on to grab for power and control, screening members' mail, romantically matching up members of the group without regard for their wishes, and, by the time she left, insisting on having sex with the female members, including those he had partnered with others.

But when she first joined the community, it felt right; things weren't so extreme. She asks herself now, "What the fuck was I thinking? I wasn't thinking. I had no forward vision, no future view." She got pregnant almost immediately, at nineteen, noting that in the counterculture world you "let go" of birth control, went natural. Still, she was "shocked to the bone" to be pregnant by a man who was "a hanger-on, a guy from the hills." It was already obvious to her that he was an alcoholic, and he "terrorized me" when she wanted to break it off, later to disappear abruptly, never meeting his daughter. During the second trimester, she told her parents that she was expecting, and they were "disturbed." Her mother was angry at her and surprisingly far less forgiving than her father.

Breast-feeding worked as a contraceptive for Maggie, since she became pregnant again only after she stopped nursing her first daughter. She gave birth again at twenty, and then carefully watched her cycles to avoid pregnancy. The group's leader was becoming more controlling, more intrusive, and Maggie knew she wanted out. She "found a new guy to hook up with" to get out of the group, finally leaving at age twenty-four, "seven months pregnant with my third."

That relationship didn't last, and Maggie went on public assistance. She enrolled in a college in a progressive community, working "under the table" as a housecleaner to support her children as a single mother. "It was hell," she says now. She lived in a poor area, where her neighbors helped her find government programs, child care, food stamps, and services for low-income families. Somehow she did it, eventually earning a bachelor's degree by age thirty.

When she finished college, Maggie moved home to Wisconsin, imagining that she would finally get the support she had missed out on as a child. Instead, tragedy struck within days as she lost a second sibling. Her family was shattered. Instead of getting support, Maggie found herself right back in the role of family nurturer, making funeral arrangements while trying to resettle her three kids as a single parent. She describes the depths of despair: "After you've lost a sister, you think nothing that bad can ever happen again, and then you get hit again. It spins you into an unreality. You know that there's nothing, absolutely nothing, you can count on."

Her parents were so disabled emotionally that Maggie moved back into their house. Her parents poured love and attention on her kids, which she felt was good for her parents and good for the kids. She stayed one school year, during Sarah's early adolescence.

From the first time her first child Sarah entered school, it was clear that she was "different" cognitively. Maggie's son, Jacob, and her other daughter, Lakota, "move at the same mental speed." Both were excellent students and are now college graduates. But Sarah has always been "spacy," "nonlinear." Friends and teachers would ask, "Have you had her tested?" but Maggie felt that her daughter had an artistic mind that just works differently. That Sarah's younger siblings breezed through school only made Sarah feel worse about herself. For years, Maggie saw Sarah as vulnerable, but she did not anticipate the difficulties that lay ahead.

Maggie planned on doing it differently, but, like her mother, she found that "I was out of touch" as her children entered the early teen stage. When Sarah was thirteen, Maggie found an apartment for the family. Sarah asked to stay at her grandparents one more year to complete middle school. Since Maggie had experienced an uprooting of sorts of her own in high school, she sympathetically allowed Sarah to do so. "Now I regret it," tearing up as if it was yesterday, not fifteen years ago. During this year, Sarah started drinking, spent time with troubled kids, and blew off school. Maggie hadn't admitted to herself how lacking her parents were as disciplinarians, and Sarah, in the family tradition, began running wild, unchecked. Maggie's parents were "of the old school of alcoholism—whatever you do, do not talk about it," and didn't tell her for months that her daughter Sarah, then fourteen, was drinking heavily.

When Maggie did find out about Sarah's alcohol abuse, it was just the beginning of her lost dreams. Sarah was among the first to wear the multicolored Mohawk that defined the punk subculture. She was shoplifting, prematurely sexually active, breaking curfew. With the benefit of hindsight, Maggie notes, "It seems stupid that as a parent you don't catch on. You do and you don't. Of course, the child is also hiding it, protecting you from the knowledge, and protecting their own wish for the sweet mommy-daughter relationship. When you catch them smoking, you both want to go along with the idea that's it's just an isolated incident." Implied in Maggie's ruminations: Was there a time when I could have changed her course?

The episodes got worse and worse. Sarah had a brief period of self-injury, scratching cuts in her skin. The "lancing of the boil" came when Sarah didn't return from a party one night and, desperate to locate her, Maggie looked in her journal for names and addresses that might help her find Sarah. Somewhat sheepishly, she admits she started reading the journal, and learned that the iceberg was gigantic. Sarah's alcoholism and criminal behavior were very serious. That day, Maggie took Sarah to an AA meeting, and by the week's end, Sarah entered inpatient treatment for alcohol addiction. She was hospitalized for five months at a facility an hour from home.

Those five months were brutal. Maggie would rush home from work, get dinner ready for her younger children, then head out for the hospital. At the hospital, she felt blamed for Sarah's alcoholism at one moment and criticized for being too maternal the next. The traditional view of Al-Anon and the conventional wisdom on codependency tells anyone who is involved with an alcoholic to "detach with love." For example, Al-Anon's leaflet "Detachment" says, "In Al-Anon we learn not to prevent a crisis if it is in the natural course of events."

Women often find detaching from children—sometimes called "tough love"—to be contrary to how they define parenting. It's our job to try to ward off danger and soothe pain. Mothers do whatever they can to keep their children safe. As a result of her alcoholism, Sarah was "a target," and Maggie would have done anything she could to prevent the tragedies her daughter suffered as a consequence of being drunk: a brutal encounter with a troubled young man, permanently lost teeth. Of course, she tried to control Sarah's drinking. Being the mother of an alcoholic teen in treatment is a catch-22: damned if you do, damned if you don't. Maggie's response to being told by therapists to detach herself from her teenage daughter's alcohol-induced problems, to let her suffer alone, was "Fuck you." What kind of mother *could* see a violent assault while drunk as a good opportunity to hit bottom?

Maggie hopes that someday Sarah will use her artistic talent. Sarah quits drinking, then relapses, over and over again. Treatment helps, so far, only temporarily. She was hospitalized a second time at age twenty, and goes in and out of Alcoholics Anonymous. She's always on the edge of a precipice, often unable to keep the simplest of jobs. Her best stretch was a two-year period in which she had her own apartment. The electricity was cut off several times, but she always got it paid up and back on.

No mother's dream for her child includes alcoholism or a career high of cashiering, a life of scrabbling for money to pay the utilities. A mother like Maggie, who has been poor herself, usually explicitly dreams of a better life for her children. And Sarah's alcoholism robbed her mother of another dream: the hope to provide a comfortable family environment. Maggie had accomplished the impossible: she became a single "welfare mother" who went to college and ended up a professional, able to bring her family back into the middle class. Just when she had it all—a good job, the family's first nice apartment—Sarah crashed. She saw Sarah as a "mocking representation of me as a teen—a caricature" that proclaimed that she hadn't achieved her dream. To make matters worse,

Sarah's "alcoholic black hole" drained time and energy that belonged to her other children, and they, too, did not have an easy adolescence. (The siblings of substance abusing, crisis-prone teens typically and understandably get placed on the back burner.)

When any mother's dream is lost, she needs to mourn. When substance abuse foreshortens a child's possibilities, the grieving occurs even as the worries and pains continue to mount. Plenty of teens do recover from substance abuse, and everyone picks up the pieces and moves on from there. When your children continue to abuse substances, however, there is no going forward. Rather than achieving independence and functionality, the movement is in reverse, as the addiction progresses and the consequences pile up. It has occurred to Maggie that Sarah's lost teeth—caused by self-neglect—represent a perverse mirroring of the time when her baby teeth fell out, and they happily counted them together. Sarah is the same age as Maggie was when she was raising three kids as a college student on a shoestring. In comparison, Sarah is "a child" who remains vulnerable, and sometimes, Maggie says, "it crushes me."

Maggie could never do what some parents of substance abusers do: disown their children, cutting off contact. But she won't "baby" or "pamper" her twenty-eight-year-old, won't catch her anymore when she falls. She draws the line differently now that Sarah is out of adolescence. "I decided she's not handicapped. She deserves a functional life, and she's capable enough to get it." She knows that Sarah can be employed, pay the rent, go to the free dental clinic, set aside money for the utilities, and *that's* her revised dream. She dreams that Sarah will do the best *she* can do. When Sarah sinks, she keeps her vision of that dream, reminding Sarah of those two years when she did it all for herself. She delights in Sarah's small successes, pleased, for example, when Sarah had a job that gave her free passes to the theater, which let Sarah treat Maggie for once.

She used to rescue Sarah, but now she won't do that financially. "I don't give her money so I don't resent her. I'm scared and worried, but not resentful." I notice that she has mentioned *not* being a resentful mother several times. Did she feel that her own mother resented her? Yes. Her mother resented her leaving home, abandoning the role of mother's helper and confidante. "I broke the pact, us against Dad-the-Asshole when I left." In this regard, Maggie has not become her mother. She remains deeply emotionally attached to Sarah, and is not angry at her for failing to meet her expectations.

Guilt usually accompanies lost dreams, regardless of what is getting in the way. Conscientious mothers are lightning quick to blame themselves for the problems of their children. Maggie, who was described to me by a mutual friend as "the best mother I know," says, "It's hard to feel good about how you raised an alcoholic—it must be something you did," even though she knows that Sarah has genes on both sides for alcoholism.

The Dream Has to Fit the Child

Maggie exhibits a key component seen in mothers successfully adapting to this key challenge: she revises the dream to suit the individual child. She lowers her aspirations for Sarah, setting them at a height she may eventually attain. Sure, she once dreamed of art school for Sarah, but now she wants her to have a job and an apartment. She dreams that Sarah will one day maintain sobriety for good. At the same time, Maggie keeps her hopes higher for her other children, Jacob and Lakota. She doesn't resent Sarah for being the outlier, but she won't let her set the bar for her siblings. They've fulfilled one ambition: Jacob and Lakota went straight to college after high school, and graduated with their age peers. One has a graduate degree, and both have interesting, fulfilling jobs.

When it comes to do-as-I-say-not-as-I-did, you wouldn't have to be a mind reader to know Maggie's hope. She wants her kids to remain childless until they are established professionally and happily partnered. She laughs when she recalls her never-ending lectures on birth control during their teen years. When she dreams of grandchildren, as she does, it's Lakota's and Jacob's children she pictures, knowing that Sarah can barely fend for herself.

Maggie feels she made colossal mistakes in her own life because she wasn't contemplative, didn't picture the consequences of her choices. She wants her children to be planners, be the "forward thinker" she wasn't at twenty. While it's obvious that Sarah is not a planner, Jacob and Lakota are. In fact, she suspects that Lakota is always working toward her next world adventure. When Maggie was pregnant with Lakota, she remembers settling Sarah and Jacob in the grassy middle of a running track, jogging in circles around them. This semi-solitary activity was what passed as time for herself in those draining days. She recalls occupying her mind during these runs with visions of travel, hoping to see the world in better, distant days. And she's conferred that aspiration to Lakota, now living in Africa, after studying in Australia. Only in her early twenties, Lakota has been to three continents outside North America, and twice Maggie has visited her on her world travels. This child *is* living Maggie's vicarious unlived dream, and perhaps that helps.

The Grief and Disappointment of Disability

There is one wish that every mother holds: let my child be normal. Let my baby have ten fingers and ten toes, let her gain weight along a healthy curve, let him walk and talk when he should. At four, let her ask "Why?" a hundred times a day; at six, let him begin reading.

Some children aren't born normal. According to the March of Dimes, one out of every twenty-eight babies is born with a birth defect, some minor, others life threatening or disabling. Some children who appear perfectly fine will go on to show significant disabilities, including autism, cognitive delay, and motor disabilities. The Center for Disease Control estimates that 17 percent of children have some form of developmental delay (including mild problems such as speech problems), and 2 percent of school-aged kids have a serious disability.

When a child is diagnosed with a significant disability, mothers are usually devastated. It's a crushing blow to realize that your child may not have a normal future, might not have a future that includes marriage, children, a good job. Even this most modest of maternal dreams—a healthy child—flies out the window.

Mothering special needs children is very stressful, and it's no surprise that in my practice I have several moms with such kids. One source of stress is the system: it's overwhelming at times to get the right diagnosis, complete comprehensive testing, find the experts, and get services from cash-strapped schools and social service agencies. The early stages are often the most emotionally difficult, when the mother hasn't had a chance to adapt to her lost dreams, the potentially changed future of her child, often in the midst of uncertainty and bureaucratic nightmares.

Andrea never suspected a problem with her daughter until she was three and a half. She looked normal and seemed fine. But in preschool, Brianna was beginning to seem different from her classmates. The preschool shrugged it off, predicting that she'd grow out of her language delay and difficulty playing with other kids. But as the months went by, Andrea had a growing sense that something was wrong. When she raised the subject with her husband, he would accuse her of being "too mommy-ish" about it, saying that she should just stop comparing Brianna to the other kids and forget about it. She couldn't stop, couldn't ignore Brianna's odd speech pattern, as she repeated certain phrases over and over again, and used far fewer words than her peers.

I suggested that she make an appointment with her pediatrician to evaluate Brianna developmentally. Unfortunately, the doctor thought there might be problems, and she referred Andrea to a special testing center for kids. With the doctor's recommendation, Andrea's husband was still skeptical, but he no longer actively opposed an evaluation or belittled Andrea's fears. Brianna went through comprehensive testing at age four and a half, a difficult task requiring many trips and lots of coaxing to get her cooperation. Sometimes Andrea could see that Brianna was doing poorly, and she'd explain repeatedly that her little girl was being "silly," hoping that the testing psychologist would give Brianna the benefit of the doubt. The evaluation took several months to complete. Anxiously waiting for this kind of assessment is agonizing. Once the possibility of trouble has been raised, you want answers immediately.

Unhappily, the answers were terrible. Brianna has developmental delays in language, speech, fine motor, and gross motor. Her IQ scores are in the mild range of mental retardation. The center referred the family to the public schools, noting that she was eligible for kindergarten-readiness developmental services. Andrea and her husband were stunned. It took them a few months to make the call to the school, and still, Andrea burst into tears at the meeting with the special education coordinator. Brianna began getting services aimed at her motor and language problems, and Andrea was sure that the problems would clear up by kindergarten. She knows that IQ tests may be unreliable in preschoolers, and feels certain that Brianna would score much higher if she was in better spirits during the testing.

Andrea is grieving. Elisabeth Kübler-Ross first described a system of five stages of mourning to characterize the sequence of emotional reactions to dying. Her system is now widely used to understand the process of grieving any significant loss. In general, individuals mourning go through (1) denial, (2) anger, (3) bargaining,

(4) depression, and (5) acceptance, although some get stuck at a particular stage and do not make it through the developmental progression. Denial goes hand in hand with shock: this can't be true. Denial generally involves believing an alternate scenario with a better outcome. When Andrea's husband criticized her for being obsessed with Brianna's development, he was in denial. How much better it would be if he were right, that she was making too much of nothing. With the test results, she entered a denial of her own. Andrea may be right about the IQ test, but even if Brianna underperformed, the whole picture is not promising. Children get silly when they can't complete tasks, and Brianna's cognitive delay may have made her act silly, rather than vice versa. Brianna is the daughter of highly educated professionals who had every reason to dream of college and graduate school, and even if Brianna's test is off the mark, the best-case scenario is probably low normal intelligence. "Silliness" is a better alternative scenario.

Despite the popular notion that therapists want everyone out of denial, it isn't true. Brianna is an only child born after infertility treatment, and parents often put their dreams and hopes into an only child with a greater intensity than in larger families. The shock is more shocking, perhaps, with no siblings to carry the parents' dreams. Denial is a problem if it interferes with getting Brianna services. The opposite behavior can be even more problematic, if a mother gives up on her child, comes to see him as damaged goods. Andrea and her husband deserve some time to absorb the impact, and Brianna deserves lots of time and help to be the best she can be.

Unfortunately, despite the services she received before starting school, Brianna fared poorly in kindergarten. She was obviously lost, unable to participate in lessons about letters, days of the week, counting. Her social deficits left her out of group play, and her language delay became more evident. Within a few months, Andrea accepted the school's recommendation to take Brianna out of kindergarten and place her in a special education classroom with a developmental curriculum.

By this time, Andrea had moved into the anger stage. She was furious at the preschool that minimized Brianna's problems. The testing center and the public school staff have been nurturing and supportive, and she hasn't wanted to kill the messenger, as some parents do. The preschool dropped the ball, should not have dismissed her difficulties so casually. But her anger is disproportionate, enormous. If anyone mentions the name of the preschool, her blood boils. She can't drive on the street where it's located. For six months, she vents about the preschool, and she knows that it's excessive, even as she struggles to let go.

She moves in and out of bargaining. She bargains with the public school: Brianna can go to the special education program if they tell her it will help her get back into regular kindergarten. She bargains with the universe: she will spare no expense, take Brianna to any expert, practice exercises with her at home, read her forty books a day if it might help.

As the denial and anger dissipate, she sees more clearly how delayed Brianna is, and it breaks her heart. One session, sobbing, she hands me a paper with what is supposed to be a circle drawn by Brianna, and it's the jerky, faint scribble of a two-year-old. Witnessing the despair a mother feels when she realizes that her child is not normal leaves me wishing that every parent could stay in denial forever, rather than experience such pain.

Acceptance of a child's disability is a complicated process. Ideally, the mother, like Andrea, is grieving her lost dreams, *not* her differently abled child.* It doesn't mean you accept less than the best your child can receive, and it doesn't mean you aren't angry or depressed at times. Mothers who have accepted their child's disability are often still angry, at everything from the cost of prescriptions to the insensitivity of a teacher. A mother's job includes advocating for her child, being sure that no institution or individual

---

* Don't Mourn for Us," by Jim Sinclair, presented at the 1993 International Conference on Autism, http://ani.autistics.org/dont_mourn.html

writes her child off. She must constantly balance a realistic assessment of her child's disability with a hopeful expectation for progress and development. Unless you've been there, it's hard to appreciate the hassle of the mountainous paperwork, phone calls, monitoring, scheduling and rescheduling, meeting with educators, speech, physical, or occupational therapy appointments, and medical care that is required to parent a special needs child. You can still feel plenty awful when you've truly grieved your lost dreams. But when you've achieved an internal process of accepting that this beloved child will struggle, perhaps suffer, and that's the way things are, then you're well on the way to healthy coping.

Andrea is in early acceptance emotionally. Practically speaking, she hasn't missed any recent opportunity to help Brianna. But she doesn't ask or push for information that isn't volunteered by a professional. If the school doesn't say that Brianna may need special education next year, she isn't going to ask. If the doctor doesn't explain why she has these problems, so be it. I've suggested she go online to look for an Internet support group, or explore groups in her community, and she politely declines. She's not ready to hear anyone else's story, not ready to risk sinking back into despair if she learns something she doesn't want to know. In time, I think she may find that the support of mothers who have shared her journey would be helpful.

Achievement by Proxy: When It's Too Much

Most of us know a "stage mother" of one sort or another. This is the mother who pushes her child with a fervor born of her own excessive need to have her child admired. Dads sometimes do it on the playing field: the volunteer basketball coach who has his son practice two hours before every game, slamming his clipboard on the bench, cursing, when the ball is stolen from his child. At the high school my children attend, so many parents insist on having their children "upgraded" into the honors track that the school has adopted a policy of refusing to allow students to switch until the end of the semester if their parents have demanded an override of the school's assessment. The school will honor the parents' request, but it's the child who is punished for the sins of the parent. If you decline the lower track they think your kid belongs in, tough luck if the school is proved right and your child struggles academically in the honors track. The school won't switch them back again in order to discourage pushy parents.

"Achievement by proxy" is the label that therapists, coaches, and teachers apply when driven parents cannot accept their children's actual accomplishments and abilities. There's a mom in my community who is notorious for badgering any teacher who fails to give her child an A, taking it up with the middle school principal any time her son is not the recipient of an academic honor. I suspect that we are quick to gossip about this mother because her actions strike a nerve: every one of us knows the urge to live vicariously through our children. Who wouldn't want her child to make straight A's? What star athlete's mom isn't proud? But mostly we control it, know that it's our shadow side when we aren't satisfied with the acclaim awarded our children. The mother who can't resist her impulse to pressure her child to do more, win more, get more praise, score higher, broadcasts the message that he isn't good enough the way he is.

Other mothers get vicarious pleasure by seeking affirmation of their children's good looks. No doubt part of the national preoccupation with the tragic death of JonBenet Ramsey was our collective horror at seeing so striking an example of a stage mother. The daughter of a former Miss West Virginia, JonBenet won five junior pageant contests by the time she was six. As Barbara Walters, on the ABCNews show *20/20,* noted, JonBenet had been called a "six-year-old-Lolita," heavily made up, photographed and videotaped in a sexually suggestive manner. It's hard to imagine that a kindergartner's own dreams would be either so sexualized or so organized, and difficult to conclude other than that JonBenet's mother relived her glory days through her.

At locker rooms, beauty salons, the office watercooler, women told one another, "I would never let my child enter a beauty pageant at that age." "No way!" Perhaps we needed mutual reassurance because we saw in this mother a sliver of that shadow self, the one that wants our child crowned princess. For most of us, the urge to live through our children is a place we visit on occasion, not where we live. We know that our child doesn't have to be the prettiest girl in the state in anyone's eyes but ours. The nation of mothers needed to remind itself that there's a big difference between the infrequent vicarious twinge, and what you actually do with your children.

One of my patients was herself a child beauty contestant, later a teen model. She certainly doesn't believe it was her dream, and has no fond memories of the long drives, boring waits, and tense competitions. Since her family is well-to-do, no argument could be made that her mother enrolled her for the potential scholarships or modeling fees. Instead, Wendy feels that it was all about her mother's need for admiration. If anything went wrong at a pageant, her mother erupted in anger as if it happened to her. As I hear about Wendy's mother, I put her on the short list of Mothers with Really Bad Boundaries. She sneaks in and rearranges her adult daughter's furniture repeatedly, phones several times a day, sometimes hanging up when she feels neglected, shows up unannounced, refuses to honor Wendy's wish to limit her kids' sugar intake, and, ironically, criticizes her mothering relentlessly.

Wendy should be at high risk for repeating the cycle, for investing too much in her children's talents, gifts, and successes. That's the model she grew up with. And her two children have remarkable gifts. Her son and daughter, both adopted from Guatemala, are simply gorgeous. Her five-year-old son William just entered kindergarten reading the Harry Potter books easily. William also stands out in a crowd for his prodigious musical abilities. If she had any tendency to live vicariously through her child, she's got a terrific candidate. He's so academically talented that I encourage her to look into one of the private Chicago area schools for gifted children, concerned that he'll be bored when his classmates are learning their ABCs. But she enrolls him in the neighborhood school, in part because she worries that to do otherwise would be the academic equivalent of enrolling a kindergartner in a beauty competition. She wants her children to have an ordinary childhood, never to feel pressure to achieve on behalf of their parents.

Wendy breaks the cycle of achievement by proxy because she remains conscious of her mothering plan. She refuses to live her dreams through her children. She isn't bending over backward to ignore his gifts: her son's advanced music studies give him a great outlet for his brilliance. She's proud, but never boastful. And she chose the neighborhood school because she feels it will give him what he most needs: social competence. Like many highly gifted children, her son is socially awkward with his peers. When he tries to play with his classmates, either they quit because they don't understand the highly elaborate rules of his complex fantasy games, or William gets frustrated with them. His reading skills make him noticeably different; William has a mild motor delay that makes it difficult for him to engage in the physical games his peers play, or to perform well at T-ball or soccer. With his powerful intellect, William is, unfortunately, all too sensitive to his own social difficulties. While Wendy feels that he'd be more like everyone else at a gifted school, she believes he will benefit from learning how to get along in the real world. If the balance changes as he advances in school, she'll reconsider. Unlike her own mother, Wendy gives the same attention to the areas where William needs help as she does to his gifts. It doesn't threaten her own self-esteem to recognize his human imperfections.

I think she has it just right, and it's a tribute to her frequent self-examination. In one sense, she is living vicariously through William, but in the best possible way. Poorly mothered herself, her dream is that he should chase his own dreams, free of parental overinvolvement, or narcissistic enmeshment. She encourages his talents, but attends carefully to his deficits, because she wants to help him be the best he can be, for himself. As she sees it, it's about him, not her.

Conclusion

The critical challenge of adapting to revised or lost dreams begins at birth and continues into a child's adulthood. No mother has the perfect child, and life may be a series of small vicarious disappointments as the perfectly imagined fetus becomes an adult with a spectrum of abilities and disabilities, strengths and weaknesses. Indeed, as children enter adolescence, the competition gets stronger and the possibilities narrow. The three-year-old who was adorable in her pink tutu turns out to have no natural rhythm. The best free-thrower on the third-grade basketball team may not have what it takes to get an athletic scholarship, or even play on the high school varsity team. The middle school musical star gets cast in the chorus at high school. The precociously early reader will have thirty high school classmates whose SAT scores will be just as good.

Ideally, an adapting mother helps support her child as he experiences disappointment, and encourages the child's actual talents and goals. For those with more than one child, the need to modify dreams for each child individually, to resist the urge to compare, will also continue over the life cycle of mothering. The mother who is coping well tailors her aspirations to that which her real child can achieve. She keeps the bar high, but not impossibly so.

Signs of Poor Adaptation to Revised Dreams

1. Excessive anxiety about your child's rank, academic placement, athletic performance, or recognition for performing or fine arts.

2. Emotionally experiencing your child's disappointments and victories as if you yourself had lost or won them.

3. Engaging in criticism, mockery, or blame when your child fails to achieve or perform as you had hoped. Belief that what counts *is* whether you win or lose, not how you play the game.

4. Belief that your child can or should be spared disappointment, which might manifest in attempts to soothe a disappointed child by criticizing the judging authority, accusing the other team of cheating, or belittling a child's competitor.

Strategies for Successful Adaptation

1. Grieve, if needed, lost dreams, moving beyond anger and denial to loving acceptance and advocacy for your child.

2. Appreciate and acknowledge each of your children's unique talents, dreams, and goals, as they are, not as you wish them to be. Accept the shadow self who secretly wishes for an Olympic athlete, a fifteen-year-old college freshman, a child movie star, but don't let her be in charge.

3. Compassionately soothe your child when he or she is disappointed, while expressing genuine pride and supporting achievable goals. Remain aware that disappointment is an opportunity to build character by focusing on effort, not outcome.

4. Attend to your own unlived dreams: take an art class, learn to play piano, travel, study a new language.

8

Adversity
The Eighth Key Challenge

> The media ply parents with endless stories of violence, loss, disease and disaster involving children. There are no boundaries on the universe a mother must monitor . . . she is never able to rest assured that she has adequately surveyed the territory.
> —Janna Malamud Smith, *A Potent Spell*

One constant in mothering: children *are* in danger. The vulnerability of the infant is obvious, but children's increasing independence is inevitably accompanied by an expanding list of potential harms. Mothers sweat the big stuff. The toddler who can electrocute himself with a fork and an outlet becomes the six-year-old who could wander off at the mall. The third grader who could be hit by a car while roller skating becomes the ninth grader who could be mugged on public transportation. The sixteen-year-old driver who forgets to look both ways before turning into traffic becomes the college student who might be the victim of date rape or alcohol poisoning. Mothers also sweat the small stuff, and the medium stuff. We worry about the party our child was not invited to, the teacher known for her harsh tongue, whether a cell phone will increase our child's safety or just make her more materialistic, if that headache is a brain tumor, how much calcium our milk-hating child consumes. I could fill a book with lists and lists of things I myself have worried about in the course of raising three children, from an unflattering yearbook photograph to a child's hospitalization. I've even worried about whether being too worried is harmful to them.

Maternal protectiveness is, no doubt, to some extent programmed biologically in our mammalian brains. Still, in 1871, when Charles Darwin assumed that "Every one knows how strong the maternal instinct is," he couldn't have imagined that sociobiologists would debate the topic into the twenty-first century. Anthropologist Sarah Blaffer Hrdy, among others, wonders how much of what we observe in mothers is that which we expect or wish to observe, challenging "mankind's assumption . . . [that] self-sacrificing motherhood was what women were for." Law professors Michelle Oberman and Cheryl Meyer point out the critical role that lack of environment and social support plays when mothers not only fail to function as protectors but actually harm their children. And, of course, fathers also understand parental protectiveness and vicarious fear.

This chapter won't address the roots of a mother's wish to protect her child from harm, but rather will explore how mothers face the critical challenge when bad things do happen. In the age of perfectionism, for every mother who does grievous harm to her child, there are countless mothers who turn chance or fate into a maternal failing. Any harm that comes to their child must, somehow, be their fault. They didn't watch carefully enough, they failed to anticipate disaster, they owed a karmic debt that their beloved child is paying off.

A mother who drank too much, once, before she knew she was unexpectedly pregnant, blames herself for the mild neonatal jaundice her baby experienced nine months later; no reassurance from the pediatrician soothes her. Another blames herself for the broken arm her child acquired at school: why didn't she move to an area with better playground supervision? The mother who dropped her child off at school and went running for an hour beats herself up when she misses a call from the school office letting her know that her son was complaining of a minor stomachache—what kind of good mother would forget to carry her cell phone 24/7?

Perfectionism Raises the Bar

Mothers even worry about things that didn't go wrong but *might* have. Renee blames herself for not believing the neighborhood gossip about a family down the block whose child her five-year-old twins liked. Renee (see Chapter 2), who grew up the ward of the irresponsible aunt about whom everyone in the neighborhood gossiped, was committed to not judging a child by her parents' behavior. She welcomed the neighbor girl as her own children's playmate, and saw no problems when she visited for playdates. But when the neighbor girl was discovered with another child, unclothed, those kids quickly became the talk of the town. It might have been natural curiosity, or it might reflect an exposure to sexually inappropriate behaviors at home. But Renee was horrified, angry at herself. The girl *could* have encouraged *her* twins to undress, possibly experiment sexually. She blames herself for failing to discourage the twins' friendship with this child at the outset—even though Michael and Madison in fact were not involved in the undressing incident and are entirely unharmed. She convicts herself of an imaginary victimless failure to protect: to her, close calls count when it comes to maternal self-reproach. That's how high the bar is.

Early in my career, I would have attempted to reassure Renee. It's natural to want to comfort worried moms who are doing just fine. "How could you possibly be at fault for something that didn't even happen?" I might have offered. To another mother, I'd point out that accidents are called accidents for a reason. Or the ultimate me-too consolation: yep, one of my kids had lice and I know how it makes you feel like a bad mother. This is what I got from the women in my life as I became a mother: encouragement that I was up to the job, but in the world of mothering, shit happens.

But I know better now. Reassurance may work for the mother who fundamentally feels adequate in her mothering. But with perfectionism as the new standard, especially but not exclusively for a poorly nurtured woman such as Renee, it is hard to know exactly what your best is. Premature reassurance frequently, paradoxically, annoys the anxious, overprotective mother. It's an empathic failure, a minimization of her experience of herself to suggest that she isn't blowing it. Early in therapy, the vigilant unmothered mother wishes only to become a better mother. To suggest that she might already *be* a better mother than she realizes leaves her convinced that she's in the hands of an idiot, a touchy-feely shrink who tells anyone that she's okay. Likewise with the brand-new mother, overwhelmed by all that she doesn't know about keeping this vulnerable creature safe.

With such a mother, my initial goal is to help her question her assumption about her own mothering. As a goal, it seems both lofty and humble. It is humble in its easily grasped truth: no mother is all-powerful; hindsight is always twenty/twenty. How easy, it would seem, to point out so simple a fact. It is lofty in that Renee's perfectionism has an intractability born of a ferocious rejection of her experience of nurturing: to strive for divine infallibility is the only way she knows how *not* to be the aunt who raised her. Since accidents, hurt feelings, disappointments happen to all children, it is always easy for an anxious woman to find evidence of her failure to protect.

Instead of offering reassurance, now I try to mirror the impossible goal of predicting the unpredictable. "I am not entirely clear about where you think you went wrong," I ask, inviting Renee to find the data that prove her hypothesis that she, like her aunt, fell asleep at the wheel. Retelling the details may force her to examine her belief that she was irresponsible. Only as she herself scientifically dissects the story does she come to acknowledge that she is not to blame for something that didn't even happen.

At times, just the simple fact that I do not recoil in horror is soothing. This is what happens when thriving mothers share their stories with one another: they get sympathy without judgment or criticism. That I do not stand up, dramatically insist that this negligent mother leave my office at once, and never, ever come back, is so surprising, so discordant with her imagined verdict, that a little chip of a boulder-sized guilt evaporates. This must occur over and over, this chiseling, this refusal to abhor her mothering, before the insecure woman can begin to judge her own mothering as anything but a hanging judge.

Over time, I nudge Renee toward a gentler perception of her role in the physical and emotional bruises that her sons acquire in the normal course of childhood. I believe that you feel responsible, I tell her, believe that you are certain you couldn't survive if anything bad happened to them and you blamed yourself, and I'm aware of what a burden that must be. How hard each moment of mothering must be with so much at stake all the time. She tears when I say this; it *is* harder for her.

Becoming Aware of the Impossibility

I ask my patients to listen closely to their words. Do you hear what you've just said? You're describing this accident as if you let something slip, as if it's your fault. Is there another explanation for the outcome, I ask? Does the fact that you *feel* guilty and responsible mean that you *are* guilty and responsible? If therapy goes well, my patient comes to experience her conviction of inadequacy as a symptom, rather than a fact. She may start with a small victory:

Julie slipped at flag football and needed two stitches, but I stopped as soon as I started beating up on myself. You'd have been proud of me; I am—that's a huge victory.

Very gradually, I might add a gentle teasing: after you figure out how to prevent all childhood accidents, the world needs you to get cracking on peace in the Middle East. To joke about exorbitant maternal expectations is risky business. If the patient is convinced that her internal job description is achievable, it is as if I am mocking her. She feels the humiliation of the child who said something serious, only to have the adults in the room laugh at a joke she neither intended nor understands. But if she has come to see the belief that she must do better than the best she can do as crazy-making, we will laugh together. By joking about a mother's inability to perfectly protect her child, we rebel together. Impossible standards: no, thank you.

Protecting Your Child from Mean People

One unlikely-to-deflect threat that mothers of daughters consistently worry about: mean girls. To some extent, this is a result of increased attention to the problem of adolescent female aggression. Books such as *Queen Bees and Wannabes: Helping Your Daughter Survive Cliques, Gossip, Boyfriends, and Other Realities of Adolescence*; *Odd Girl Out: The Hidden Culture of Aggression in Girls*; and *Reviving Ophelia: Saving the Selves of Adolescent Girls* have raised maternal consciousness about the harsh reality of girls' social lives.

But when I talk to my girlfriends about girl aggression, watch my daughters navigate early adolescent social groups, and listen to my patients worry about the impact of cliques on their daughters, I think our worry is not simply trendy. Mothers naturally wish they could protect their children from that which they themselves suffered, and most of us can remember the pain of being excluded or put down by another girl during our teen years. Some of us also remember with shame being mean to someone lower on the totem pole than we found ourselves.

Carolyn is obsessed with her daughter's social life, and she knows she's gone over the top. She suffers from anxiety problems that predate her daughter's birth twelve years ago, and she is only too aware of her tendency to ruminate about worst-case scenarios. Her background has a big impact on the way she has experienced her daughter's early adolescence. Carolyn was essentially ignored growing up, the too-good girl whose sister drained all the attention. Her father, a very successful businessman and a womanizer, was always somewhere else. She describes her mother as a helpless waif, a woman who constantly found life to be overwhelming. Although she did not work outside the home, she delegated basic parental functions to housekeepers, none of whom stayed long enough to become satisfactory substitute nurturers.

Dysfunctional families such as Carolyn's often have at least one symptomatic teenager who reacts with anger or chaos to parental neglect in ways that demand attention. Carolyn's sister developed self-cutting and alcohol abuse. She was always in crisis, repeatedly psychiatrically hospitalized, and Carolyn was told again and again how her mother depended on her to be "good." Carolyn got the message loud and clear: make no demands. She was praised for invisibility, expected to meet her own needs. She did: she remembers being the only girl at her private school who took three buses to get there, and she believes that her parents never once attended one of her many gymnastic meets. Now that she is in the driver's seat, it hurts with fresh pain to picture herself at ten having to change buses twice while her mother stayed home, sleeping in or playing tennis. She loves her mother, and easily imagines how hard it was to put up with her father's infidelities, his detachment, and her sister's difficulties, but still, she cannot understand why her mother couldn't spare the half hour to drive her to school in the morning.

Like many unmothered mothers, Carolyn made a vow to herself in those days: she'd be like other mothers she saw: actively involved. She is. A stay-at-home mother of three (Jessica, fourteen; Ryan, eleven; and Matthew, nine), she is the epitome of the capable soccer mom. She is the room parent who calls you on a snow day, the church volunteer who organizes the candy sale, the one other mothers count on to arrive on time when it's her turn to drive car pool to softball.

Jessica is an equally competent child. She has the gifts we'd want for our teenagers: beauty, brains, and athletic determination. What she doesn't have is a seamless social life in the junior high school she attends in one of Chicago's affluent north suburbs. If you do the math, chances are extremely slim that your daughter is the queen bee. Carolyn's daughter is socially successful in that she has a group of friends, participates in a number of after-school activities, and is a good student who is well liked by her teachers. Carolyn dismisses Jessica's accomplishments, instead obsessing on any indication that Jessica has been socially slighted. Carolyn knows exactly who the premiere girl is—Brooke—and she seeks out opportunities to assess Jessica's social status. If Brooke doesn't ask Jessica to be in her mother's van at car pool, Carolyn calls other moms to find out which girls Brooke selected to ride to field hockey with her. She uses her network of mom-girlfriends to find out who was at Brooke's Halloween party, who sat together at the football game, the exact order of when each girl got cut from cheerleading tryouts, who danced with the popular boys at the seventh-grade social, or what kids went together to the opening day of the latest teen flick.

The ridiculous thing about Carolyn's obsession is that she isn't a shallow person at all, but you'd never know it from her preoccupation with her daughter's social status. She doesn't believe that Jessica would be a better human being if she was at the top of the heap, but she does believe that Jessica would be spared the pain and ickiness of cliques if she were Brooke's best friend. If you ask her what kind of person she'd like her daughter to be, she'd tell you all the right things: compassionate, kind, sensitive to other people's feelings. She knows I have a daughter several years older than Jessica, and just as she fantasizes that I'm the perfect mother, she imagines that my daughter is the most popular girl in school. I tell her the truth: I'd be horrified if my daughter were the queen bee. I would not want a child with the ruthlessness it takes to stay on top of the heap. Be careful what you ask for, I advise. They call them mean girls for a reason, I say, and why do you want Jessica inside that circle?

Still, I would be lying to say that I've never worried about my daughters' social standing. I know exactly where I want my girls: on the B+ list. I want them spared the humiliation and adolescent angst of being ostracized, but I don't want them powerful or unkind enough to ostracize others. I also know that while I can help my children be kind, I cannot help my children be popular. Jessica is on the B+ list, and I wish I could help Carolyn let it be. It's painful for Carolyn to be unable to detach herself from the roller coaster that marks the typical adolescent girl's social life. What's worse is that her daughter is onto her. When her mother grills her every time she comes home from a party or a school outing, she knows exactly what her mother is doing. She used to tell her mother the details, but now she slams her door, calls her mother "psycho," or complains to her father.

Carolyn thinks she wants to know the details so she can help Jessica; she's fighting the powerlessness that she has over cliques. She kids herself that she can reverse things by complaining to other moms if her daughter is excluded from the A list, or by throwing a party and inviting the most popular kids, or by managing to give Jessica the right suggestions about how to approach Brooke and her inner circle. I imagine that Jessica hears the following message: you're failing at the popularity game, you're disappointing me. She fails to help Jessica cope because she's too involved in futile micromanaging.

Even when a child is hurting, even when a mother cannot protect her child from adversity, she always has the opportunity of soothing. Picture for a moment a pain we rarely fault ourselves for:

the toddler who falls while taking his first wobbly steps. Instinctively, a mother picks up the crying child, sings or rocks or kisses the child until the boo-boo goes away. Carolyn's preoccupation with her daughter's social status interferes with her ability to do the adolescent equivalent of soothing the pain. By telegraphing her anxiety to Jessica, Carolyn keeps her from being able to turn to her mother for comfort. Jessica might be protecting Carolyn from getting upset, or she might be angry at her mother's intrusiveness, but either way she sees that she cannot turn to her mom for comfort around these issues. In a classic case of overcompensation, Carolyn's grandiose plan to protect her daughter from adversity backfires. By trying too hard to control Jessica's social standing, she creates a distance that prevents her from giving Jessica what she most needs: comfort and loving adult guidance on how to cope with the almost ubiquitous pain of female adolescence.

Cheryl (see Chapter 4) had a different way of handling her son's adolescent angst. Charles Jr. was hit by a bat playing Little League, and his front teeth were discolored as a result. He also wears glasses, still the teen kiss of death. When he told his mother that other teens were making fun of his appearance, she addressed what she thought was reasonable, working out a financial plan with his father to get some cosmetic dental repair work done. Glasses were another matter: she acknowledged his discomfort, but let him know that she didn't feel buying expensive contacts to be more stylish was warranted. She did one of the hardest things for a mother to do: she sat with it. The message she gave Charles Jr. was "It's painful but I think you're strong enough to cope with being teased about glasses."

Yvonne (see Chapter 6) had an experience with adversity that she says all African-American mothers fear: racism touching your children. She notes, "For African-American boys, the initiation into manhood is being pulled over by policemen." In fact, she had to witness a scene in which her sons were assumed to be criminals when the family went shopping at a grocery store in an almost exclusively white suburb. Her grocery store routine was that she and her husband would shop, while her sons, avid readers, browsed the magazine section. One day, she recalls, "I was strolling past the magazine aisle, and I see them being accused by a big security guard of trying to steal a book. I know they're not perfect, but they don't lie, and they know we'll buy them books. I said 'They'll tell you the truth. Ask them.' My older son said, 'I was going to ask you to buy this book.' The security guard replied that he saw them at the store all the time, and knew they were trouble. Yvonne was furious, because since the store wasn't one they frequented, it was literally impossible that her sons had been there stealing books in the past. The security guard made one of two errors: either he thought all African-American teenaged boys looked alike, or thought they all stole so it didn't really matter. In either case, he treated them differently than white kids whose parents were shopping there, and it was terribly painful for her.

She was too upset, certain she'd lose her cool, so her husband handled it. She says that since he grew up in Africa, he sees the world through "rose-colored glasses. He doesn't see prejudice." He calmly convinced the store manager that the security guard made a mistake, and the family quickly left. She comforted herself and her children by acknowledging the terrible injustice. "The world judges you constantly. People will see you in a certain way, and you can't let their interpretation affect you." When they hung by her side in future shopping trips, she understood why, but reminded them that they are not responsible for other people's erroneous opinions. The world is not a perfect place, and neither Cheryl nor Yvonne is blind to their inability to protect their children from its bruises.

When Adversity Passes Through You to Your Children

The children of mothers with heritable mental illnesses face a real risk: inherited psychiatric illness. Their genes are no phantom menace. These mothers do not limit their fantasies to keeping their children safe from the normal wear and tear of childhood. Their wish is that their children do not suffer as they have suffered. Hilary is one such mom. I treated her years ago, before she moved to San Francisco. She checks in by phone now and then, keeping me updated about her therapy with a new doctor. Her issues, until lately, have been about her difficulties standing in for her hopelessly unmothering mother. The oldest of five siblings, she has been filling in for as long as she can remember. At age nine, her two-year-old sister found her way to her bed rather than her mother's when scared in the night. Like Jessie of the Boxcar Children, by her early teens, she was overseeing laundry, lunches, and homework for all. She was the source of comfort when her mother threw a glass against the wall, screamed curses, or disappeared for days, as happened periodically due to hospitalization for depression or alcoholic binges.

The presence of a single caretaker, an aunt, a neighbor, a grandparent, or a father, can boost the unmothered child's resilience. A kind and soothing adult who says, in words or deeds, that this is not how it is supposed to be, can be all that it takes for a child to emerge from such chaos with self-esteem. The unmothered mother may unconsciously use that nurturing adult as her role model, a well to draw upon in defining her own quest for good mothering. Hilary and I never found any such caretaker in her background. Instead, she always struck me as a miraculously capable mother. Unmothered in the extreme, she somehow emerged from the ashes with an innate ability to care for others, a gloriously feathered maternal phoenix.

Hilary is, I'd guess, the brightest patient I have ever known. I have often wondered whether her inexplicable nurturing gifts weren't somehow secondary to her phenomenal brain power. Perhaps as a child, a voracious early reader, she derived vicarious mothering at the hands of Beverly Cleary or Laura Ingalls Wilder. Most deprived children, when glimpsing a seemingly abundant world, blame themselves, feel that they haven't been good enough, smart enough, quiet enough, or pretty enough to deserve a better mom. Did a precocious ability to abstract allow her to witness her unmothered existence without the shame that adds insult to injury? Did her intellectual power let her create an internal model of a caretaker, a blueprint for how to raise her siblings? I can't easily explain how she knew, without being nurtured, how to nurture. She just did.

Blessings can become curses, of course, and our work together centered on cutting the apron strings for her often overly dependent adult siblings. It's hard enough to push the birds out of the nest when it's time, and they're your birds, and you think they're probably ready to fly. Her sibling birds were, not surprisingly, a little weak, and hanging on to the only mother they know. When she phoned, she told me that she continued working with her new therapist toward extracting herself from her tendency to rush to the sibling rescue, at no small cost to her marriage and her actual children. She shared that she was learning to sort through how to differentiate the request to drive a twenty-three-year-old college graduate to a job interview, because he might oversleep the alarm without her help, from the need to oversee the retrieval of a sister who, without benefit of luggage or money, had just taken a bus to Hollywood in a manic belief that she was the next Julia Roberts.

With both parents afflicted with chronic, persistent mood disorders, I had considered Hilary relatively lucky. Despite her clear risks, she experienced not a touch of postpartum depression. Later, when her children were in preschool, she had mild depression, which responded robustly to a sprinkle of Prozac. Compared to siblings who had been hospitalized for the very issues she had witnessed in her parents, Hilary felt doubly blessed. Not only was her inherited disease about as mild as it comes, she had a supportive, loving marriage, economic stability, a substance-abuse-free household, and her kids were, understandably, thriving.

Alas, her new psychiatrist called with terrible news. She explained that Hilary's oldest child, who had just hit puberty, had been touched by the family illness. For the first time, this unmothered mother, a contender for the Most Improved Second Generation Mother competition, could not stop an oncoming train. And in Hilary's view, it was her fault. Her genes had harmed her adored child.

Typically, her initial reaction was: fix the problem. Many mothers know this reaction to crisis: get through it, make sure everyone is safe, then fall apart on your own time. Automatically, Hilary went into research mode, quickly finding an exceptional child treatment center in San Francisco. As always, she did a beautiful job for her daughter, finding a perfect match for her. Her daughter's physician reassured her: Toni's problems were minor, nothing that would in any way interfere with a perfectly normal adolescence.

And then, her doctor recounted, Hilary fell apart. Fell apart in a way she had never done in her life. She became severely depressed. She sobbed incessantly, trying to hide out in her bedroom so that her kids wouldn't see her cry. Becoming tearful in front of her children was horrifying to her, a catastrophic loss of control that she experienced as tantamount to her mom throwing a glass at the wall when she didn't like what you were wearing.

Depression is bad, but the type of depression Hilary got, melancholic depression, is awful. Hilary had an agitated, melancholic depression. She could barely make it through the three or four days until her next appointment, calling me long distance for reassurance that she'd recover. I told her again and again, you'll get better. Your doctor will find the drugs. You'll beat this depression, whatever it takes. This is not reassurance about being a good mom. It is reassurance about carrying on.

If you have agitated depression, you've thought about suicide. It is the obvious solution to your pain. Because suicide can be seductive in the midst of excruciating depression, her new doctor was afraid that Hilary might persuade herself that this would be acceptable. The possibility of suicide is a paradoxical comfort for severely depressed people: if the way I feel doesn't go away, I can end my suffering. Others find that thoughts of death are relentless, intrusive, unwanted. But Hilary once told me that she felt that the most self-indulgent thing a mother can do is to attempt suicide. Her mother had threatened it repeatedly, and that's an emotional tattoo that can't be removed. Still, as her depression lingered, any doctor would worry that she would be unable to sustain her belief that suicide would destroy her children, or might even come, falsely, to believe that her children would be better off without her.

For mothers with melancholia, the usual thing that stands between them and suicide is their children. The more children a mother has, the less likely she is to commit suicide. You can lie to yourself with one child: he'll remarry, he'll find the child a stepmother who, unlike me, will take proper care of my beloved child. In the mind's desperate effort to rationalize the most heinous of maternal crimes, suicide becomes a gift one gives one's deprived children. Its destruction is denied. But by the time you get to three or four kids, there is no way to tell yourself that an alternate caretaker will step in, that your children would do anything but suffer in your death. Mothers of four or more children are the least likely to kill themselves, and it surely is not because more kids protect against the most severe forms of mental illness. They just make it impossible to sustain the self-deception that it's all for the best.

Hilary's new psychopharmacologist prescribed medicines from each of the major classes of psychotropic medication, from the newest epilepsy drugs, which often act as mood regulators, to the most old-fashioned antidepressants. During her calls, she told me that some provided relief; others made her worse, mimicking symptoms of depression as they clouded her concentration, or made her feel restless. Her therapist and physician shared a belief in the biological foundation of Hilary's illness. We have an expression in my field for this type of predisposition: her family tree lights up like a Christmas tree. But even as I, too, believed this, I also spoke to the psychologist seeing Hilary for therapy. The new therapist was struck by the meaning of her child's illness to her, as a precipitating event. No parent would want a child to experience even mild anxiety, but her anguish was wildly out of proportion to her daughter's distress, and noticeably more marked than that experienced by her child's other parent, the one with the clean genetic history. The psychologist felt that the trigger to this profound depression was the agony of the ultimate maternal powerlessness: faulty DNA. Hilary is a mother whose life's work has been to protect her children from the chaos she experienced time and again growing up, only to find that there was nothing she could do to ensure that her children were invulnerable to the family curse.

Hilary's therapist tried to get her to see the obvious: her genes, in the different environment she herself provides as their mother, aren't so devastating. Her children have never once been terrified by a parent's volatility. Her daughter quickly recovered, returning easily to the world of worrying about boys and drama club tryouts and whether the music teacher has favorites.

Hilary's depression was like an offering of herself as a sacrifice to the gods: take me, leave my child alone. It's hard not to notice the way in which Hilary unconsciously re-created her childhood. Because she felt on the verge of tears, she avoided her children. Convinced that to see their mother cry would evoke the pain she endured when one or both of her parents would erupt in a fit of drunken rage, she withdrew from them, afraid to tell them for months that she was ill. In attempting to protect them from her imagined defective mothering, for the first time, she stumbled as a mother in one of the most common ways parents falter. She kept a secret that everyone knew.

Hilary's story deserves a tidy ending. Her therapist wanted her to see what she saw: a young woman who by age seven had already learned to parent better than she had been mothered. She might share her mother's depressive illness, but she would not replicate her mothering. She hoped that Hilary might even come to realize how fortunate her daughter is: she was given to exactly the right set of parents, who immediately detected and got help for the mood disorder. In the end, although both the new psychiatrist and the psychologist became convinced that the igniting flame was primarily psychological—her dashed hopes to provide a bulletproof childhood for her kids—once afire, the illness burned on its own. The medicines gradually kicked in, hope and peace returned, and eventually, without benefit of the "ah-hah" moment therapists and patients crave, she got well.

As often happens in my practice, life imitates therapy. At times, I think this is simply what happens when you help mothers with mothering: your own mothering issues come up. In the midst of Hilary's inability to protect her child, one of my children experienced a pain that sooner or later most people suffer: heartache (obviously a far less significant adverse event than illness). His first love, the kind of girl any mother would choose for her son, a ten-karat diamond of a young woman, had to move across the country with her family. Her new home was remote, not a quick or inexpensive flight away for love-struck teens. For all practical purposes, the romance was over, and it had not died a natural death. Teenagers feel deeply, and there is no love like your first love. He was devastated.

My own devastation took me by surprise. The art of therapy is experiencing other people's pain with empathy, while maintaining a healthy distance. I feel sorrow six or eight times a day, really feel it, and yet I walk away whole. When my son was suffering so acutely, I felt the sorrow but couldn't get a grip on the objectivity, on the boundary between his pain and mine. Like Hilary, my first impulse was to cry in my bedroom lest the kids think I'd wigged out—they knew it wasn't *my* girlfriend who was leaving town.

I got a grip by realizing what I *had* lost: the ability to put myself between an emotional train and my child. This was a pain I could not deflect or absorb on his behalf. I was watching my child suffer, and I was helpless. The train was coming, the train came, it hit hard, and he hurt.

I bounced back when I told him that I would take his sadness if

I could only find a way to do so. Voicing the impossible maternal wish, standing in the futile yet universal urge to protect one's child from life's bruises, I admitted defeat. The days when I could kiss a boo-boo and make it all better were long gone. I couldn't make this one better. Once I surrendered, I could find soothing words. There isn't and shouldn't be a shortcut for losing someone you love. *This is really awful. You will feel better. You won't always feel as bad as you do right this moment.*

Teenage boys, even psychiatrist's kids, don't talk about their feelings with their moms, so I don't really know what helped him bounce back. He did bounce back, and in the cellular age—free long distance after ten p.m. and on weekends—the romance limped along.

Conclusion

For most, there is no threat like that of harm befalling one's child. Mothers commonly describe the profound attachment they feel to their children in terms of sacrifice: I'd give my life for this person, I'd throw myself in front of a moving train to save my child, I'd take food from my mouth to feed this baby. When new mothers talk about the first wave of consciousness of their deep connectedness with their infant, they often couch it in terms of anxiety, fear, disorientation. The feeling is as close to pain as it is to sweetness. Love that powerful renders you vulnerable in the extreme.

But you can't live there. You can't view the world as a constant threat to your child's well-being, and thrive. You aren't likely to raise a resilient child if you're convinced she's too fragile to cope with the ordinary bumps of life.

I was reminded by my son's adversity: we can do certain things that keep our kids safe and happy. We can make them wear seat belts, feed them well, read to them at bedtime. But sooner or later, sorrow will touch our kids. You can count on it. We have to hope that when it does, they can count on us to listen, to validate, to offer a vision of better days ahead. It's the best we can do.

Since no mother can guarantee her child a pain-free life, or deflect all of life's potential blows, mastering the challenge requires self-acceptance, and relinquishing grandiose fantasies of maternal omnipotence. It requires a mother to accept that she has not failed in her duty to protect her child just because something bad happens.

Signs of Poor Adaptation to Adversity in a Child

1. Belief that your child's first eighteen years can or should be pain free.

2. Inability to be reassured when something goes wrong, because you cannot distinguish the blows you can deflect from the ones you cannot.

3. Emotional reasoning: deciding that because you feel guilty, you are guilty.

4. Feedback from your child that she/he attempts to protect you from your emotional reactions to her or his disappointments, difficulties, or emotional trauma, or feels criticized when she or he tells you about those issues.

Strategies for Successful Adaptation

1. When you become aware of feeling guilty or at fault for adversity that touches your child, generate a mental or written list of alternative explanations for the conclusion that you're responsible. If necessary, picture yourself help-

ing a close friend or sister with exaggerated self-blame, and review what you would say to reassure her if you were the observer and she was the mother feeling guilty.

2. Examine the basis of your sense of responsibility when adversity arises. If you do not have control over the situation, lower your expectations for yourself. Study the Serenity Prayer—"God grant me the serenity to accept the things I cannot change; the courage to change the things I can; and the wisdom to know the difference"—until you can achieve a clearer, more balanced view of the situation.

3. Focus on the exceptional value and unique role of a mother in soothing and comforting a child who is experiencing illness, harm, or hurt.

4. Seek out the support of mothers facing similar difficulties. For example, join a self-help group for parents of children with diabetes, attend school meetings for parents with children receiving special education services, compare notes with the mother who is waiting next to you at the emergency room, have coffee with a mother who has helped her child through a similar difficulty.

9

Saying Good-bye
The Ninth Key Challenge

*We shift gears constantly, as we meet our offspring
in an elusive dance of change. We find ourselves relentlessly
retracing old paths one week and discovering new ways
of getting along the next.*
—Karen Levin Coburn and Madge Lawrence Treeger, *Letting Go*

Mom, you've had eighteen years to teach me values. Chill.
—Sam Raskin, one month prior to starting college

Mothers commonly discuss launching their children into adulthood in terms of pain. Kathleen, who struggled to find a good school fit for her children (see Chapter 6), hoped that as a divorced mother, she'd have an easier time, because she'd already "practiced." "I knew many lonely nights when the girls were at their dad's house," she recalls. Still, when her daughter Ciara's departure for college approached, the pain was visceral. "I was a basket case when she graduated high school. It weighed on my body, my grief became physical. I had to tell myself, let it be painful. It is what it is. Let it be sad."

When grief becomes somatic, it's the mind's attempt to defend against intense emotional pain. Humans naturally resist feeling powerful, painful emotions. Most of us would choose to have a stomachache if the alternative is despair. Bereavement and loss are the daily bread of any psychotherapist, and we pretty much all offer the same guidance: there is no shortcut through grief. The only way to fight the fire is to walk right smack through the middle of it. Kathleen knew that her bodily distress was disguising her sorrow, and she knew that her task was to let herself stop fighting the feeling of loss.

Once she began to experience her emotions, Kathleen used a number of better psychological defense mechanisms to cope. She used altruism to help soften the pain, telling herself, "Ciara is a gift to the world. It would be selfish to try to keep her [for myself]." For many mothers, letting go is the ultimate maternal sacrifice—better for the child than for the mother. Kathleen centered herself in creative imagery: "Like the poets say, life is to be lived." She wrote poetry about children leaving a garden, and she visualized Ciara as a chrysalis becoming a beautiful butterfly. She also remained vigilant about slipping into thinking traps. Catching herself reasoning with her emotions rather than her common sense ("I feel abandoned therefore I am being abandoned."), she reminded herself, "My daughter was going on a great adventure, and she will tell me about it." Only partly playfully, she set her bottom line: "When you come back from college, will you still hug me?" Ciara does.

Anticipating the Loss

Just as older teens prepare for independence, mothers begin to get ready for the inevitable departure of a child. Anticipation of loss is often worse than the loss itself. For some, the mental preparation for a child's departure is like watching the guillotine blade poised for months, waiting for it to eventually drop. Coping generally only begins *after* the feared event has occurred—in the meantime, you just fret about how bad it might be. Many women describe a tremendous surge in anxiety about safety during the last one or two years of high school; others note a significant uptick in parent-child conflict in response to "senioritis."

Marla is in the anticipatory stage. When her son Nick, seventeen, first started driving to school, he checked in daily if he wasn't coming straight home. But one Friday, after borrowing his father's car for school, he didn't call, and his phone went to voice mail. He sauntered in that evening around six-thirty looking for dinner, and Marla "completely lost it. I yelled and screamed and threatened to take back his cell phone, never let him use the car again, peel his fingernails off one by one, you name it, I promised it."

Nick, knowing that he had a heavy weekend of studying ahead of him, impulsively decided to go to an after-school movie with a friend. He used his own babysitting money to pay for the ticket, went with a kid Marla liked, and returned in time for his dad to use the car if he needed it when he got off the train from work. In his mind, he had been the model of adolescent responsibility. He accuses Marla of being a control freak. It was the first time as a mother that Marla had absolutely no idea where he was and could not reach him. She immediately went to worst-case scenarios (he's buying drugs and got caught in a drive-by shooting, he's bleeding on the side of a road after a car accident, he's been arrested, etc.). Nick was angry—he's a good kid who has never been in any trouble, and her first thought is that he's buying drugs?

Her relief was followed by rage at his thoughtlessness—she blamed him for putting her through the agony of picturing him dead or in trouble. Her emotional state was identical to that of the mother who cries in relief while simultaneously upbraiding a toddler who almost ran in front of a car, a reaction almost any mother understands viscerally: thank God you're okay and now I'd like to kill you for making me worry. She couldn't think straight for a while, but as she let the incident percolate, she realized that she had held Nick responsible for her exaggerated worrying. Knowing him, there were any number of more logical scenarios that she could now picture: he had become engrossed in conversation at an espresso bar, his cell phone was sitting in his backpack in the car trunk, the battery ran out after he neglected to recharge it, or, as turned out to be the case, he got involved in a social activity and forgot about her.

Nick and Marla are simultaneously rehearsing leaving home. In less than one short year, Marla will go from occasionally not knowing what Nick is doing to *usually* not knowing. He may stay up all night studying, crash at a party after having too much to drink, take off with a friend to a rock concert in a town two hours away, or volunteer to work the three a.m. shift at a homeless shelter, and she won't have a clue. She will, without question, lose the security of frequent reassurance that all is well with her child.

When Marla blames Nick for making her upset, she's briefly lost the me-other delineation (see "healthy mothering boundaries" in Chapter 1). She cannot ask that he be responsible for the anxiety that his approaching leave-taking engenders in her. The parent and child aren't experiencing the same emotional event. The typical mother's anticipatory stage emotions are mostly loss and fear, perhaps with a little pleasure and satisfaction mixed in. For the typical child, leaving home is mostly satisfaction and pleasure, with a little loss and fear mixed in. Nick is appropriately excited about the prospect of being on his own.

Marla knows that she is supposed to applaud her child's steps toward independence, just as she did when he first went to kindergarten. She also knows that although he would never admit it, he's scared, too. She realizes that although he said he just forgot, subconsciously, he might have been taking a mini-dry run, practicing being on his own. If he's to imagine going across the country to college, she thinks, he just may need to reassure himself that he can handle three hours of complete independence. This helps her meet the challenge of this impending stage: it was once her job to be vigilant; now it is her job to let him succeed in pulling away from her safety net.

I hope that Marla enters this rehearsing for independence stage with a vision of the best outcome: moving from being Nick's physical safety net to being his emotional safety net and sounding board, when, as they will, bad things happen. If Marla were to ask my opinion, I'd want her to go one step further than zipping her lip about her fear. During the time that Nick is experimenting with a new independence, he may well screw up, or simply find that things don't go as he expects. Each time Nick messes up during the year before leaving, if Marla goes overboard with threats, shame, blame, or punishment, Nick learns that secrecy is a better plan. On the other hand, if she responds to his slips as opportunities to help him develop better internal judgment, she gives herself the possibility of active mothering during the year before college by inviting him to access her wisdom without accessing shame or retribution.*

If a child must push her mother away in order to feel grown up enough to leave home, she will. Some high school seniors will push hard against their mothers regardless of what the mother does. Ironically, those teens may be the most deeply attached; they fight their buried fears of being on their own by staging dramatic battles that serve to reassure them that Mom is so worth leaving, that her cozy nest isn't all that great. But now and then, mothers can soften the conflict by refusing the bait. By biding her tongue the next time something worrisome happens, Marla refuses to accept being cast as the Mom You're Better Off Without.

If a mother is to successfully launch her young adult child, she will have to find a way to bear the discomfort of knowing all the terrible things that can happen in the Big Bad World, and to tolerate a certain amount of bad behavior as part of rehearsing to leave

---

* I am referring here to the pretty good kid who slips on occasion, not the more troubled adolescent with a serious substance-use disorder, academic failure or true aimlessness, anorexia nervosa, et cetera, who likely needs more aggressive intervention.

home. As author Judith Viorst notes in *Necessary Losses,* "A normal adolescent isn't a normal adolescent if he acts normal." A mother cannot and should not ask her child to forgo experimentation with autonomy because it would be easier on her—it isn't in that child's long-term interest. Insisting on controlling your teen's every move may mean that the adolescent child never gets drunk, smokes a cigarette, blows off an exam, has sex, drives without a seat belt, misses a deadline, fails to meet an obligation, underperforms on the athletic field, or skips breakfast. More likely, if your child appears perfect, it means that he or she is hiding normal adolescent behavior, or, of more concern, that the child will not develop the internal self-control that she will need once she no longer lives under your roof. You do not want your child to be the overprotected kid in the freshman dorm who goes wild, mistaking "independence" for "anything goes."

No, They Aren't All Grown Up Yet

The other challenge for Marla in the year that precedes Nick's departure for college: settling for having done a good-enough job. Every mother is a perfectionist when it comes to launching a child. Frantic efforts to get the cake just right are normal, and yet they are as doomed as any other maternal quest for perfection. Some mothers find themselves trying to surgically implant caution in the year before a child leaves home. Sylvia jumps on every opportunity to warn her seventeen-year-old daughter about the risk of sexual assault, with stories about girls she knew in college who were date-raped. Every time her daughter goes out at night, Sylvia warns her about where she parks, reminding her to be alert when she gets in and out of the car. She cuts stories out of the paper, often noting, "I'm sure she thought it couldn't happen to her—you never do until it does." Mary Ellen's fixation is substance abuse, pointing out how stupid Uncle John looked when he got drunk at a family gathering, calling her son in to watch television stories of celebrities in rehab, reminding him about how a neighbor's child dropped out of college when he got into drugs. Others focus on life skills: how to do laundry, stay on a budget, read a map. Some mothers try to perfect interpersonal skills: here's how you resist peer pressure, date, make new friends, get out of a bad relationship.

When it comes to fretting about kids leaving home, part of what makes it especially difficult is that many of us recall only too vividly all the stupid things we did in our youth, the bullets we dodged, and perhaps a few that hit. Recalling our own experiences with the danger that accompanies early-adult independence and undeveloped judgment is in no small part why it is so incredibly difficult to have our children leave the nest. We *know* that good judgment often only follows bad experience. Being only human, we want our kids to do as we say, not as we did. When it comes time to leave, no mother feels that her child is *perfectly* ready for independence—it's only a question of where you fall on the anxiety spectrum, how imperfect your mothering seems to have been, how vulnerable your not-all-grown-up child appears to be.

Then Again, It Might Be Worse Than You Feared

Debbie's child needed a lot of support freshman year. Debbie never considered leaving home to be synonymous with "separating." At age eighteen, she herself "fled precipitously," never returning home once college began. Yet at forty-nine, she wouldn't describe herself as completely emotionally separated from her own mother, although I think she gives herself too little credit. She felt so enmeshed with her own mother as a younger woman that when she was pregnant, she was terrified that if she had a daughter she wouldn't know how to establish healthy boundaries. Never released to independent adulthood by her mother, she feared she would not know how to let go of a girl. This is another example of the poorly mothered woman's manifesto: Please don't let me be like her.

In the be-careful-what-you-wish-for-mode, her hopes were answered. The married mother of two boys, she now sometimes feels that she "lives in a men's locker room." And she found that her fantasized separation from a male child wasn't exactly a cakewalk. A year and a half after her older son went to college, she's still struggling to find the right balance, working to "just sit still" while he navigates what has turned out to be a rocky entry into young adulthood.

Debbie is quite psychologically sophisticated and introspective. Her husband is a clinical psychotherapist; she is a professor who specializes in the psychoanalytic study of literature, and she's had plenty of therapy herself, trying to overcome the wounds of being unmothered. When she says her mother has a narcissistic personality disorder, she knows of what she speaks.

Narcissists make terrible mothers. By definition, a narcissist cannot genuinely empathize with her child. Narcissistic mothers demand attention and admiration in the absence of cause, and are typically highly manipulative and arrogant. Despite their egotism and sense of entitlement, narcissists are exquisitely sensitive to criticism, and as mothers, regularly rage at perceived slights from their children. Children of narcissists learn early to reverse roles, serving as the parent's mirror. They cope by learning to avoid the rage and shame that failing to comply with their mothers' expectations precipitates. It's a deeply ingrained way of relating. The narcissistic mother has a hole in the bottom of her cup, and the child's frantic and often lifelong efforts to boost her mother's self-esteem is doomed to fail. Teens of narcissists don't rebel overtly, because they've already learned that emotional abuse and humiliation are the price of even the slightest move toward independence. For the narcissistic mother, it's always about her.

Because normal adolescent autonomy enrages a narcissistic

mother, her children typically leave home by escape, just as Debbie did. Subconsciously, they know plans made openly will be sabotaged. When she left for college, she promised to return, but Debbie had no intention of coming back. She reveled in getting away from the burden of being her mother's supplier of self-esteem, but thirty years later, she isn't emotionally untangled. She and her two sisters dread every holiday, taking turns letting her mother ruin their family events. Narcissists are envious people, and Debbie's mother's jealousy of the loving relationship Debbie has with her sons comes out in nasty snipes and shocking criticism. Debbie would "never even consider" turning to her for emotional support. A good encounter with her mother means that she wasn't emotionally trashed.

Outsiders wonder why children of narcissists don't just "divorce" their monstrous parents. What seems easy to an outsider is far more complicated to the insider. One simple explanation is that children love their parents, even emotionally handicapped ones. Most of us only get one mother, and bad is generally preferred to none at all. Perhaps more important, the entanglements run very deep. Narcissists begin "training" their children very early to gratify their demands, and to suppress their own emotional needs. By adulthood, the daughter of a narcissist has had thousands of experiences in which sacrificing her own desires has resulted in a calmer, more "motherly" mother. As the child grows into adulthood, she sees the bottomless insecurity of her mother, for whom haughty arrogance is a defense against an inner fragility. The sensitive child, like Debbie, often comes to understand that her mother is terribly defective; she cannot fail to notice that her mother eventually alienates all others whom she touches. Premature responsibility for the well-being of a mother, what psychotherapists call "parentification" of the child, results in a daughter who feels obligated to care for her mother.

Debbie's mother is blind to the resentment and guilt her behavior generates. By definition, she lacks the ability to put herself in her daughter's emotional shoes. She feels no responsibility for kindness and goodwill toward her offspring. It would no sooner occur to her to refrain from telling a daughter who gave birth three days ago that she's looking fat than it would to reflect on her child's emotional experience of leaving home. She simply doesn't go there, which means if you're reading this and genuinely reflecting on your own child's experience of leaving home, you aren't a narcissist.

Daughters of narcissists have a very challenging task becoming mothers. On the one hand, they've been caretakers since early childhood, and they often enter motherhood with excellent nurturing skills. However, many, like Debbie (and Naomi in Chapter 1), worry that their own children are harboring the secret resentment toward them that they carry toward their own mothers. Debbie, for example, just assumed that her boys would leave home in the same abrupt way—in a rush, thrilled to be gone, exhilarated by shedding a burdensome mother. "I was really afraid my son would never come back," she recalls. "I thought he'd go to school and we'd never see him again."

Debbie's oldest son is very bright, and yet he struggled in school, troubled in part by attention deficit disorder with hyperactivity. "He was the antithesis of the kind of kid I had to be," she says. She was the perfect little girl; Seth was always in trouble. He was "very reactive," immune to negative feedback. In grade school, he was "the kind of kid who required a lot of parental involvement," she says euphemistically. By high school, he had settled down behaviorally, wasn't always in trouble anymore, but his grades were erratic. If he felt a homework assignment was "stupid," he simply didn't do it. He had a game going to see if he could get B's without exerting any effort. The night before earning a perfect SAT score, he was surprised when she told him he would need pencils for the test. He had given the college entrance examination no thought whatsoever.

In addition to being intellectually capable, Seth is athletic. He was recruited into an academically competitive school in a nearby state to play basketball, a seduction that any high school senior is bound to enjoy. On the day Debbie and her husband drove Seth to his dorm, the coach called him to welcome him to the university. Things looked promising for Seth. Typically, Debbie and Seth had different reactions. He was excited, and "it hit me harder than I expected it to. There was the sadness of knowing that part of my life was over," Debbie recalls.

Seth's early enthusiasm about starting college quickly evaporated, and he began instant-messaging his parents with complaints. The basketball coaches were ignoring him, he said. They chalked it up to anxiety: they aren't supposed to talk to you until formal try-outs, they reassured him. "They're paying attention to the other freshman basketball players," Seth noted. Debbie "hung on every IM [instant message] exchange. I could tell he was agitated, and I couldn't stand the pain." She encouraged him to socialize more, go to activities, but he complained that everyone was already drunk when the parties started, and she certainly didn't want him to feel he had to drink to make friends. They visited him in October, and "my husband and I just looked at each other—it was clear he was miserable." On November 1, basketball tryouts began, and Debbie optimistically predicted that he'd finally find his niche, things would get better. On November 3, as Seth somehow sensed from Day One, he was cut from the team. The coaches *had* changed their minds about his basketball prospects, after Seth had turned down other offers to enroll at a college that then broke its seductive promise.

No parent would suffer such a vicarious blow easily, but Debbie and her husband were terrified. Clinical depression, including suicide, runs in both families. They couldn't help worrying that this would be the last straw for Seth, even as they realized that particular fear was one of those things that go bump in the night, since Seth showed no suicidal tendencies himself. But Seth was so unhappy that even in the absence of a life-threatening reaction, Debbie and her husband realized it was time to quit insisting that he'd eventually adjust. They asked him to try to finish the semester, making it clear that he could return home at any point. "He was stunned. He expected us to make him stick it out the whole year." Seth did complete the semester, with two trips back home for TLC.

Debbie seems unaware of how her reaction to her son's crisis could not have been more unlike how her own mother would have handled it. Most parents naturally have a personal investment in their child's academic and athletic success, and Seth was at a college any mother could brag about. If Debbie truly had the poor boundaries she feared, she would have experienced Seth's failure to cope with the disappointments of his first college semester as a reflection on herself, or insisted he stay so that she could maintain the image of having a perfect child. She might have blamed him for getting cut from basketball, and she would have confused what was best for her with what was best for him. Instead, she supported him in extracting himself from a very poor college fit, and in his disappointment at being inexplicably rejected athletically.

She immediately set to worrying about what he would do when he came home. "I was afraid he'd come back and fester," she says. To her surprise, Seth returned with greater maturity. He landed a job and two nearby apartment mates who, while young, were responsible and likable. She says, "They're almost grown-ups." Seth has the best of both worlds—independence, but in some sense, it is a "semi-separation." He grocery shops, cooks for himself, and he's found a social group that doesn't center on alcohol, while remaining connected to his parents. The situation, she says, "is teaching us and him how to do autonomy."

Her greatest pleasure is in watching Seth take full responsibility for his college transfer applications. Last time, Debbie and her husband were involved in every detail, from providing pencils for his SAT exam to talking with the coaches. This time, Seth is doing it all. He's written his own essay explaining why he left the first college, and he alone is talking to coaches. He is only considering schools within an hour or two of home.

Debbie has several explanations about why she thinks it is going so much better this time around. She doesn't rule out the simple biological explanation that a year of "brain development" helped him settle. But she also feels an elaborate dance has taken place. She was forced to separate emotionally from his pain, and by doing so, he has been able to acknowledge his need for a gentler, more gradual separation from her. She says "I spent twenty years of parenting trying to unlearn feeling whatever the person I loved was feeling. My mother expected me to mirror her feelings, and I do it naturally. As a result, perhaps I'd been excessively enmeshed with my boys. If Seth felt like shit, I felt like shit. The hardest thing I know is watching my kid in pain and not being able to fix it."

She used humor to help overcome her tendency to feel-and-fix his problems. "We have a family joke, 'Don't do anything, just sit there.'" That's not her way—her instinct is to rescue, bolster, compensate—anything but just sit there. Seth's disastrous semester taxed her capacity to just sit there, but she finally got it. She remembers once when he was instant-messaging his misery. She was responding with one suggestion after another—do this, try that, feel this way, don't feel like that—which he would promptly "shoot down." Finally it clicked for her: just sit there. In that moment, she changed her behavior, quit trying to fix it for him, and she recognized that not only did she not have to internalize Seth's distress, perhaps he didn't really want her to.

In addition to letting go of his misery, Debbie also had to let go of her emotional investment in his success. "My hurdle was letting it be about him. His experience in college isn't mine, it's his. My husband and I aren't aloof, but we're letting go." In this victory, Debbie has positively distinguished her mothering from that which she received. She is not a mother who defines herself in terms of her child, and she does not demand that her child be responsible for her emotional well-being. She says that she cannot predict how the next college year will go, because she has internalized the knowledge that his college experience is *his* college experience.

Seth appears to have responded to her newfound "sitting there" by becoming more comfortable with his ongoing need for mothering. It's almost as if he himself had fled his need for connection, promptly crashed, and then, in seeing that his parents could separate themselves from him ("try to finish the semester but only if you can"), was able to find a distance (one mile) that worked better for him emotionally. In a twist one might expect from an O. Henry story, by letting go, Debbie is rewarded by Seth's connectedness. She pulled back; he stepped forward.

She gives him the gift of a separating mother: pleasure in his autonomy. One day, he was planning to stop by to visit his parents. He called his mother and asked, "Do you need me to stop at Panera to pick up dinner for tonight?" She teases him, acknowledging his maturation: "Excuse me, isn't that *my* role?" And she accepts his offer. "It was lovely," she sighs.

And Sometimes It's Terrifying

Carlotta, the mother of a twenty-year-old son who has left home and a seventeen-year-old on the verge, answers the question "When do you stop worrying about them?" with "Not yet." She compares herself with her female friends, "I see others still worrying, so at least I know I'm not the only one." She worried about them leaving the suburbs to hang out in the city: don't accidentally make gang signs, don't get into fights, don't drink, she warned. In an attempt to alleviate her anxiety, one of her sons told her he has a crowbar in his car. Her reaction: "Great, then someone can use it on you." Some of her most irrational worries are obviously just that, but Carlotta is more than entitled to be an excessively worried mother: her older son is a solider in Iraq.

You wouldn't have predicted that Michael would enlist in the air force at age eighteen. He was a good student at a high school where almost all the graduates attend college; his parents are educated professionals, and he could have attended several colleges affiliated with the hospital where Carlotta is a nurse, tuition-free. The only obstacle to Michael leaving home for college was a deep, early passion for airplanes. Michael's first word was "Mama"; his second word, "Dada"; his third word, "airplane." In grade school, while other boys read comic books and watched *Power Rangers*, Michael read books on military history. Every weekend, his father indulged his passion and took him to the city airport, where they watched planes land and take off for hours. By eight or nine years of age, Michael could look at an airplane and tell you what kind of engine it had. Later, he bought a scanner to listen to air traffic control chatter.

During his senior year of high school, he refused to complete college applications, even though every single one of his boyhood friends was going off to college. Carlotta blamed herself. "What did I do wrong?" She worried that Michael was angry that his parents had gotten divorced not long before, but he denied it, and she reminds herself that his passion started well before the divorce. She envied other mothers. "I never saw myself as wanting to keep up with the Joneses, but it was hard to see his friends going off to college."

Michael enlisted within weeks of graduating from high school. He took an aptitude test, and to his delight, he was selected for training as an air traffic controller. Because the specialized training is only offered periodically, he expected to start boot camp as late as a year after enlisting. But then, on September 11, 2001, the World Trade Center was attacked, and Michael ended up leaving home two months earlier than expected. Carlotta's separation was instantaneous: the air force called and said "Come tonight." In the rush to get supplies together, she recalls thinking that it felt like getting him ready for summer camp rather than boot camp. Then *whoosh*—he was gone. "Of course, he never cleaned his room before he left."

Boot camp felt like a ripping away of her son, and, in retrospect, it seems to Carlotta that it's supposed to be that way. You can't contact your child by phone during the first two weeks, and then you get only a minute on the phone. In case of emergency, she was told that she could only contact the American Red Cross, not the base. Soldiers in boot camp may only leave for the death of a parent or sibling, end of discussion. For the first time, she was out of touch, only getting brief letters he scribbled in the bathroom stall. Needless to say, she worried in overdrive. One specific fear: she was afraid that he was being physically abused, but later, she believed him when he said the toughening-up process of boot camp was "emotional." He told her later that they'd get in the face of the recruits and yell, "You're not Mommy's boy anymore." Carlotta's take: "They are breaking the ties to Mom. When you leave boot camp, your order of duty has changed. It's God, Country, and Family, in that order."

Carlotta, her other son, and her ex-husband attended Michael's boot camp graduation together. "We wanted to show him that he has a committed family and that we still get along." Carlotta was helped by a mixture of male and female support. Her ex-husband and her brother (both of whom had served in the military) pointed out that Michael was a man now, and that the military experience had been formative for them. Her girlfriends "completely understood" her angst, and encouraged her: "You pray that they're independent of you, and when they are, you have to let them go."

Perceiving Your Child's Autonomy

Like Debbie, struck by her son's offer to pick up dinner on the way over, Carlotta had an "ah-hah" moment, when she realized in a flash that Michael was growing up. Visiting him at the base where he was studying air traffic control after boot camp, she noticed right away that he had packed his own lunch for his shift. He also had microwave popcorn and a DVD to watch during his break. She thought to herself, "This guy can take care of himself." Like many mothers, she had a moment of realizing that he was independent when she saw him doing for himself what she had done for him for so many years: feed himself. Food is such a symbol of maternal caretaking that a child's self-reliance is readily noticed.

Other mothers notice that a child home from college has put gas in the car she used, folded the towels that were in the dryer rather than dumped them on the laundry room floor, stopped at the market for milk when they noticed the supply was running low. These ah-hah moments are about a child taking responsibility for himself, and sometimes even for his mother. They are so deeply powerful because they are about the previously invisible mother becoming visible. Children do not notice the tasks a mother performs hundreds or thousands of times on their behalf, and the average mother has clocked hours and hours being taken for granted. Juice regenerates itself in the refrigerator, correct bus change grows on trees, lunches are left by the fairies, clean sheets magically appear, mittens are delivered by elves just when you need them. When a mother observes her child casually performing one of these invisible tasks, she recognizes that a huge transformation has occurred. It's a pivotal developmental moment to become visible to your child. Ideally, you feel pride and validation: the child gets it, understands the labor that went into the love, knows now what she's done for her for so many years.

Children grow away from their mothers in fits and starts, and in the same moment that Carlotta saw her son's maturation, the teenager reappeared. He was worried that his mother might have embarrassed him by complaining that he didn't have an upcoming holiday off. She responded to him adult to adult by teasing: "You mean I shouldn't have called your supervising officers a bunch of assholes?" Then she returned to reassuring mom: "Ask your brother, he'll confirm I didn't say anything." Still, Carlotta noticed that her son had left the worst of adolescence behind. Michael had been a very typical teenager, pushing back at his mother as he emotionally rehearsed leaving home during the last few years of high school. "It was the typical teen stuff," she says, "talking back, being belligerent." When she visited him at the training base, he was thoughtful, sensitive, caretaking of her. As an independent young man, he had no reason to be a jerk just to prove his autonomy. She recalls comments such as "Here, Mom, you don't have to do that." And, unlike his younger, still-pushing-away brother, he gave her the ultimate adult child gift: a kiss and hug in public.

Carlotta relaxed after seeing Michael's maturation at boot camp graduation. She felt he would be okay on his own. When the United States invaded Iraq, she didn't worry. He wasn't a pilot or a mechanic, so she believed he wouldn't be sent there. Mind you, this is a mother who worried that her well-behaved suburban kids would somehow get shot by mistakenly flashing gang signs while driving into the city, so I can't help thinking she was in denial. She quieted any doubts by asking Michael, who replied, "Mom, they only send qualified people. I'm in training."

A month or two later, "My mother's intuition gave me a bad feeling." She called and asked Michael directly: are you going to Iraq? He paused and then replied, "Yes, I signed up." He delayed telling her because he knew she would be upset. She was hopeful that the war would end before his turn came up. There were several more qualified air traffic controllers in line before him, but it didn't turn out that way. One had a heart attack, another developed migraines, and suddenly, Michael was headed to Iraq. *He* was thrilled, calling her within the first few days to excitedly report, "I've done more air traffic control here in the first three days than I did in a year and a half of training." When he mentioned going "sightseeing" in Iraq, she worried about his sense of invulnerability, noting, "I guess this is why they send twenty-year-olds to war."

Carlotta's girlfriends mobilized around her to support her when he left for Iraq. Her best friend from childhood called her the day he left and said that she, too, hadn't slept all night. Carlotta felt "Hey, I'm not alone with this." Others stopped in to visit frequently during the first few days, "to sit with me." A very dear friend was dying of breast cancer, and her visit meant a good deal to Carlotta, "because it was such a special effort." Another friend invited her to her vacation home to be together for Mother's Day. She coped in other ways: her doctor gave her sleeping pills for the first two weeks he was in Iraq, and she threw herself into her work. She works with very ill cancer patients, and caring for others in desperate straits gave her an outlet for her nurturing needs. To her surprise, since she isn't very religious, the chaplain at the Catholic hospital where she works had "care notes" that helped her, including one she carries, "when someone you love is in harm's way." She realized, "I'm part of a big caring institution," and dusting off her spirituality helped her cope.

When Michael first left for Iraq, Carlotta mothered as if her son were riding a bike for the first time. "I know his cousins were sending him e-mails that said, 'You're cool, man, have fun.' I was writing, 'A doctor at the hospital who is from the Middle East told me to tell you to be sure to wash your fruit before you eat it so that you don't get leishmaniasis." On the day that I interviewed her in her home, she was baking chocolate chip cookies to send to him, something she hadn't done in years. Sure, Michael can make his own lunch and direct war planes to land safely, but no one but Mom makes Mom's homemade cookies.

Like Debbie, Carlotta uses her own departure from the nest as a point of reference. Debbie worried that all children leave home the way she did, without a backward glance, and her goal is that of an unmothered mother: *be* different from her mom. Carlotta's mom was pretty good, but she wants to *do* the letting-go challenge differently than she herself experienced. Carlotta felt well nurtured and happy as a kid, but she thinks her mom botched the launching phase. At that point, her mother, a survivor of the Great Depression, "used money to control." As an example, her mother refused to pay a penny for Carlotta's wedding unless she was in charge—her church, her invitation list, et cetera. Things were "her way or you leave. It was always in the back of my mind with my boys—it pushed me away from her." Although in later years they became close again, Carlotta wanted to avoid creating a home environment that her children would be anxious to flee. She has a goal that I believe she is meeting. She doesn't want to control her children as they attempt to leave the nest. Her other son is considering a nearby college, and may choose to live at home rather than the dorm. She's pleased that he has "no sense of 'I can't wait to get the hell out of here.' "

Carlotta can look back on the rocky time in which Michael was "belligerent" with perfect twenty/twenty hindsight, and yet those were tough times. One thing that got her through: she didn't take it personally, didn't (usually) blame herself. Mothers will, from time to time, examine the success or failure of their mothering through the lens of their children's achievements, as Carlotta did when she wondered what *she* did wrong that her son wasn't going to college like all his friends. The developmental challenge here is knowing, really knowing, that your child is not solely the product of you. The normal parent has some narcissistic investment in her child— that's what parental pride is. The challenge is to avoid black-and-white thinking, at either end of the spectrum. The high school student who patented a new scientific discovery and tutored at a homeless shelter prior to enrolling at Stanford was not perfectly mothered any more than the high school student who got caught drinking underage was necessarily badly mothered. Carlotta is flourishing under difficult circumstances because she has an achievable goal. Her goal is not to be a perfect mother, but to do better than her mother did.

Finishing the Cake

Carlotta is also thriving because she has come to welcome collateral cake-finishers: the boot camp that helped him separate, the military training that taught him self-reliance. He isn't all grown up, but he's getting there with help from others.

Audrey had a more difficult time letting go of active mothering. Her almost-finished cake seemed like a huge glop of gooey batter, and it was her fault. Audrey was a neglected child who developed a classic case of "empty nest syndrome," becoming clinically depressed a few months after her daughter left home at age nineteen. Her own mother was an angry alcoholic, and Audrey, while anxious every step of the way, knew that she had done a far better job of mothering than she had experienced firsthand. But her daughter's departure triggered tremendous anxiety. Had she done enough? What if Tina, who hadn't yet had a romantic relationship, never dated? What if she couldn't figure out a major? Why did she call every day for a week, then not at all for the next week? How would an only child learn to share a dorm room? Why didn't she complain to the professor when her teaching assistant gave her an unfair grade? Each of these questions were embedded in Audrey's self-doubt as a mother: Did I nurture someone who would be able to enjoy an intimate romantic relationship? Did I raise someone who knows what she wants out of life? Did I make her too needy, or too independent?

In psychotherapy for this bout of depression, Audrey revisited an issue she thought long dead: her own need to mourn the mother she never had. Her old belief that the only way to counter terrible mothering was to be a perfect mother reappeared because Tina's leaving home felt to Audrey as if her last chance to get it right was now gone. Her sense of inadequacy surged because Tina, like any child leaving home, wasn't all grown up. Audrey was also looking through the lens of her own experience: she, like Debbie, fled home, never to return. She didn't know how to interpret Tina's on-again, off-again telephoning pattern because she had never viewed a phone call to her own mother as anything but a chore. She herself hadn't been without a boyfriend since age thirteen, because she'd learned too young to turn elsewhere for affection. Her own experience growing up with an inadequate mother could not serve as a barometer of how her own daughter was doing because her daughter grew up in a loving, predictable home. This time in her mothering career was the other bookend, a time to reflect back on how she had done with that task. As she appraised her own performance, and her daughter's more typical start-and-stop entry into adulthood, she saw more clearly that her job wasn't, in fact, close to being done.

If you step outside of your experience being a mother, you may recognize that you have a need for being mothered that hasn't ended. If your mother is good enough, and still alive, you probably know that you have moments when she has something unique that you want. She may be the first one you called when you found out you were pregnant, or the first you told about your divorce. Her validation, praise, support, and/or unconditional love may be a touchstone that you seek out in good times or bad. If you were partly or significantly unmothered, you may find that you remain sensitive to the emotional sustenance that is missing, perhaps noticing what your husband or friends get from their mothers that you do not.

Recognizing your own ongoing mothering needs, met or unmet, will help you see that mothering adult children is a change. It is not an end any more than it is a continuation of business as usual. Women who have successfully grown into mature relationships with their mothers are better able to sustain a hopeful vision when it is their turn to become the mother of adults. Those who were suffocated into adulthood, or, conversely, neglected from childhood, are more vulnerable to difficulties with imagining what parenting adults well looks like. Audrey's depression lifted as she realized that she would have a lifelong loving relationship with her daughter. Another patient was reassured at freshman parent orientation when the student health center nurse noted, "Don't worry. We haven't had a seriously ill student yet who didn't immediately ask us to call Mom. Yours won't be the exception."

Boomerang Children

Audrey turned out to have a mothering relationship with an adult child that she had never imagined: Tina came back home to live after graduating from college, while searching for a job. The nineteen-year-old girl who had left home declaring her independence came back at twenty-three in vacation mode, expecting three hot meals and freshly folded laundry. Audrey sat Tina down and went over the list she called "A Welcome Home Plan," which included rules such as "You are welcome to join your parents for dinner if you have asked to do so and we have agreed," and "After arranging a time with us to use the washer and dryer, please have your laundry completed within four hours." Audrey wanted to avoid the friction that often accompanies the return of an adult child to the nest, but, more important, she wanted to discourage an emotional regression that might hinder her daughter's pursuit of appropriate independent living. Much as both parties might enjoy a brief period of mommy-care, when any healthy adult child returns home to live, the child is generally best served when the mother supports his move back toward independence.

U.S. Census Bureau statistics indicate that the number of adult children living at or returning home has been increasing over the past several decades. The return of so-called boomerang children has led to what has been termed "the cluttered nest" or "the not-so-empty nest." I'd encourage all mothers who have adult children returning home to do as Audrey did: clarify specific expectations, roles, and boundaries. Like Tina, boomerang children return home during transitional times—between college and graduate school, while job hunting, or during the first few months of marital separation. Old habits die hard, and mothers and children can all too easily fall back into old caretaker-caretakee roles. It's the same force that makes you feel fifteen again when you sleep in your old twin bed at your parent's house. Audrey did a great job of parenting a "boomerang" child, in part because she finally made peace with the mothering job she had done.

Gloria is having a much harder time letting her adult son go. Eric, thirty-one, finished his pediatrics residency two years ago. Unfortunately, his marriage failed soon after, and he, squeezed by student loans and the financial toll of divorce, moved home for several months when the marriage ended. Gloria hadn't seen up close quite how busy her son's professional life was, and she did everything she could to help Eric get through those terrible first months. He moved into his old bedroom, and they converted another room into a bedroom for his three-year-old son. Gloria, with the best of intentions, cooked dinner for him every night, did his laundry, and backed him up anytime he needed to run to the hospital when it was his parenting time with his son.

Eventually, Eric moved into his own place. Gloria has not let go of the hands-on mothering, becoming more and more intrusive over time. Not long ago, at a family bar mitzvah, a relative told her "He's a big boy now, Mommy" after she suggested that he not order a second glass of wine before driving home. She scrutinizes his decisions, suggesting that it's too early to get serious about a new girlfriend, pushing him to seek counseling before getting remarried. She tries to get him to slow down at work, and lets him know when she feels he isn't parenting effectively. Taken point by point, her suggestions are not bad, but they simply are not appropriate to make to a thirty-one-year-old accomplished man. I've tried to help her identify better boundaries, but, so far, she can't seem to stop herself, even when she can stand back and see in hindsight that she's crossed a line.

Gloria practices Orthodox Judaism, and is deeply ashamed that her son is divorced. She blames herself for it. She isn't clear what she did or didn't do to cause it, but she believes that he would have chosen a better match for himself if she had been a better mother. I am struck by the poignant irony: she is failing *now,* as she tries desperately to overcompensate for some imperfection she didn't recognize years ago. Every time she offers to organize his son's birthday party, tells her grandson to "tell Daddy you missed him when he went to the hospital this morning," suggests that he lacks the judgment to know when he's had too much to drink, or criticizes his dating choices, she conveys the belief that he cannot make good decisions by and for himself, that he needs her to function now that he's a single parent. I suspect that Gloria, along with feeling guilty, is very angry at her son for disappointing her hopes and dreams for him. The golden child, the well-educated doctor in a recently immigrated family, has not delivered on the promise of being the Perfect Son, and she is frantically trying to glue the pieces back together again. She's struggling, but I'm optimistic about her willingness to share these struggles with me, prefaced as they are each time by her rationalization of why this time her intrusion was the only thing she could do. It tells me that she is preparing to change, getting closer to forgiving herself and him for human imperfection, and truly letting go.

Conclusion

There's no dressing it up; the developmental challenge of saying good-bye to one's child is simply hard, whether it's the first time or the last. This challenge has elements of each and every one of the previous challenges. A mother launching a child will need to develop a new maternal identity—that of adult mother to adult child—and a new identity as a nonmother, or a less active mother. Her child's forays into autonomy may be accompanied by unloving thoughts, as many a child's preparations for leaving the nest include behaviors, words, or eye-rolls, that could bring a saint to her knees. As the child leaves, the mother's relationship with her partner, and/or her child's father, will also shift. Separation issues flare up, with a new twist, as the stakes of independence increase. For the mother of the college-age student, limits will almost certainly include, at a minimum, financial limits, as the reality of college costs and teen spending habits collide. The relationship with the imperfect college, employer, or military institution that one's child enters has even less room for maternal input than high school; there is no PTA meeting in the army, no employer-parent conference. You get the tuition bill, but your child's university won't even send your child's report card to you without her written permission. At the same time that you're adjusting to all these changes, your child is fashioning his own dreams, and possibly having those dreams battered or bruised by reality.

Is it any wonder that many a mother dreads this final critical challenge of motherhood? It may help to remind yourself that while it feels as if you have only a few months to teach your child everything he needs to know before he leaves, in fact, as my son pointed out, you've spent eighteen years getting him ready.

One of the earliest challenges of motherhood is to avoid judging your inside—your maternal identity—by other mothers' outsides. At this final challenge of mothering, it is helpful psychologically to avoid judging your inside—your maternal report card—by your child's outside. You will have a much better sense of who your child has turned out to be, and if you must, how you did as a mother, when he is twenty-five or thirty. At eighteen, your child has an agenda of differentiation from you, and will, as a normal and healthy aspect of maturation, try on and discard different identities before settling into being himself. Try to believe that you've done well enough, and be a sounding board during these shifts in identity, rather than a critic of your child or yourself.

Signs of Poor Adaptation to Saying Good-bye

1. The empty nest syndrome—clinical symptoms of anxiety, depression, insomnia, psychosomatic symptoms, or excessive substance use at the time a child leaves home.

2. Interpreting your child's normal and healthy autonomy-seeking behavior as a personal rejection of you, your mothering, and/or the values you have encouraged. Likewise, interpreting your near-adult or adult child's success or failure as if it is your own success or failure.

3. Age-inappropriate caretaking. Ask friends, teachers, therapists, or wise people you know to help you assess whether your level of involvement is too little, too much, or in the broad range of middle. Some clues that you're too involved: writing your child's college application essays, editing their college papers, contacting their employer, rescuing them repeatedly from things they can handle on their own.

4. Frantic efforts to "finish the cake" by attempting to stuff into your departing child all the adult wisdom and judgment you should have had back when you were their age.

Strategies for Successful Adaptation

1. Just sit there.

2. Do not fight the grief (or elation, or both) that you feel about your child leaving home. Expect to feel the bitter along with the sweet, and root out statements that begin with "I should feel _____ about my child leaving home."

3. Let others help you see the adult your baby is becoming. Listen to what teachers, friends, employers, and family members have to say about what they see that you do not see in your child's readiness to move to a new stage of independence.

4. Remember that a shared roof is neither necessary nor sufficient for love. Do not mistake a child's entry into adulthood for a lost relationship. Let in what others who have gone before you have to say about the pleasures of a relationship with an adult child.

10

Conclusion

There is a hell of a lot more to being a mother
than most people suspect.
—comedienne Roseanne Barr

We should tell each other this stuff.
—Lynette, *Desperate Housewives*

Do not believe a thing because many people speak of it . . .
Do not believe what you yourself have imagined . . .
After examination, believe what you yourself have tested and
found to be reasonable, and conform your conduct thereto.
—Buddha

Mothering isn't just about our children; it's about us, too. No mother enters the journey with all the answers, yet most of us feel that we should. I can't think of another profession that has such impossible expectations, where the standard of competency is entering the job already knowing everything.

We don't have to accept the myth of the all-knowing, perfect mother. We have a choice to stand back, reflect, and embrace the realities. As an observer of, guide to, and participant in motherhood, I've learned that motherhood is sometimes great, and sometimes awful. Motherhood changes you. It can make you a better person, and it will expose every vulnerability you have. Your mother's model will sometimes inspire you, other times frighten you. Good mothers think about mothering, and try to do their best. Good mothers try to reproduce the best part of how they were raised, while seeking to overcome the missteps their own moms made.

Mothers will often feel inept, inadequate, awkward. Mistakes are inevitable. You are not the only one feeling what you're feeling, even if everyone you know swears otherwise. Good mothering does not require self-loathing, shame, constant vigilance, or flawless children. Good mothering requires consciousness and courage to objectively evaluate how you are doing.

It seems so simple, and yet so elusive a truth: of course we grow as mothers. The myth of the perfectly formed mother is so very seductive. It offers us the promise of certainty in an inherently uncertain endeavor: if there is such a thing as a perfect mother, then I can get there. I can buy the books, study harder, take the exam, get the certification that it seems everyone else already has. But the myth of knowing it all, of being already all grown up as a mother, is a siren's song that lures you to a shipwreck. Like the sailors on Ulysses' ship, we must plug our ears to the sirens' song in order to get where we want to go.

Growth is accompanied by growing pains. Yes, it may be alarming to acknowledge how much you don't know about mothering when you first arrive at a critical challenge, or frustrating to realize that you've circled back to an issue that you stumbled over the first time around. Acknowledging imperfection or uncertainty does not make us weaker as mothers—it makes us stronger as individuals seeking higher ground. Until you shed the burden of trying to become the mythical Perfect Mother, you won't be able to truly reflect on your performance, to notice when and how and why you could or should change how you mother. And you won't know when you're doing just fine, and should stay on course.

After years of observing moms who are flourishing, sometimes despite the odds of early or unwanted parenthood, a painful childhood, or countless social problems that make motherhood more difficult, I've learned and relearned the value of honest conversation. Mothers need to talk truthfully with one another. We who mother in modern, industrialized cultures are perhaps the most isolated mothers in human history. We lack the village community of women who would have guided us, shown us their truths about mothering. We are isolated in our scattered urban and suburban homes, isolated from our extended families, isolated when we fear sharing our experience of motherhood, and isolated by a cultural mythology that is heavily invested in sugar-coating motherhood.

We have a choice to reject the isolation, refuse the expected secrecy of motherhood's challenges. When another mom gives us the glossy version, we can say, "Okay, so now tell me how it really is." We can reach out to the new mother, tell her about what we're still learning about motherhood, even as we seek the encouragement of those who go before or side by side with us.

And we can look to the wisdom of those who went before us, perhaps not waiting until we ourselves are grandmothers to understand Yoko Ono's comment at seventy: "Motherhood is extremely complicated and difficult, though I suppose some mothers would say it's as natural as breathing." Sometimes it *is* as natural as breathing, and sometimes it is extremely difficult.

And when it's difficult, we can find courage in another wise woman's comments about letting ourselves be human:

> Yes, Mother, I can see you are flawed. You have not hidden it.
> That is your greatest gift to me.
> —Alice Walker

Bibliography

Introduction

Crittenden, Anne. *The Price of Motherhood: Why the Most Important Job in the World Is Still the Least Valued.* New York: Henry Holt and Company, 2001.

Douglas, Susan J. and Meredith W. Michaels. *The Mommy Myth: The Idealization of Motherhood and How It Has Undermined All Women.* New York: Free Press, 2004.

Smith, Janna Malamud: *A Potent Spell: Mother Love and the Power of Fear.* Boston: Houghton Mifflin Company, 2003.

Warner, Judith. *Perfect Madness: Motherhood in the Age of Anxiety.* New York: Riverhead Books, 2005.

Wolf, Naomi. *Misconceptions: Truth, Lies, and the Unexpected on the Journey to Motherhood.* New York: Anchor Books, 2003.

Chapter 1

Black, Jan and Greg Enns. *Better Boundaries: Owning and Treasuring Your Life.* Oakland, CA: New Harbinger Publications, 1997.

Brill, Amy. "No bottle feeders, no spankers," in "Mothers Who Think," www.salon.com, March 31, 2000. See also letters that followed, www.salon.com, April 4, 2000.

Enright, Robert D. *Forgiveness Is a Choice: A Step-By-Step Process for Resolving Anger and Restoring Hope.* Washington, DC: American Psychological Association, 2001.

Robin, Peggy. *When Breastfeeding Is Not an Option: A Reassuring Guide for Loving Parents.* Rocklin, CA: Prima Publishing, 1998.

Rogers, Carl. *On Becoming a Person: A Therapist's View of Psychotherapy.* Boston: Houghton Mifflin, 1961.

Sears, William and Martha Sears. *The Attachment Parenting Book : A Commonsense Guide to Understanding and Nurturing Your Baby.* Boston: Little, Brown and Company, 2001.

Stern, Daniel N. and Nadia Bruschweiler-Stern. *The Birth of a Mother: How the Motherhood Experience Changes You Forever.* New York: Basic Books, 1998.

www.forgiving.org

www.gentlechristianmothers.com, formerly www.gentlemothering.com

www.imperfectparent.com

Chapter 2

Gabbard, Glen. *Psychodynamic Psychiatry in Clinical Practice,* Third Edition, Washington, DC: American Psychiatric Press, Inc., 2000.

Lamott, Anne. "Mother Rage: Theory and Practice," in salon.com, at www.salon.com/mwt/lamo/1998/10/29lamo.html, and *Operating Instructions: A Journal of My Son's First Year.* New York: Ballantine Books, 1994.

Mead-Ferro, Muffy. *Confessions of a Slacker Mom.* Cambridge, MA: Da Capo Lifelong Books, 2004.

Stone, Katherine. "My Turn: I Was Scared I Might Hurt My Baby." *Newsweek,* June 7, 2004.

Chapter 3

Belkin, Lisa. *Life's Work: Confessions of an Unbalanced Mom.* New York: Simon & Schuster, 2003.

Gottman, John M. and Nan Silver. *The Seven Principles for Making Marriage Work : A Practical Guide from the Country's Foremost Relationship Expert.* New York: Three Rivers Press, 2000.

Pearson, Allison. *I Don't Know How She Does It.* New York: Alfred A. Knopf, 2002.

Sansom, Ian. *The Truth About Babies.* London: Granta Publications, 2002.

Thayer, Elizabeth and Jeffrey Zimmerman. *The Co-Parenting Survival Guide: Letting Go of Conflict After a Difficult Divorce.* Oakland, CA: New Harbinger Publications, 2001.

www.thebowencenter.org/conceptds.html

www.coloradodivorcemediation.com/family/schedules.asp

Young, Cathy. "The Mama Lion at the Gate," www.salon.com, June 12, 2000.

Chapter 4

Burns, David D. *The Feeling Good Handbook.* Rev. Ed. New York: Plume, 1999.

Edelman, Hope. *Motherless Mothers: How Mother Loss Shapes the Parents We Become.* New York: HarperCollins, 2006.

Fromm, Erich. *The Sane Society.* New York: Henry Holt and Company, 1955.

Chapter 5

Covey, Steven. *The Seven Habits of Highly Effective People: Powerful Lessons in Personal Change.* New York: Simon and Schuster, 1989.

Darling, Nancy. Parenting Style and Its Correlates, http://www.athealth.com/Practitioner/ceduc/parentingstyles.html

http://psychologytoday.psychtests.com/tests/lc_access.html

MacKenzie, Robert J. *Setting Limits with Your Strong-Willed Child: Eliminating Conflict by Establishing Clear, Firm, and Respectful Boundaries.* New York: Three Rivers Press, 2001.

Mellor, Christie. *The Three-Martini Playdate: A Practical Guide to Happy Parenting.* San Francisco: Chronicle Books, 2004.

Steinberg, Laurence. *The Ten Basic Principles of Good Parenting.* New York: Simon and Schuster, 2005.

Steinberg, Laurence. *You and Your Adolescent: A Parent's Guide for Ages 10–20.* New York: HarperCollins, 1997.

Warner, *Perfect Madness.*

www.parenting.com/parenting/article/0,19840,647543,00.html

Chapter 6

Delpit, Lisa. *Other People's Children: Cultural Conflict in the Classroom.* New York: New Press, 1995.

Kindlon, Dan and Michael Thompson. *Raising Cain: Protecting the Emotional Life of Boys.* New York: Ballantine, 2000.

Sadker, David and Myra Sadker. *Failing at Fairness: How America's Schools Cheat Girls.* New York: Touchstone, 1994.

Thompson, Michael and Teresa Barker. *The Pressured Child: Helping Your Child Find Success in School and Life.* New York: Ballantine, 2004.

Chapter 7

http://specialchildren.about.com/cs/parenting/

Levine, Madeline. *The Price of Privilege: How Parental Pressure and Material Advantage Are Creating a Generation of Disconnected and Unhappy Kids.* New York: HarperCollins, 2006.

Rosenfeld, Alvin and Nicole Wise. *The Over-Scheduled Child: Avoiding the Hyper-Parenting Trap.* New York: St. Martin's Press, 2000.

Sinclair, Jim. "Don't Mourn for Us," presented at the 1993 International Conference on Autism, http://ani.autistics.org/dont_mourn.html

www.irsc.org/ (Internet Resources for Special Children)

Chapter 8

Darwin, Charles. *The Descent of Man.* 1871. New York: Penguin, 2004.

Hrdy, Sarah. *Mother Nature: Maternal Instincts and How They Shape the Human Species.* New York: Ballantine, 1999.

Meyer, Cheryl and Michelle Oberman, *Mothers Who Kill Their Children: Understanding the Acts of Moms from Susan Smith to the "Prom Mom."* New York: New Press, 2001.

Pipher, Mary. *Reviving Ophelia: Saving the Selves of Adolescent Girls.* New York: Random House, 1994.

Simmons, Rachel. *Odd Girl Out: The Hidden Culture of Aggression in Girls.* Orlando, FL: Harcourt Books, 2002.

Smith, *A Potent Spell.*

Wiseman, Rosalind. *Queen Bees and Wannabes: Helping Your Daughter Survive Cliques, Gossip, Boyfriends, and Other Realities of Adolescence.* New York: Three Rivers Press, 2002.

Chapter 9

Coburn, Karen Levin and Madge Lawrence Treeger. *Letting Go: A Parents' Guide to Understanding the College Years.* Fourth Ed. New York: Quill, 2003.

Hopkins, Jim. "Why grown kids come home." *USA Today.* January 11, 2000.

Hotchkiss, Sandy and James F. Masterson. *Why Is It Always About You?: Saving Yourself from the Narcissists in Your Life*. New York: Free Press, 2003.

The Talk of the Town. *The New Yorker.* May 19, 2000.

Viorst, Judith. *Necessary Losses: The Loves, Illusions, Dependencies, and Impossible Expectations That All of Us Have to Give Up in Order to Grow.* New York: Fireside, 1986.

Walker, Alice. *Possessing the Secret of Joy.* Orlando, FL: Harcourt Brace and Company, 1992.

Acknowledgments

For being the best teachers a student of mothering could have, I thank Sam, Abby, and Molly Raskin.

I'm deeply grateful to Anne Edelstein, without whom this book would not exist. Her involvement and encouragement at each stage of the manuscript helped me find the book within. Once again, I am reminded how lucky I am to have her as my friend and agent.

Heartfelt thanks, too, to Susanna Porter, my editor, for applying her skill, wisdom, and dedication to this book, which is much the better for it. To others seen and unseen at Ballantine, thank you.

I am indebted to the women who shared their stories with generosity and courage, and honored by the women in my practice who trust me with their most precious struggles.

Thanks, too, to the early readers who read and commented on multiple early drafts: Jill Baskin, Lisa Groves, Jinger Hoop, Paula Machtinger, and Suzy Sachs. Thanks also to them, and to Susan Axelrod, Karen Gillette, Marianne Green, Vanessa Klugman, and Naomi Levy for indulging me in countless honest, insightful, and supportive conversations about the experience of motherhood.

Finally, thanks to Matt Terebessy and Abby Raskin for their research and careful attention to detail. Gene, thank you for everything.

About the Author

VALERIE DAVIS RASKIN, M.D., maintains a private practice in the Chicago area. A former clinical associate professor of psychiatry at the University of Chicago's Pritzker School of Medicine, she also co-founded the Pregnancy and Postpartum Treatment Program at the University of Illinois at Chicago College of Medicine. She has been honored by Postpartum Support International for her contributions to increasing awareness of emotional health related to childbearing. She is the author of *This Isn't What I Expected: Overcoming Postpartum Depression*, *When Words Are Not Enough: The Women's Prescription for Depression and Anxiety*, and *Great Sex for Moms: Ten Steps to Nurturing Passion While Raising Kids*. She is the mother of a young adult and two teenagers.